Contents

In selecting material for this book, the authors focused on concepts and principles that are important to developmental theorists and to educational practitioners. The result is a text that is uniquely useful to those who are interested in practical applications of developmental scholarship.

Educational Implications of Vygotsky's Ideas

Vygotsky's work and the recent theoretical advances it has inspired yield numerous implications for classroom practice, including the following:

■ *Help students acquire the basic conceptual tools of various academic disciplines.* Through such disciplines as science, mathematics, and social studies, our culture passes along key concepts (e.g., molecule, negative number, democracy), symbols (e.g., H_2O, π, ∞), and visual representations (e.g., graphs, maps) that can help growing children organize and interpret the physical and social worlds in which they live. Literature, poetry, music, and fine arts help children impose meaning on the world as well—for example, by capturing the thoughts and feelings that characterize human experience.

■ *Present challenging tasks, perhaps within the context of cooperative activities.* To promote students' cognitive development, teachers should present some classroom tasks and assignments that students can perform successfully only with assistance—that is, tasks within students' zone of proximal development. To some extent, students with different zones of proximal development may need different tasks and assignments, which makes a strong case for providing as much individualized instruction as possible.

In some instances, students can accomplish challenging tasks only with the assistance of more skilled individuals, such as adults or older students. But at other times, students of equal ability can work together on difficult assignments, thereby jointly accomplishing tasks that none of them might be able to do on their own. In such situations, the students are essentially providing scaffolding for one another's efforts. Cooperative learning groups and other activities in which students work collaboratively can be highly effective in promoting both cognitive development and classroom achievement (Brown & Palincsar, 1989; Lou et al., 1996; Stevens & Slavin, 1995).

■ *Scaffold students' efforts.* When teachers provide the challenging tasks so important for cognitive development, they should also provide sufficient scaffolding to enable students to accomplish those tasks successfully. Here are some examples of how a teacher might scaffold a new and difficult task:

• Demonstrating the proper performance of the task in a way that students can easily imitate
• Dividing the task into several smaller, simpler pieces
• Providing a structure, set of steps, or guidelines for performing the task
• Asking questions that get students thinking in appropriate ways about the task
• Keeping students' attention focused on the relevant aspects of the task
• Giving frequent feedback about how students are progressing
(Gallimore & Tharp, 1990; Good et al., 1992; Rogoff, 1990; Rosenshine & Meister, 1992; Wood et al., 1976)

Educational Implications. Throughout every chapter, you will find extensive discussion of the relevance of this material to teachers and others who work with children. Most major topics contain sections that examine in depth the educational implications of the developmental research and theory being presented. The student comes away not only understanding current views of concepts such as children's theory construction or attachment but also seeing the relevance and application of these ideas to working with children.

Development and Practice. In addition to consistent discussion of application throughout the text itself, the authors provide "Development and Practice" features that offer concrete educational strategies for facilitating student development. To help students move from research to practice, each strategy is followed by an actual example of a teacher using that strategy in a classroom.

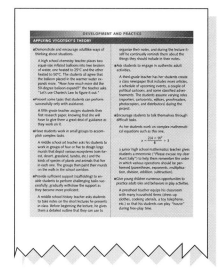

Observation Guidelines. To work productively with children and adolescents, one must first be able to accurately see them. Knowledge of development provides an essential lens through which teachers must look if they are to understand children. One of the foundational goals of this text is to help teachers observe developmental nuances in their students. To this end, throughout the book, the authors give readers "Observation Guidelines." These offer specific characteristics to look for in students, present illustrative examples, and provide specific recommendations for teachers.

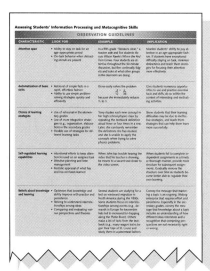

Another central focus of this text is to extensively illustrate concepts and research with examples of real children and adolescents. Authentic case studies begin and end each chapter, and there are often separate, shorter vignettes within the bodies of chapters. In addition to these types of illustrations, the text, much more than any other similar text, also makes frequent use of real artifacts from children's journals, sketchbooks, and school assignments. It is among real children and adolescents and in the midst of the work that children and adolescents produce that developmental content becomes meaningful to teachers. More than any other text, *Child Development and Education* brings this educational context to life.

Case Studies. Each chapter begins with a case that, by being referenced throughout the chapter, is used to help illustrate and frame that chapter's content. A chapter ending case provides readers with an opportunity to apply chapter content to an instructional setting. A series of questions that accompany each of these end-of-chapter cases help the reader in this application process.

Artifacts from Children and Adolescents. The frequent use of actual artifacts provides another forum for illustrating developmental abilities and issues. Throughout the text, actual examples of children's and adolescents' artwork, poetry, and school assignments are integrated into discussions of various concepts and applications. Not only do these artifacts offer readers authentic illustrations of chapter content, but they also help place developmental research and theory directly within an educational context.

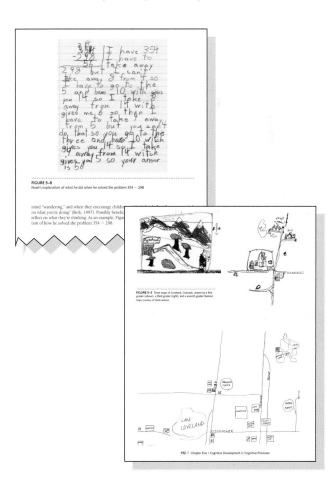

The other core goal of *Child Development and Education* is to help readers come to a broad conceptual understanding of the developmental field, to make them aware of the foundational ideas and issues that frame the field, and to provide them with a broad sense of how and when children develop. Throughout all of its chapters, the book consistently examines three core developmental issues—the relationship between biological and environmental influences on development, universality and diversity of developmental changes, and whether developmental changes are qualitative or quantitative. Though organized topically, the book also provides an overview of developmental changes from a chronological perspective.

Basic Developmental Issues. Every chapter examines ways in which development is the complex product of interacting forces—nature, nurture, and the children's own efforts. The authors also spotlight circumstances that reveal fairly universal developmental trends and areas marked with substantial diversity. Finally, the text analyzes developmental changes for their underlying nature: do they take the form of dramatic qualitative changes, or are they the outcome of many small, trend-like quantitative changes?

Developmental Trends. The book is organized around substantive topics of development to allow for an in-depth examination of each area of development. In the context of this topical approach, however, the authors also identify the unique characteristics of students during particular periods of growth. In the narrative, the authors frequently provide detailed chronological examples of children's abilities to give teachers a flavor of what children can do at specific ages. In each chapter, a "Developmental Trends" table summarizes typical features of four developmental periods: early childhood, middle childhood, early adolescence, and late adolescence. You will also note that these tables explain common types of individual and group differences and provide instructional implications.

Child Development and Education

Symoen, age 9

Cognitive Development 1: Piaget and Vygotsky

CASE STUDY: WHALE WATCHING

Six-year-old Kerry and her mother are talking about their family's recent whale-watching expedition:

Mother: And we went with, who'd we go with?
Kerry: David.
Mother: David. Who else?
Kerry: And Nana and Papa.
Mother: And who else? Daddy went too, didn't he?
Kerry: Yeah.
Mother: Yeah. Who else?
Kerry: That's all.
Mother: Oh, and Auntie Karen and Uncle Pete, right?
Kerry: Yeah.
Mother: And David's two brothers.
Kerry: Mmhm.
Mother: We went whale watching and um I think it turned out to be a disaster because it was rough out there and we got kind of seasick. We did see whales, but not as good as we wanted to.
Kerry: I saw one.
Mother: Yeah, we saw them. They're big, huh?
Kerry: [Nods.]
Mother: How many were there?
Kerry: About thirteen.
Mother: About thirteen! There were only two or three!
Kerry: No, there wasn't, because they were runnin' back and forth like fifty times! (Hemphill & Snow, 1996, p. 182)

KERRY HAS ALMOST CERTAINLY learned something about the animal world from her whale-watching experience. By observing whales in the flesh, she has probably acquired a better understanding of the characteristics and behaviors of whales than she could gain from a verbal description, picture book illustration, or videotape. At the same time, Kerry's interpretations of what she observed may not be entirely accurate. For instance, Kerry and her mother disagree about the number of whales that the group saw, and one of them—perhaps both of them—counted incorrectly. Furthermore, Kerry can recall certain aspects of the expedition, such as the specific people who accompanied her, only with her mother's assistance.

The conversation between Kerry and her mother gives us a brief glimpse into how a young child thinks about a particular event; in other words, it illustrates cognition in action. More generally, **cognition** encompasses all the mental activities in which a person engages, including perception, categorization, understanding, inference drawing, logical reasoning, problem solving, imagination, and memory. Such processes change and evolve in many ways over the course of childhood and adolescence; for instance, Kerry's comprehension of her experiences with the animal kingdom will almost certainly improve as she grows older.

To some extent, cognitive development is a function of physiological maturation. As you discovered in Chapter 3, the brain undergoes a series of genetically controlled changes during childhood and adolescence, and such changes almost certainly allow increasingly sophisticated thinking processes over time. Yet environmental events—both informal experiences (e.g., play activities with age-mates and encounters with new, intriguing objects) and more formal, planned interventions (e.g., whale-watching trips and classroom lessons)—also play a key, in fact *essential,* role in the development of children's and adolescents' cognitive capabilities.

The nature and course of cognitive development are the focus of Chapters 4, 5, and 6. In this chapter, we consider two early theories—those of Jean Piaget and Lev Vygotsky—that have greatly enhanced our understanding of how children's thinking changes with age. In the following two chapters, we look more closely at the development of cognitive processes (Chapter 5) and the nature of intelligence (Chapter 6).

Piaget's Theory of Cognitive Development

Children of different ages often think and reason very differently about the situations they encounter and the phenomena they observe. Consider, for example, a 6-year-old and an 8-year-old in a study by Piaget (1952a). The experimenter (Exp) shows the children a box that contains about a dozen wooden beads; two of them are white and the rest are brown. The 6-year-old, whom we'll call Brian,[1] responds as follows:

Exp:	Are there more wooden beads or more brown beads?
Brian:	More brown ones, because there are two white ones.
Exp:	Are the white ones made of wood?
Brian:	Yes.
Exp:	And the brown ones?
Brian:	Yes.
Exp:	Then are there more brown ones or more wooden ones?
Brian:	More brown ones.
Exp:	What color would a necklace made of the wooden beads be?
Brian:	Brown and white. (Here [Brian] shows that he understands that all the beads are wooden.)
Exp:	And what color would a necklace made with the brown beads be?
Brian:	Brown.
Exp:	Then which would be longer, the one made with the wooden beads or the one made with the brown beads?

cognition
The various mental activities in which a person engages.

---

[1]Piaget identified individuals in his studies by abbreviations. We've substituted names throughout the text to allow for easier discussion.

Brian:	The one with the brown beads.
Exp:	Draw the necklaces for me.

Brian draws a series of black rings for the necklace of brown beads; he then draws a series of black rings plus two white rings for the necklace of wooden beads.

Exp:	Good. Now which will be longer, the one with the brown beads or the one with the wooden beads?
Brian:	The one with the brown beads. (dialogue from Piaget, 1952a, pp. 163–164)

The experimenter gives 8-year-old "Natalie" the same problem:

Exp:	Are there more wooden beads or more brown beads?
Natalie:	More wooden ones.
Exp:	Why?
Natalie:	Because the two white ones are made of wood as well.
Exp:	Suppose we made two necklaces, one with all the wooden beads and one with all the brown ones. Which one would be longer?
Natalie:	Well, the wooden ones and the brown ones are the same, and it would be longer with the wooden ones because there are two white ones as well. (dialogue from Piaget, 1952a, p. 176)

Brian has difficulty with a question that, to us, seems ridiculously simple. Even though all the beads are wooden and only some (albeit the majority) are brown, he concludes that there are more brown beads. Natalie, who is 2 years older, answers the question easily: Logically there *must* be more wooden beads than brown beads. Natalie exhibits **class inclusion,** the recognition that an object can belong both to a particular category and to one of its subcategories simultaneously.

In the early 1920s, Swiss biologist Jean Piaget began studying children's responses to a wide variety of problems, including the class inclusion problem just described (e.g., Piaget, 1928, 1952a, 1959, 1970; Piaget & Inhelder, 1969). He was particularly curious about the nature of knowledge and how children acquire it, borrowing from a branch of philosophy known as *genetic epistemology.* To determine where knowledge comes from and the forms that it takes at different age levels, he observed the everyday actions of infants and children and drew inferences about the logic that seemed to be influencing their behavior. He also pioneered the use of a procedure he called the **clinical method,** whereby he gave children a variety of tasks and problems (among them the "wooden beads" problem just illustrated) and asked a series of questions about each one. Piaget tailored his interviews to the particular responses that children gave, with follow-up questions varying from one child to the next, as a way of probing into the specific reasoning processes that the children were using. The results of his studies provide many unique insights about how children think and learn about the world around them.

Key Ideas in Piaget's Theory

From his observations of children in problem-solving situations, Piaget derived several concepts and principles related to the nature of cognitive development. Among the most central ones are the following:

■ *Children are active and motivated learners.* Piaget believed that children do not just passively observe and remember the things they see and hear. Instead, they are naturally curious about their world and actively seek out information to help them understand and make sense of it. They continually experiment with the objects they encounter, manipulating things and observing the effects of their actions. For example, we think back (without much nostalgia) to the days when our children were in high chairs, experimenting with (picking up, squishing, pushing, rolling, dropping, and throwing) their food as readily as they might eat it.

■ *Children organize what they learn from their experiences.* Children don't just assemble the things they learn into a collection of isolated facts. Instead, they gradually construct an overall view of how the world operates. For example, by observing that food, toys, and other objects always fall down (never up) when they are released, children begin to construct a rudimentary understanding of *gravity*. As they interact with family pets, visit zoos,

class inclusion
Recognition that something simultaneously belongs to a particular category and to one of its subcategories.

clinical method
Procedure whereby a researcher probes a child's reasoning about a task or problem, tailoring questions to what the child has previously said or done.

look at picture books, and so on, they develop an increasingly complex understanding of *animals*.

In Piaget's terminology, the things that children learn and can do are organized as **schemes**—groups of similar thoughts or actions. Initially, children's schemes are largely behavioral in nature, but over time they become increasingly mental and, eventually, abstract. To illustrate, an infant may have a scheme for putting things in her mouth, a scheme that she uses in dealing with a variety of objects, including her thumb, her toys, and her blanket. A 7-year-old may have a scheme for identifying snakes, one that includes their long, thin bodies, their lack of legs, and their slithery nature. As a 13-year-old, Jeanne's daughter Tina had her own opinion about what constitutes *fashion*—a scheme that allowed her to classify various articles of clothing on display at the mall as being either "totally awesome" or "really stupid."

Piaget proposed that children use newly acquired schemes over and over in both familiar and novel situations. In the process, they also refine the schemes and begin to use them in combination with one another. Eventually, they integrate individual schemes into larger systems of mental processes, or **operations,** and such integration allows children to think in increasingly sophisticated and logical ways. For instance, 8-year-old Natalie's reasoning about the "beads" problem shows greater integration than 6-year-old Brian's: Although both children understand that some beads are both brown and wooden, only Natalie takes both characteristics into account *simultaneously* to conclude that there must be more wooden beads than brown beads. Brian apparently can consider only one characteristic at a time; as a result, he compares the brown beads only with the *remaining* wooden beads (the white ones) and thereby concludes that there are more brown ones.

■ *Children adapt to their environment through the processes of assimilation and accommodation.* Children's developing schemes allow them to respond in ever more successful ways to their environment. Such **adaptation** occurs as a result of two complementary processes: assimilation and accommodation.

Assimilation is a process of dealing with an object or event in a way that is consistent with an existing scheme. For example, an infant may assimilate a new teddy bear into her putting-things-in-the-mouth scheme. A 7-year-old may quickly identify a new slithery object in the backyard as a snake. A 13-year-old may readily label a classmate's clothing as being either quite fashionable or "sooooo *yesterday.*"

But sometimes children cannot easily interpret a new object or event in terms of their existing schemes. In these situations, one of two forms of **accommodation** will occur: Children will either modify an existing scheme to account for the new object or event or else form an entirely new scheme to deal with it. For example, the infant may have to open her mouth wider than usual to accommodate a teddy bear's fat paw. The 13-year-old may have to revise her existing scheme of fashion according to changes in what's hot and what's not. The 7-year-old may find a long, thin, slithery thing that can't possibly be a snake because it has four legs. After some research, the child develops a new scheme—*salamander*—for this creature.

Although children's schemes change over time, the two processes through which their schemes are acquired and modified—assimilation and accommodation—remain the same throughout the course of development. Assimilation and accommodation typically work hand in hand as children develop their knowledge and understanding of the world. Children interpret each new event within the context of their existing knowledge (assimilation) but at the same time may modify their knowledge as a result of the new event (accommodation). Accommodation rarely happens without assimilation: People of any age can benefit from (accommodate to) new experiences only when they can relate those experiences to their current knowledge and beliefs.

■ *Interaction with one's physical environment is critical for cognitive development.* New experiences are essential for cognitive development to occur; without them, the modification of schemes—accommodation—cannot take place. By exploring and manipulating the world around them—by conducting many little "experiments" with various objects and substances—children learn the nature of such physical characteristics as volume and weight, discover principles related to force and gravity, acquire a better understanding of cause-effect relationships, and so on. Activities such as "fiddling" with sand and water, playing games with balls and bats, and experimenting in a science laboratory help children construct a more complete and accurate un-

scheme
In Piaget's theory, an organized group of similar actions or thoughts.

operation
In Piaget's theory, an organized and integrated system of thought processes.

adaptation
Developmental process of responding to the environment in an increasingly effective manner.

assimilation
Dealing with a new event in a way that is consistent with an existing scheme.

accommodation
Dealing with a new event by either modifying an existing scheme or forming a new one.

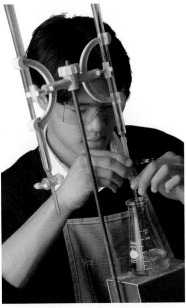

derstanding of how the physical world operates. The following anecdote from preschool teacher Frances Hawkins illustrates:

> Tommy . . . had built a tower on a base of three regular blocks on end, with a round, flat piece of Masonite on top. Then on top of this were three more blocks and Masonite, supporting in turn a third story. Each story was defined by round, flat pieces of Masonite in the structure. The tower was already taller than Tommy, and he had a piece of triangular Masonite in hand and was gently testing the tower's steadiness against his taps. Small taps and the tower would lean, settle, and become still. Again and again he varied the strength and place of the taps; watched, waited, tapped again, and finally—on purpose—did hit hard enough to topple the structure. Then the entire process of building the tower and testing it was repeated. (Hawkins, 1997, p. 200)

■ *Interaction with other people is equally critical.* As you will soon discover, young children often have difficulty seeing the world from anyone's perspective but their own. By conversing, exchanging ideas, and arguing with others, they gradually begin to realize that different individuals see things differently and that their own view of the world is not necessarily a completely accurate or logical one. Elementary school children may begin to recognize logical inconsistencies in what they say and do (e.g., recall Brian's insistence that there were more brown beads than wooden beads) when someone else points out those inconsistencies. And through discussions with classmates or adults about social and political issues, high school students slowly modify their newly emerging idealism about how the world "should" be.

■ *The process of equilibration promotes progression toward increasingly more complex forms of thought.* Piaget proposed that children are sometimes in a state of **equilibrium**: They can comfortably explain new events in terms of existing schemes. But this equilibrium doesn't continue indefinitely. As children grow, they frequently encounter situations that they cannot adequately explain in terms of their current understanding of the world. Such situations create **disequilibrium,** a sort of mental "discomfort" that spurs them to try to make sense of what they observe. By replacing, reorganizing, or better integrating their schemes (in other words, through accommodation), children eventually become able to understand and explain previously puzzling events. The movement from equilibrium to disequilibrium and back to equilibrium again is known as **equilibration.** Equilibration and children's intrinsic desire to achieve equilibrium promote the development of more complex levels of thought and knowledge.

Let's return to the case of Brian and the "beads" problem presented earlier. The experimenter asks Brian to draw two necklaces, one made with the wooden beads and one made with the brown beads. The experimenter hopes that after Brian draws a brown-and-white necklace that is longer than an all-brown necklace, he will notice that his drawings are inconsistent with his

equilibrium
State of being able to explain new events in terms of existing schemes.

disequilibrium
State of being *unable* to explain new events in terms of existing schemes.

equilibration
Movement from equilibrium to disequilibrium and back to equilibrium; a process that promotes the development of increasingly complex forms of thought and knowledge.

statement that there are more brown beads. Brian should therefore experience disequilibrium, perhaps to the point where he will reevaluate his conclusion and realize that all the brown beads *plus two white ones* must necessarily be more than the brown beads alone. In this case, however, Brian apparently is oblivious to the inconsistency, remains in equilibrium, and so has no need to revise his thinking.

■ *Children think in qualitatively different ways at different age levels.* Piaget was a *stage theorist:* He proposed that children proceed through four stages of cognitive development and that their thinking and reasoning processes are qualitatively different at each one. These qualitative changes in children's thinking are due both to neurological maturation and to the increasing integration of their knowledge and thought processes. We turn now to the nature of Piaget's stages.

Piaget's Stages of Cognitive Development

Piaget's four stages of cognitive development are as follows:

1. Sensorimotor stage (birth until about 2 years)
2. Preoperational stage (2 years until about 6 or 7 years)
3. Concrete operations stage (6 or 7 years until about 11 or 12 years)
4. Formal operations stage (11 or 12 years through adulthood)

These stages are briefly summarized in Figure 4–1.

Piaget believed that each stage builds on the accomplishments of any preceding stages, so that children must progress through the four stages in the same, invariant sequence. Furthermore, he suggested that the stages are *universal*—that they describe the cognitive development of children throughout the world.

FIGURE 4–1 Piaget's stages of cognitive development

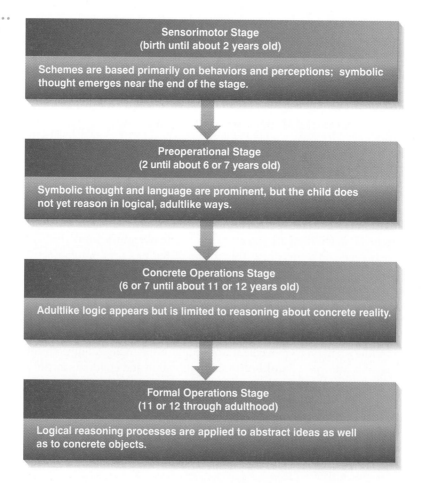

Sensorimotor Stage
(birth until about 2 years old)

Schemes are based primarily on behaviors and perceptions; symbolic thought emerges near the end of the stage.

Preoperational Stage
(2 until about 6 or 7 years old)

Symbolic thought and language are prominent, but the child does not yet reason in logical, adultlike ways.

Concrete Operations Stage
(6 or 7 until about 11 or 12 years old)

Adultlike logic appears but is limited to reasoning about concrete reality.

Formal Operations Stage
(11 or 12 through adulthood)

Logical reasoning processes are applied to abstract ideas as well as to concrete objects.

As you will discover later in the chapter, many psychologists question the notion that cognitive development is either as stagelike or as universal as Piaget believed. Nevertheless, Piaget's stages do provide insights into the nature of children's thinking at different age levels, and so we will look at them in depth. Note that the ages associated with each stage are *averages*; some children may reach a stage at a slightly younger age than average, and others may reach it at an older age. Furthermore, some children may be *transitional* from one stage to the next and so display characteristics of two adjacent stages during the same time period.

Sensorimotor Stage (Birth Until Age 2) Imagine this situation:

We show a colorful stuffed clown to 6-month-old Elena. Elena reaches for the clown in much the same way that she reaches for her teddy bear and her stacking blocks. She then drops it and squeals in delight as it falls to the floor. We pick up the clown and, as Elena watches, put it inside a box so that it is no longer visible. At this point, Elena seems to forget about her new toy and turns to play with something else.

Elena readily applies several schemes to the clown, including reaching-and-grasping, letting-go, and visually-following-a-moving-object. In the early part of the sensorimotor stage, children's schemes are based primarily on behaviors (e.g., grabbing, dropping) and perceptions (e.g., visual tracking). According to Piaget, children in this stage are not yet capable of *mental* schemes that enable them to think about objects beyond their immediate view. Elena acts as if she cannot think about a clown she cannot actually see. In other words, out of sight, out of mind.

Later in the sensorimotor stage (at about 18 months, according to Piaget), a child develops **symbolic thought,** the ability to mentally represent and think about objects and events in terms of internal, mental entities, or *symbols*. For example, Elena will eventually be able to think about a clown she has just seen without having it directly in front of her. Such symbolic thinking marks the beginning of true thought as Piaget defined it.

As infants experiment with their environments in a trial-and-error fashion, other important cognitive capabilities emerge as well. One important acquisition is **object permanence,** the realization that physical objects continue to exist even when they are removed from view. For instance, whereas 6-month-old Elena forgets about the toy clown once it is put in a box, a 12-month-old will know where the clown is and open the box to get it.

Furthermore, after repeatedly observing that certain actions lead to certain consequences, children in the sensorimotor stage acquire an understanding of cause-effect relationships. Accordingly, they begin to engage in **goal-directed behavior:** They behave in ways that they know will bring about desired results. (Whereas Elena lets go of the clown to see what will happen, an older baby or toddler might drop the clown *intentionally,* knowing in advance that it will fall to the floor and waiting eagerly to see it happen.) Older sensorimotor children also begin to combine behaviors in new and creative ways to accomplish their goals. They frequently "experiment" with such combinations in their minds first, predicting what will happen if they do such-and-such and then transforming their plans into action.

The acquisitions of the sensorimotor stage, including symbolic thought, object permanence, and goal-directed behavior, are basic building blocks on which later cognitive development depends.[2] At the same time, growing children don't entirely discard sensorimotor ways of interacting with the environment. Even as adults, we continue to use the behavioral and perceptual schemes we acquired as infants (reaching and grasping, following a moving object with our eyes, etc.), and sometimes trial-and-error experimentation is the only way to interact with a new and puzzling object.

Preoperational Stage (Age 2 Until Age 6 or 7) The ability to represent objects and events mentally (i.e., symbolic thought) gives children in the preoperational stage a greater "world view" than they had during the sensorimotor stage. They can now recall past events and envision future ones, and so they can begin to tie their experiences together into an increasingly more complex understanding of the world.

---

[2]Piaget described the sensorimotor stage as having six substages—substages that are probably of greater interest to new parents than to teachers. If you are interested in learning about the substages of the sensorimotor stage, we refer you to Piaget (1952b), Flavell (1963), or Flavell, Miller, and Miller (1993).

symbolic thought
Ability to represent and think about external objects and events in one's mind.

object permanence
Realization that objects continue to exist even after they are removed from view.

goal-directed behavior
Planful behavior intended to bring about an anticipated outcome.

Language skills virtually explode during the early part of the preoperational stage. The words in children's rapidly increasing vocabularies provide labels for newly developed mental schemes and serve as symbols that enable them to think about objects and events even when such things are not directly in sight. Furthermore, language provides the basis for a new form of social interaction: verbal communication. Children can express their thoughts and receive information from other people in a way that was not possible during the sensorimotor stage.

The advent of symbolic thought reflects itself not only in rapidly expanding language skills but also in the changing nature of children's play. Young children often engage in fantasy and make-believe, using either realistic objects or reasonable substitutes to act out the roles and behaviors of those they see around them. Piaget proposed that such pretend play enables children to practice using newly acquired symbolic schemes and familiarize themselves with the various roles they see others assume in society. The following incident involving 5-year-olds Jeff and Scott illustrates:

> In a corner of Jeff's basement, the boys make a dining area from several child-sized tables and chairs. They construct a restaurant "kitchen" with a toy sink and stove and stock it with plastic dishes and "food" items. They create menus for their restaurant, often asking a parent how to spell the words but sometimes using their knowledge of letter-sound relationships to guess how a particular word might be spelled.
>
> Jeff and Scott invite their mothers and fathers to come to the new restaurant for lunch. After seating their "customers," the boys pretend to write their meal orders on paper tablets and then scurry to the kitchen to assemble the requested lunch items. Eventually they return to serve the meals (hamburgers, French fries, and cookies—all of them plastic—plus glasses of imaginary milk), which the adults "eat" and "drink" with gusto. After the young waiters return with the final bills, the adults pay for their "meals" with nickels and leave a few pennies on the tables as tips.

With the emergence of symbolic thought, then, young children are no longer restricted to the "here and now" and so can think and act far more flexibly than they have previously. At the same time, preoperational thinking has some definite limitations, especially as we compare it to the concrete operational thinking that emerges later (see Table 4–1). For example, Piaget described young children as exhibiting **preoperational egocentrism,** the inability to view situations from another person's perspective.[3] Young children may have trouble understanding why they must share school supplies with a classmate or why they must be careful not to hurt someone else's feelings. They may play games together without ever checking to be sure that they are all playing according to the same rules. They may also exhibit **egocentric speech,** saying things without considering the perspective of the listener. They may leave out critical details as they tell a story, giving a fragmented version that a listener cannot possibly understand. As an illustration, an adult in Piaget's laboratory once told a story and asked young Giovanna to retell it:

The original:
Once upon a time, there was a lady who was called Niobe, and who had 12 sons and 12 daughters. She met a fairy who had only one son and no daughter. Then the lady laughed at the fairy because the fairy only had one boy. Then the fairy was very angry and fastened the lady to a rock. The lady cried for ten years. In the end she turned into a rock, and her tears made a stream which still runs today. (Piaget, 1959, p. 82)

Giovanna's version:
Once upon a time there was a lady who had twelve boys and twelve girls, and then a fairy [had] a boy and a girl. And then Niobe wanted to have some more sons. Then she was angry. She fastened her to a stone. He turned into a rock, and then his tears made a stream which is still running today. (p. 102)

preoperational egocentrism
Inability of a child in Piaget's preoperational stage to view situations from another person's perspective.

egocentric speech
Speaking without taking the perspective and knowledge of the listener into account.

---

[3]Bjorklund and Green (1992) have suggested that young children's egocentrism, rather than being a limitation, may actually have an adaptive function. A common finding in studies of human learning is that people can remember information more easily when they see its relevance to their own lives.

TABLE 4–1 Preoperational Versus Concrete Operational Thought

PREOPERATIONAL THOUGHT	CONCRETE OPERATIONAL THOUGHT
Preoperational egocentrism Inability to see things from someone else's perspective; thinking that one's own perspective is the only one possible. *Example:* A child tells a story without considering what prior knowledge the listener is likely to have.	**Differentiation of one's own perspective from the perspectives of others** Recognition that different people see the same things differently; realization that one's own perspective may be incorrect. *Example:* A child asks for validation of his own thoughts (e.g., "Did I get that right?").
Confusion between physical and psychological events Confusion of external, physical objects with internal thoughts; thinking that thoughts have physical reality and that objects think and feel. *Example:* A child is afraid of the "monsters" in a dark closet and worries that a doll will feel lonely if left alone at home.	**Distinction between physical and psychological events** Recognition that thoughts do not have physical reality and that physical objects don't have psychological characteristics such as "feelings." *Example:* A child realizes that imagined monsters don't exist and that dolls have no thoughts or feelings.
Lack of conservation Belief that amount changes when a substance is reshaped or re-arranged, even though nothing has been added or taken away. *Example:* A child asserts that two rows of five pennies similarly spaced have equal amounts; however, when one row is spread out so that it is longer than the other, she says that it has more pennies.	**Conservation** Recognition that amount stays the same if nothing has been added or taken away, even when the substance is reshaped or re-arranged. *Example:* A child asserts that two rows of five pennies are the same number of pennies regardless of their spacing.
Irreversibility Lack of awareness that certain processes can be undone, or reversed. *Example:* A child doesn't realize that a row of five pennies previously made longer by extra spacing can be shortened back to its original length.	**Reversibility** Ability to envision how certain processes can be reversed. *Example:* A child moves the five pennies in the longer row close together again to demonstrate that both rows have the same amount.
Reliance on perception over logic Dependence on how things appear when drawing conclusions. *Example:* A child hears a story about a girl whose uncle gives her a baby rattle as a gift. Though sad about the age-inappropriate gift, the girl in the story smiles so that she won't hurt her uncle's feelings. When looking at a picture of the smiling girl, the child concludes that the girl feels happy (Friend & Davis, 1993).	**Reliance on logic over perception** Dependence on conceptual understandings when drawing conclusions. *Example:* A child hearing the same story and seeing the picture of the smiling girl concludes that the girl *looks* happy but actually feels sad (Friend & Davis, 1993).
Centration Focus on a single physical dimension when comparing two or more objects. *Example:* When water is poured from a tall, thin glass into a short, wide glass, a child claims that there is now less water than before. He is focusing on the lesser height of the water in the second glass, without considering that the second glass is also wider than the first.	**Decentration** Consideration of two or more dimensions of objects simultaneously; recognition that one dimension may compensate for another. *Example:* A child recognizes that water poured from a tall, thin glass into a short, wide glass is still the same amount of water. He understands that the greater width of the second glass makes up for its lesser height.
Single classification Ability to classify objects in only one way at any given point in time. *Example:* A child denies that a mother can also be a doctor.	**Multiple classification** Recognition that objects may belong to several categories simultaneously (includes *class inclusion*). *Example:* A child acknowledges that a mother can also be a doctor, a jogger, and a spouse.
Transductive reasoning Reasoning that involves combining unrelated facts (e.g., inferring a cause-effect relationship simply because two events occur close together in time and space). *Example:* A child believes that clouds make the moon grow (Piaget, 1928).	**Deductive reasoning** Drawing an appropriate logical inference from two or more pieces of information. *Example:* A child deduces that if Jane is taller than Mary, and if Mary is taller than Carol, then Jane must be taller than Carol.

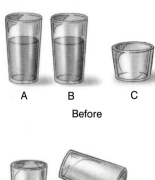

A   B   C
Before

A   B   C
After

FIGURE 4–2 Conservation of liquid: Do glasses A and C contain the same amount of water after the water in B is poured into C?

Notice how Giovanna never explained who "she," "her," and "he" were—things that couldn't possibly have been obvious to a listener.

In Giovanna's rendition of the story we find one reason why, from Piaget's perspective, social interaction is so important for cognitive development. Someone listening to the child's story might express confusion about who was angry and who turned into a rock. Repeated feedback from other people helps children learn that their thoughts and feelings are unique to them—that their perception of the world is not always shared by others and, in some cases, may not even reflect the true state of affairs.

Preoperational thinking is also *illogical* (at least from an adult's point of view), especially during the preschool years. As an example, recall Brian's insistence that there were more brown beads than wooden beads, an error that reflects single classification (see Table 4–1). Here is another example of the "logic" of children exhibiting preoperational thought:

We show 4-year-old Lucy the three glasses in Figure 4–2. Glasses A and B are identical in size and shape and contain an equal amount of water. We ask Lucy if the two glasses of water contain the same amount, and she replies confidently that they do. We then pour the water in Glass B into Glass C. We ask her if the two glasses of water (A and C) still have the same amount. "No," Lucy replies. She points to glass A: "That glass has more because it's taller."

Lucy's response illustrates a lack of **conservation:** She does not realize that because no water has been added or taken away, the amount of water in the two glasses must be equivalent. Young children often confuse changes in appearance with changes in amount. Piaget suggested that, in general, children in the preoperational stage depend more on perception than on logic when they reason.

As children approach the later part of the preoperational stage, perhaps at around 4 or 5 years of age, they show early signs of being logical. For example, they sometimes draw correct conclusions about conservation problems (e.g., the water glasses) or multiple classification problems (e.g., the wooden beads). They cannot yet explain *why* their conclusions are correct, however; they base their reasoning on hunches and intuition rather than on any conscious awareness of underlying logical principles. When children move into the concrete operations stage, they become increasingly able both to make logical inferences and to explain the reasoning behind their conclusions.

Concrete Operations Stage (Age 6 or 7 Years Until Age 11 or 12) At about age 6 or 7, children's thinking processes become integrated into *operations* that allow them to pull their thoughts and ideas together more effectively than they have before. As a result, concrete operational thought is more advanced than preoperational thought in a number of ways (see Table 4–1). For example, children now realize that their own thoughts and feelings are not necessarily shared by others and may reflect personal opinions rather than reality. Accordingly, they know that they can sometimes be wrong and begin to seek out external validation for their ideas, asking such questions as "What do you think?" and "Did I get that problem right?"

Children in the concrete operations stage are capable of many forms of logical thought. For instance, they show conservation: They readily understand that if nothing is added or taken away, amount stays the same despite any changes in shape or arrangement. (Hence, they would have no trouble with the water glasses problem that Lucy struggled with.) They also exhibit **multiple classification:** They can readily classify objects into two categories simultaneously. (Recall 8-year-old Natalie's ease in solving the wooden beads vs. brown beads problem.) And they demonstrate **deductive reasoning:** They can draw logical inferences from the facts they are given.

Children continue to develop their newly acquired logical thinking capabilities throughout the elementary school years. For instance, over time they become capable of dealing with increasingly more complex conservation tasks. Some forms of conservation, such as conservation of liquid and conservation of number (the latter illustrated by the "pennies" problem in Table 4–1), appear at age 6 or 7, but other forms may not appear until several years later. Consider the task involving conservation of weight depicted in Figure 4–3. Using a balance scale,

conservation
Realization that if nothing is added or taken away, amount stays the same regardless of any alterations in shape or arrangement.

multiple classification
Recognition that objects may belong to several categories simultaneously.

deductive reasoning
Drawing a logical inference about something that must be true given other information that has already been presented as true.

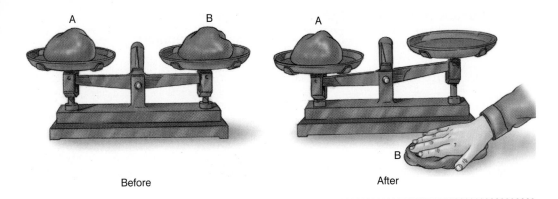

Before   After

FIGURE 4–3 Conservation of weight: Balls A and B initially weigh the same. When Ball B is flattened into a pancake shape, how does its weight now compare with that of Ball A?

an adult shows a child that two balls of clay have the same weight. One ball is removed from the scale and smashed into a pancake shape. Does the pancake weigh the same as the un-smashed ball, or do the two pieces of clay weigh different amounts? Children typically do not achieve conservation of weight—that is, they do not realize that the flattened pancake weighs the same as the round ball it was previously—until sometime around age 9 to 12 (Sund, 1976).

Although children displaying concrete operational thought show many signs of logical thinking, their cognitive development is not yet complete (see Table 4–2). They have difficulty thinking about proportions and ratios, formulating and testing hypotheses, and separating and controlling variables—processes central to adult forms of mathematical and scientific reasoning. They also have trouble understanding and reasoning about abstract ideas. In mathematics, this weakness may be reflected in their confusion about such concepts as *pi* (π), *infinity,* and *negative number.* In social studies, it may limit their comprehension of such abstract notions as democracy, communism, and human rights. Finally, children who show concrete operational thought are likely to have difficulty reasoning about ideas that involve hypothetical situations or contradict reality.

A Piaget (1928) study with children of various ages illustrates. In it, the experimenter presents this problem: *Someone said, "If ever I kill myself from despair I won't choose a Friday, because Friday is a bad day and would bring me ill luck." What's silly about that?* Several children respond:

9-year-old:	People can kill themselves every day; they don't need to kill themselves on a Friday.
9-year-old:	Friday is not unlucky.
10-year-old:	Perhaps Friday will bring him good luck.
11-year-old:	He doesn't know if it will bring him ill luck. (responses from Piaget, 1928, pp. 63, 65)

The true "silliness" of the situation is, of course, that people who commit suicide don't have to worry about any subsequent bad luck. Yet many elementary school children fail to make the connection; instead, they deny that Friday is a bad day or reject the idea that people can or might kill themselves (Copeland, 1979).

Formal Operations Stage (Age 11 or 12 Through Adulthood) Consider this task:

An object suspended by a rope or string—a pendulum—swings indefinitely at a constant rate. Some pendulums swing back and forth very quickly, whereas others swing more slowly.

One or more of four variables might affect a pendulum's oscillation rate (i.e., how fast it swings): the weight of the suspended object, the force with which the object is pushed, the

TABLE 4–2   Concrete Operational Versus Formal Operational Thought

CONCRETE OPERATIONAL THOUGHT	FORMAL OPERATIONAL THOUGHT
Dependence on concrete reality Logical reasoning only about concrete objects that are readily observed. *Example:* A child has difficulty with the concept of negative numbers, wondering how something can possibly be less than zero.	**Ability to reason about abstract, hypothetical, and contrary-to-fact ideas** Logical reasoning about things that are not tied directly to concrete, observable reality. *Example:* A child understands negative numbers and is able to use them effectively in mathematical procedures and problems.
Inability to formulate and test multiple hypotheses Identifying and testing only one hypothesis when seeking an explanation for a scientific phenomenon. *Example:* When asked what makes a pendulum swing faster or more slowly, a child states that the weight of the pendulum is the determining factor and disregards any observations she has made that contradict her hypothesis.	**Formulation and testing of multiple hypotheses** Developing and testing several hypotheses about cause-effect relationships related to a particular phenomenon. *Example:* When asked what makes a pendulum swing faster or more slowly, a child proposes that weight, length, and strength of initial push are all possible explanations and then tests the effects of each variable.
Inability to separate and control variables Confounding two or more variables when attempting to confirm or disconfirm a particular hypothesis about a cause-effect relationship. *Example:* In testing possible factors influencing the oscillation rate of a pendulum, a child adds more weight to the pendulum while at the same time also shortening the length of the pendulum.	**Separation and control of variables** Testing one variable at a time while holding all others constant, in an attempt to confirm or disconfirm a particular hypothesis about a cause-effect relationship. *Example:* In testing factors that influence a pendulum's oscillation rate, a child tests the effect of weight while keeping string length and strength of push constant and then tests the effect of length while keeping weight and push constant.
Lack of proportional reasoning Lack of understanding about the nature of proportions. *Example:* A child cannot make sense of the procedure his teacher demonstrates for converting fractions to ratios.	**Proportional reasoning** Understanding proportions and using them effectively in mathematical problem solving. *Example:* A child works easily with proportions, fractions, decimals, and ratios.
Lack of combinatorial thought Difficulty identifying all possible combinations of several objects, such that various combinations are identified in an unsystematic, random fashion. *Example:* A child asked to identify the ways in which four objects (A, B, C, D) might be combined generates four combinations (AB, CD, AD, ABCD) and then cannot think of any more.	**Combinatorial thought** Systematic identification of all possible combinations of several objects. *Example:* A child asked to identify possible combinations of four objects generates all 15 possibilities (A, B, C, D, AB, AC, AD, BC, BD, CD, ABC, ABD, ACD, BCD, and ABCD).

height from which the object is initially released, and the length of the string that holds the object. Design an experiment that can help you determine which of these factors affect(s) a pendulum's oscillation rate.

To identify the one or more factors that influence oscillation rate, you must *separate and control variables:* You must test one factor at a time while holding all others constant. For instance, to test the hypothesis that weight makes a difference, you should try different weights while keeping constant the force with which you push each weight, the height from which you drop it, and the length of the string. Similarly, if you hypothesize that the length of the string is a critical factor, you should vary the length of the string while continuing to use the same weight and starting the pendulum in motion in the same manner. If you carefully separate and control the variables, then your observations should lead you to conclude that only *length* affects a pendulum's oscillation rate.

Piaget and his colleague Bärbel Inhelder asked children of many ages to tackle the pendulum problem. The following two examples, with children we'll call Craig and Emily, illustrate how children of different ages responded to the problem.

Craig, age 10, begins his experimentation with a long string and a 100-gram weight. He then shortens the string and changes to a 200-gram weight, which he drops from a higher point.

Exp: Did you find out anything?
Craig: The little one goes more slowly and the higher it is the faster it goes.

He puts the 50-gram weight on the same short string.

Craig: The little weight goes even faster.

He then ignores what he just observed.

Craig: To go faster, you have to pull up [shorten] the string, and the little one goes less fast because it is less heavy.
Exp: Do you still wonder what you have to do to make it go faster?
Craig: The little weight goes faster.
Exp: How can you prove it?
Craig: You have to pull up the string. (dialogue from Inhelder & Piaget, 1958, p. 71)

Emily, age 15, at first believes that each of the four factors is influential. She studies different weights with the same string length (medium) and does not notice any appreciable change.

Emily: That doesn't change the rhythm.

She then varies the string length, using the same 200-gram weight.

Emily: When the string is small, the swing is faster.

Finally, she varies the dropping point and then the strength of the push, each time using the same medium length string and the same 200-gram weight.

Emily: Nothing has changed. (dialogue from Inhelder & Piaget, 1958, pp. 75–76)

Notice how Craig changes weight and length simultaneously when he experiments, and he has difficulty separating the two variables even when he draws his conclusions (e.g., to prove that weight makes a difference, he says that "You have to pull up the string"). In contrast, Emily systematically tests each of the four variables in isolation from the other three, and she correctly concludes that only length makes a difference.

According to Piaget, several abilities essential for sophisticated scientific and mathematical reasoning emerge in formal operations (see Table 4–2). Three of these—reasoning logically about hypothetical ideas, formulating and testing hypotheses, and separating and controlling variables—together allow adolescents to use the *scientific method,* in which several possible explanations for an observed phenomenon are proposed and tested in a systematic manner. Only with formal operational thinking can people address and answer questions about cause-effect relationships in a truly scientific fashion.

Capabilities in mathematics are also likely to improve once formal operational thinking develops. Abstract problems, such as mathematical word problems, should become easier to solve. Students should become capable of understanding such concepts as *negative number* and *infinity*; for instance, they should now comprehend how temperature can be below zero and how two parallel lines will never touch even if they go on forever. And because they can now use proportions in their reasoning, they can study and understand fractions, ratios, and decimals, and they can use such proportions to solve problems.

Because adolescents capable of formal operational reasoning can deal with hypothetical and contrary-to-fact ideas, they can envision how the world might be different from, and possibly better than, the way it actually is. (Brady's cartoon in Figure 4–4 is an example.) As a result, they may exhibit some idealism

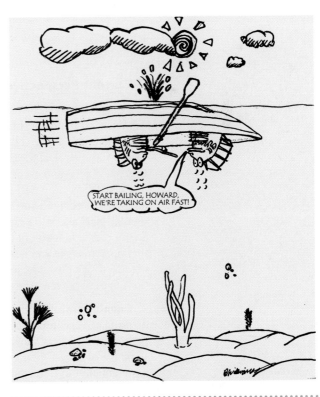

FIGURE 4–4 One characteristic of Piaget's formal operations stage is the ability to imagine alternatives to reality. At age 14, Brady Williamson drew this cartoon (partly by computer, partly by hand) of two fish rowing a boat upside-down at the water's surface.

Piaget's Theory of Cognitive Development | **113**

about social, political, religious, and ethical issues. For example, secondary school students often argue that they should be allowed to wear anything they want to school, no matter how skimpy or suggestive their fashion choices might be. They may reject their parents' political or religious affiliations and seek out alternative belief systems. Many secondary school students begin to show concern about world problems and devote some of their energy to worthy causes such as the environment, world hunger, or animal rights. Curiously, however, their devotion may sometimes be more evident in their talk than in their actions (Elkind, 1984).

As adolescents become increasingly able to reason about abstract, hypothetical, and contrary-to-fact ideas, they also become increasingly idealistic about how the world should be.

Idealistic adolescents often present recommendations for change that seem logical but aren't practical in today's world. For example, they may argue that racism would disappear overnight if people would only just begin to "love one another," or they may propose that a nation should disband its armed forces and eliminate all its weaponry as a way of moving toward world peace. Piaget suggested that adolescent idealism reflects **formal operational egocentrism,** an inability to separate one's own logical abstractions from the perspectives of others and from practical considerations. It is only through experience that adolescents eventually begin to temper their optimism with some realism about what is possible in a given time frame and with limited resources.

Current Perspectives on Piaget's Theory

Piaget's theory has inspired hundreds of research studies concerning the nature of children's cognitive development. In general, research supports Piaget's proposed *sequence* in which different abilities emerge (Flavell, 1996; Siegler & Richards, 1982). For example, the ability to reason about abstract ideas emerges only after children are already capable of reasoning about concrete objects and events, and the order in which various conservation tasks are mastered is much as Piaget proposed. Researchers have discovered, however, that Piaget was not always accurate regarding the *ages* at which various abilities appear. They have found, too, that children's logical reasoning capabilities may vary considerably from one occasion to another and are, in part, a function of previous knowledge and experiences, education, and culture. Furthermore, many researchers question the stagelike nature of cognitive development that Piaget described. We turn now to these issues; we then identify some of Piaget's enduring contributions to developmental psychology.

Capabilities of Infants A growing body of research indicates that Piaget probably underestimated the thinking capabilities of young infants. By 5 months of age, infants look surprised when objects vanish unexpectedly, supporting the idea that they have some understanding of object permanence earlier than Piaget believed (Baillargeon, 1994). Mental representation of observed events (i.e., symbolic thinking) also emerges sooner than Piaget proposed. Infants as young as 9 months can remember actions that adults perform (e.g., shaking a plastic egg, pushing a button on a box) long enough to imitate them 24 hours later (Meltzoff, 1988).

Some developmental theorists argue that infants' brains are "preprogrammed" to a certain degree—that infants are born already possessing some basic knowledge, or at least some preliminary

formal operational egocentrism
Inability of an individual in Piaget's formal operations stage to separate one's own abstract logic from the perspectives of others and from practical considerations.

intuitions, about their world (e.g., Baillargeon, 1994; Spelke, 1994). For instance, even very young infants seem to know that an object maintains its existence and shape as it moves, that one object can influence another only when the two come into contact, and that two objects cannot occupy the same space at the same time (Spelke, 1994). This idea of preprogrammed knowledge or inclinations, known as **nativism,** is particularly prevalent in theoretical views of language development; hence, we will encounter it again in Chapter 7.

The proposal that some knowledge is "built in" has been a source of considerable controversy among developmental theorists. Ultimately, we must await further research to determine the extent to which the human brain is hard-wired with what it either "knows" or is prepared to learn easily.

Capabilities of Preschoolers Preschool children are probably more competent than Piaget's description of the preoperational stage would indicate. Children as young as 3 or 4 years old are not completely egocentric; in many situations, they *can* take another person's perspective. For example, they recognize that an object looks different when viewed from different angles, and they can identify such emotions as sadness or anger in others (Lennon, Eisenberg, & Carroll, 1983; Newcombe & Huttenlocher, 1992).

Preschoolers also think more logically than Piaget suggested. They can draw logically valid deductions; for instance, they often make appropriate inferences when they listen to stories (Donaldson, 1978; Gelman & Baillargeon, 1983). Children as young as 4 sometimes show conservation; they are more likely to answer a conservation problem correctly if the transformation occurs out of sight, so that they are not misled by appearances (Donaldson, 1978; Rosser, 1994). And many supposedly preoperational children can correctly solve multiple classification problems if words are used to draw attention to the entire group; for example, many 4- and 5-year-olds realize that, in a *forest* of eight pine trees and two oak trees, there must, of course, be more trees than pine trees (Gelman & Baillargeon, 1983; Resnick, 1989; Rosser, 1994).

Why have Piaget and more recent researchers sometimes found conflicting results? Theorists have offered several explanations. One possibility is that the children in Piaget's studies sometimes misinterpreted the wordings of his problems (Reyna, 1996; Rosser, 1994). For example, when water is poured from a short, fat glass into a tall, skinny one, a child might say that the tall one has more water because she misconstrues the word *more* to mean "higher." Sometimes, too, a problem may have more pieces (e.g., more pennies in a conservation-of-number task) than a child can reasonably keep track of and remember (Gelman, 1972).

On some occasions, children may simply say what they think an adult expects them to say (Winer, Craig, & Weinbaum, 1992). For instance, when a researcher asks the same question twice (e.g., "Do the two glasses have the same amount of water?" and later, "Do they *still* have the same amount?"), children may conclude that a change *must* have occurred; otherwise, the researcher would not have repeated the question.

Capabilities of Elementary School Children Piaget may have underestimated the capabilities of elementary age children as well. Children in this age group occasionally show evidence of abstract and hypothetical thought (Carey, 1985b; Metz, 1995). As an illustration, consider this hypothetical (and therefore formal operational) situation:

All of Joan's friends are going to the museum today.
Pat is a friend of Joan.

Children as young as 9 can correctly deduce that "Pat is going to the museum today" even though the situation involves people they don't know and so has no basis in their own concrete reality (Roberge, 1970). Also, elementary school children can sometimes separate and control variables, especially when the tasks are simplified and they are given hints about the importance of controlling all variables except the one they are testing (Danner & Day, 1977; Metz, 1995; Ruffman, Perner, Olson, & Doherty, 1993).

Capabilities of Adolescents Formal operational thought processes probably emerge much more gradually than Piaget originally proposed. High school and college students often have difficulty with tasks involving such formal operational thinking abilities as separation

nativism
Theoretical perspective that some knowledge is biologically built-in and present at birth.

and control of variables, proportional reasoning, and combinatorial thought (Flieller, 1999; Kuhn, Amsel, & O'Loughlin, 1988; Pascarella & Terenzini, 1991; Siegler & Richards, 1982). Furthermore, students may demonstrate formal operational thought in one content domain while thinking more concretely in another. Evidence of formal operations typically emerges in the physical sciences earlier than in such subjects as history and geography; adolescents often have difficulty thinking about abstract and hypothetical ideas in history and geography until well into the high school years (Lovell, 1979; Tamburrini, 1982).

Effects of Prior Knowledge and Experience

Piaget believed that once children acquire a particular reasoning skill, they can apply it in virtually any context. It is becoming increasingly apparent, however, that for people of all ages, the ability to think logically in a particular situation depends on knowledge and background experiences relative to that situation. Preschoolers are less likely to exhibit the "illogic" of transductive reasoning (e.g., to say that clouds make the moon grow) when they have accurate information about cause-effect relationships (Carey, 1985a). Children as young as 4 may begin to show conservation after having experience with conservation tasks, especially if they can actively manipulate the materials of the tasks and are asked

Having a great deal of knowledge about a particular topic often allows students to engage in formal operational thought; however, the students may continue to think concretely about less familiar topics.

to discuss their reasoning with someone who already exhibits conservation (Field, 1987; Mayer, 1992; Murray, 1978). And in general, young children are more likely to think in a concrete operational rather than preoperational fashion when they are familiar with the objects they are dealing with (Ceci & Roazzi, 1994).

Formal operational thought, too, is affected by the specific knowledge and experiences that children and adolescents have acquired. Ten-year-olds can learn to solve logical problems involving hypothetical ideas if they are taught particular strategies for solving such problems (Lee, 1985). Students in the upper elementary and middle school grades are better able to separate and control variables in laboratory experiments when they have practice and guidance in doing so (Kuhn & Phelps, 1982; Ross, 1988). Junior high and high school students, and adults as well, often apply formal operational thought to topics about which they have a great deal of knowledge yet think "concrete operationally" about topics with which they are unfamiliar (Linn, Clement, Pulos, & Sullivan, 1989; Metz, 1995; Schliemann & Carraher, 1993).

As an illustration of how knowledge affects formal operational thinking, consider the fishing pond in Figure 4–5. In a study by Pulos and Linn (1981), 13-year-olds were shown a similar picture and told, "These four children go fishing every week, and one child, Herb, always catches the most fish. The other children wonder why." If you look at the picture, it is obvious that Herb is different from the three other children in several ways, including the kind of bait he uses, the length of his fishing rod, and the place where he is standing. Children who were experienced fishermen more effectively separated and controlled variables for this situation than they did for the pendulum problem described earlier, whereas the reverse was true for nonfishermen (Pulos & Linn, 1981).

One general experience that promotes more advanced reasoning is formal education: Going to school and the specific nature of one's schooling are associated with mastery of concrete operational and formal operational tasks (Artman & Cahan, 1993; Flieller, 1999). For instance, you may be happy to learn that taking college courses in a particular area (in child development, perhaps?) leads to improvements in formal reasoning skills related to that area (Lehman & Nisbett, 1990).

Effects of Culture Piaget proposed that his stages were universal, that they applied to children and adolescents around the globe. Yet research indicates that the course of cognitive development differs somewhat from one culture to another (Glick, 1975). For example, Mexican children whose families make pottery for a living acquire conservation skills much earlier than Piaget indicated (Price-Williams, Gordon, & Ramirez, 1969). Apparently, making pottery requires children to make frequent judgments about needed quantities of clay and water—judgments that must be fairly accurate regardless of the specific shape or form that the clay or water container takes. In other cultures, especially in those where children don't attend school, conservation appears several years later than it does in Western cultures, and formal operational reasoning may never appear at all (Cole, 1990; Fahrmeier, 1978). In such contexts, some logical reasoning skills may simply have little relevance to people's daily functioning (J. G. Miller, 1997).

Does Cognitive Development Occur in Stages? As you have seen, Piaget was not completely on target in terms of when certain abilities develop and, in some cases, whether they develop at all. He also overestimated the extent to which children generalize newly acquired reasoning skills to a broad range of tasks and contexts.

In light of all the evidence, does it still make sense to talk about discrete stages of cognitive development? A few theorists say yes. In particular, *neo-Piagetian* theorists have proposed stage theories that may more adequately account for current findings about children's logical thinking. However, most contemporary developmentalists believe that cognitive development is not as stagelike as Piaget proposed—that a child does not reason in consistently logical or illogical ways at any particular time period (Flavell, 1994). Although children exhibit certain developmental *trends* in their thinking (e.g., a trend toward increasingly abstract thought), their knowledge in particular domains will influence the sophistication of their reasoning.

A perspective known as *information processing theory* characterizes some of the general trends in cognitive processes that we are likely to see as children develop. We describe both information processing theory and neo-Piagetian theories (which draw from information processing theory as well as from Piaget's ideas) in Chapter 5.

Piaget's Enduring Contributions Despite the concerns we have raised, Piaget's theory has had a profound influence on contemporary theories of cognitive development. Piaget's lasting contributions to our understanding of children's thinking include the following:

■ *Cognitive development is, to a considerable degree, propelled by intrinsic motivation.* As you have seen, Piaget believed that children are naturally curious about their environment and so actively explore it to learn as much as they can. They are especially motivated when they encounter surprising or puzzling events (those that create disequilibrium). Many contemporary theories of cognition and cognitive development retain such notions of intrinsic motivation: Growing children *want* to learn more about the people, objects, and events around them and so naturally engage in the kinds of behaviors and activities that bring about increasingly more complex and accurate understandings over time.

■ *The nature of thinking and reasoning changes with age.* Whether we talk about discrete stages or more general trends, it is clear that *something* inside changes over time. Piaget explained these changes in terms of such concepts as *schemes* and *operations.* As you will discover in Chapter 5, contemporary theorists are more apt to speak of changes in working memory, long-term memory, cognitive strategies, metacognitive knowledge, and mental "theories" about the nature of living beings and inanimate objects.

■ *Piaget's stages provide a general idea of when new abilities are likely to emerge.* Piaget identified and documented many characteristics of children's thinking that researchers continue to study today. We list several of them in the Observation Guidelines table on the following page, where we also give suggestions for classroom practice.

Although we have, we hope, dissuaded you from taking Piaget's stages at face value, we urge you to keep them in mind when considering the kinds of tasks that children and adolescents probably can and cannot do at different ages. Some of these abilities and *in*abilities may be a function of knowledge and experience (or lack thereof) and therefore amenable to change under the right circumstances, whereas others (perhaps because of neurological factors) may be more dependent on time and maturation (Metz, 1997). It is important to remember, too, that children don't necessarily discard their earlier ways of thinking when they acquire more sophisticated ones. For instance, even when children acquire the ability to think abstractly, they may continue to think concretely, and occasionally in a "sensorimotor" fashion, about many of the situations they encounter.

■ *Piaget's clinical method reveals a great deal about children's thinking processes.* The many tasks that Piaget developed to study children's reasoning abilities—tasks dealing with conservation, classification, separation and control of variables, and so on—and the kinds of probing follow-up questions that he pioneered yield invaluable insights about the "logic" that children and adolescents use when they think about their world. Researchers and practitioners alike frequently use Piaget's tasks and method in their efforts to uncover how children and adolescents think and learn.

■ *Through their interactions with their physical and social environments, children construct their own view of the world.* Virtually all developmentalists share the view that manipulation of physical objects and interactions with other people are *essential* for cognitive development. Furthermore, the idea that children don't just "absorb" such experiences—that they actively try to interpret and make sense of them, and then integrate what they've learned into more general, personally constructed understandings—plays prominently in many contemporary views of learning and cognition. The view that people construct rather than absorb knowledge is generally known as **constructivism.** More specifically, because it focuses on constructive processes within a single person, it is sometimes called **individual constructivism.**

■ *Children benefit only from experiences that they can relate to what they already know.* In Piaget's view, accommodation typically occurs only when it is accompanied by some degree of assimilation. New knowledge, understandings, and reasoning processes (new schemes) are typically derived from previously acquired knowledge and processes (existing schemes). Contemporary developmentalists embrace this idea of *new acquisitions being based on earlier ones* almost without exception. Developmentally speaking, new knowledge, skills, and cognitive processes don't just appear out of thin air.

constructivism
Theoretical perspective proposing that learners construct a body of knowledge from their experiences, rather than absorbing knowledge at face value.

individual constructivism
Theoretical perspective that focuses on how people construct meaning from events without the assistance of others.

Assessing Students' Reasoning Skills

OBSERVATION GUIDELINES

CHARACTERISTIC	LOOK FOR	EXAMPLE	IMPLICATION
Preoperational Egocentrism	• Describing events without giving listeners sufficient information to understand them • Playing group games without initially agreeing about rules • Difficulty understanding others' perspectives	Luisa doesn't understand why she must share a box of art materials with the other children at her table.	Let children know when you don't understand what they are telling you; ask them to share their ideas and opinions with one another.
Concrete Thought	• Dependence on concrete manipulatives to understand concepts and principles • Difficulty understanding abstract ideas	Tobey solves arithmetic word problems more easily when he can draw pictures of them.	Use concrete objects and examples to illustrate abstract situations.
Abstract Thought	• Ability to understand strictly verbal explanations of abstract concepts and principles • Ability to reason about hypothetical or contrary-to-fact situations	Ilsa can imagine how two parallel lines might go on forever without ever coming together.	Occasionally rely on verbal explanations (e.g., short lectures) with adolescents, but assess students' understanding frequently to make sure they understand.
Formal Operational Egocentrism	• Idealistic notions about how the world should be • Inability to adjust ideals in light of what can realistically be accomplished	Martin advocates a system of government in which all citizens contribute their earnings to a common "pool" and then withdraw money only as they need it.	Engage adolescents in discussions about challenging political and social issues.
Scientific Reasoning Skills	• Identifying multiple hypotheses for a particular phenomenon • Separation and control of variables	Serena proposes three possible explanations for a result she has obtained in her physics lab.	Have students design and conduct simple experiments; include experiments about issues related to their backgrounds and interests.
Mathematical Reasoning Skills	• Understanding and using proportions in mathematical problem solving • Identifying all possible combinations and permutations	Giorgio uses a 1:240 scale when drawing a floor plan of his school building.	Introduce abstract mathematical concepts and tasks (e.g., proportional reasoning, combinatorial thought) using simple examples (e.g., fractions such as ⅓ and ¼, all possible arrangements of 3 objects)

Educational Implications of Piaget's Theory and Post-Piagetian Research

Piaget's theory and the body of research it has inspired have numerous implications for teachers, including the following:

■ *Provide opportunities for students to experiment with physical objects and natural phenomena.* Children of all ages can learn a great deal from exploring the natural world in a hands-on fashion. At the preschool level, this might involve playing with water, sand, wooden blocks, and age-appropriate manipulative toys. During the elementary school years, it might entail such activities as throwing and catching balls, going on nature walks, working with clay and watercolor paints, or constructing Popsicle-stick structures.

Despite the increased capabilities for abstract thought in adolescence, high school students also benefit from opportunities to manipulate and experiment with concrete materials—

APPLYING PIAGET'S THEORY

■ Provide hands-on experiences with physical objects, especially when working with elementary school students. Allow and encourage students to explore and manipulate things.

A kindergarten teacher and his students work with small objects (e.g., blocks, buttons, pennies) to explore such basic elements of arithmetic as conservation of number and the idea that addition and subtraction are reversible processes.

■ Provide opportunities for students to share their ideas and perspectives with one another.

A high school history teacher has students meet in small groups to debate the pros and cons of the United States' decision to become actively involved in the Vietnam War.

■ Present puzzling phenomena.

A second-grade teacher crumples a paper towel and places it inside an otherwise empty glass. She asks students to predict what will happen to the towel when she places the glass upside-down in a bowl of water. Many students predict that the paper towel will get wet. The teacher performs the experiment; when she removes the glass from the water, the students discover that the paper towel is completely dry.

■ Relate abstract and hypothetical ideas to concrete objects and observable events.

A middle school science teacher illustrates the idea that heavy and light objects fall at the same speed by having students drop objects of various weights from a second-story window.

perhaps equipment in a science lab, cameras and film, food and cooking utensils, or wood and woodworking tools. Such opportunities allow them to discover laws of the natural world firsthand and to tie their newly emerging abstract ideas to the physical, concrete world.

■ *Explore students' reasoning with problem-solving tasks and probing questions.* By presenting a variety of Piagetian tasks involving either concrete or formal operational thinking skills—tasks involving conservation, multiple classification, separation and control of variables, proportional reasoning, and so on—and observing students' responses to such tasks, teachers can gain valuable insights into how their students think and reason. They can then tailor the classroom curriculum and instructional materials accordingly. Figure 4–6 presents an example of a Piagetian task that a teacher might use to probe students' reasoning processes about the concept of *area.*

To probe students' reasoning in novel situations, teachers need not stick to traditional Piagetian reasoning tasks. On the contrary, such strategies are applicable to a wide variety of academic domains and subject matter. For example, Liben and Downs (1989) showed young children (kindergartners, first graders, and second graders) various kinds of maps (e.g., a road map of Pennsylvania, an aerial map of Chicago, a three-dimensional relief map of a mountainous area) and asked the children to interpret what they saw. The children interpreted many of the symbols in a concrete fashion. For example, some correctly recognized some of the roads "because they are gray" but thought that the roads marked in red were actually painted red. The children also had trouble understanding the scales of the maps (a finding consistent with Piaget's belief that proportional reasoning doesn't emerge until early adolescence). For example, one child rejected the idea that a road could be a road because it was "too skinny for two cars to fit on," and another denied that mountains on a relief map were mountains because "they aren't high enough."

■ *Keep Piaget's stages in mind when interpreting children's behavior and developing lesson plans, but don't take the stages too literally.* Piaget's four stages are not always accurate descriptions of students' logical thinking capabilities. Nevertheless, teachers might think of the stages as giving some clues about the thinking and reasoning processes they are apt to see in students at various age levels (Kuhn, 1997; Metz, 1997). For example, preschool teachers should not be surprised to see young children arguing that the three pieces of a broken candy bar constitute more candy than a similar, unbroken bar (a belief that reflects lack of conservation). Elementary school teachers should recognize that their students are likely to have difficulty with proportions (e.g., fractions, decimals) and with such abstract concepts as *historical time* in history and *place value, negative number,* and *pi* in mathematics (Barton & Levstik, 1996; Byrnes, 1996; Tourniaire & Pulos, 1985). And high school teachers should expect to hear their adolescent students debating passionately about idealistic yet unrealistic notions about how society should operate.

Materials:
2 sheets of 8½" by 11" green construction paper
2 small toy (perhaps plastic) cows
24 sugar cubes or equal-size small wooden blocks

Procedure:
In Piaget's clinical method, the interviewer tailors questions to the particular things that a child has previously said and done, but such flexibility often comes only with considerable experience. Here we present a procedure that a novice interviewer might use in presenting a conservation-of-area task.

1. Lay the 2 sheets of construction paper side by side, and place a cow on each sheet. Say, *These two cows are grazing in their pastures. Do they each have the same amount of grass to eat?* The student will probably say yes. Place a cube on each sheet and say, *A farmer builds a barn in each pasture. Do the two cows still have the same amount of grass to eat, or does one cow have more than the other?* The student will probably say that the cows each have the same amount.
2. Add 3 more cubes to each sheet. On the first sheet, place the cubes next to the first cube so that they form a square. On the second sheet, scatter 3 additional cubes around the pasture. Ask, *The farmer builds three more barns in each pasture, like this. Do the cows still have the same amount of grass to eat, or does one have more?*

3. Place 8 more cubes on the first sheet, placing them next to the square so that the 12 cubes form a rectangle. Place 8 more cubes on the second sheet, scattering them around the pasture. Ask, *The farmer builds eight more barns in each pasture, like this. Do the cows still have the same amount of grass to eat, or does one have more?* After the student responds, ask, *How do you know?*
4. If the student says that both cows have the same amount, say, *The other day, someone told me that this cow has more to eat* (point to the cow on the second sheet). *What could you do or say to convince that person that the two cows have the same amount?*

Interpretation:
Students who have fully achieved conservation of area realize that the amount of grass is the same if the same number of barns are placed in each pasture, despite the different arrangements of the barns. To justify a "same" response, students might (a) explain that the same number of barns cover the same amount of grass regardless of their arrangement or (b) move the scattered barns in the second pasture into a rectangular shape similar to that of the barns in the first pasture. In Piaget's theory, conservation of area appears early in the concrete operations stage.

FIGURE 4–6 Conservation of area: An example of how a teacher might probe students' reasoning processes with Piaget's clinical method

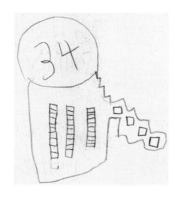

FIGURE 4–7 Noah's depiction of the number 34

Piaget's stages also provide guidance about strategies that are likely to be effective in teaching students at different grade levels. For instance, given the abstract nature of historical time, elementary school teachers planning history lessons should probably minimize the extent to which they talk about specific dates before the recent past (Barton & Levstik, 1996). Also, particularly in the elementary grades (and to a lesser degree in middle and high school), teachers should find ways to make abstract ideas more concrete for their students. As one simple example, a third-grade teacher, realizing that *place value* might be a difficult concept for third graders to comprehend, showed her students how to depict two-digit numbers with blocks, using 10-block rows for the number in the 10s column and single blocks for the number in the 1s column. We present 8-year-old Noah's drawing of "34" in Figure 4–7.

■ *Present situations and ideas that students cannot easily explain using their existing knowledge and beliefs.* Events and information that conflict with students' current understandings create disequilibrium that may motivate students to reevaluate and perhaps modify what they "know" to be true. For instance, if students believe that "light objects float and heavy objects sink" or that "wood floats and metal sinks," a teacher can present a common counterexample: a metal battleship (floating, of course) that weighs many tons.

■ *Plan group activities in which students share their beliefs and perspectives with one another.* As noted earlier, Piaget proposed that interaction with peers helps children realize that others often view the world very differently than they do and that their own ideas are not always completely logical or accurate ones. Interactions with age-mates, especially those that involve conflicts or differences of opinion, are likely to create disequilibrium and thus spur children to reevaluate their current perspectives.

Many contemporary psychologists share Piaget's belief in the importance of such **sociocognitive conflict** (e.g., Damon, 1984; Webb & Palincsar, 1996). They have offered several reasons why interactions with peers may help promote cognitive growth:

* Peers speak at a level that children can understand.
* Whereas children may accept an adult's ideas without argument, they are more willing to challenge and contest the ideas of their peers.
* When children hear competing views held by peers—individuals who presumably have knowledge and abilities similar to their own—they may be motivated to reconcile the contradictions.
(Champagne & Bunce, 1991; Damon, 1984; Hatano & Inagaki, 1991)

A study by Bell, Grossen, and Perret-Clermont (1985) illustrates the effect that sociocognitive conflict can have on young children's logical reasoning capabilities. Young children who did not yet demonstrate conservation of liquid (i.e., they stated that two differently shaped glasses contained different amounts of water) were each paired with a same-age partner and asked to play a "game" in which the two had to share equal amounts of juice. The experimenter gave the nonconserving children two glasses, one taller and thinner than the other, and asked them to pour the same amount of juice into each one. In most cases, the children poured juice to equal heights in the two glasses, which provoked disagreement from their partners. The "game" ended only after the children and their partners both agreed that they had the same amount of juice to drink. On a conservation posttest a week later, the children showed greater gains in their ability to conserve liquid than a control group who had worked with the same materials alone.

Research by Kuhn, Shaw, and Felton (1997) illustrates similar effects of peer interaction and conflict for adolescents. For five successive weeks, seventh and eighth graders met in pairs to discuss capital punishment, a topic about which many of them had strong yet varying opinions. Students were paired with different partners each week so that, over the course of the experiment, they were exposed to opinions both consistent and discrepant with their own. During the paired discussions, the students were observed asking questions that clearly challenged one another's reasoning (e.g., "What do you mean by 'justifiable'?"; "Do you think that [capital punishment] is going to stop them from doing that?"). After the fifth discussion, the researchers found that the students' reasoning about capital punishment had changed in several important ways:

* The students had a better understanding of both the pros and cons of capital punishment.
* Although few students completely reversed their positions on capital punishment, many took a less extreme stance on the issue.

sociocognitive conflict
Encountering and having to wrestle with ideas and viewpoints different from one's own.

- The students identified more reasons for believing as they did than they had before the discussions.
- The students showed greater awareness that multiple and possibly equally legitimate perspectives could exist about the issue.

When using group interaction to help students acquire more sophisticated understandings, keep in mind that students can also learn *misinformation* from one another (Good, McCaslin, & Reys, 1992). It is essential, then, that teachers closely monitor discussions and correct for any misconceptions or misinterpretations that students may pass on to their classmates.

■ *Use familiar content and tasks when asking students to reason in sophisticated ways.* Earlier we presented evidence to indicate that children and adolescents display more advanced reasoning skills when they work with topics they know well. With such evidence in mind, teachers might ask students to

- Conserve liquid within the context of a juice-sharing task (as Bell and her colleagues did).
- Separate and control variables within the context of an activity the students engage in regularly (perhaps fishing, playing sports, or riding a bicycle).
- Consider abstract ideas about subject matter that students have already studied in depth in a concrete fashion.

In Piaget's theory, cognitive development is largely an individual enterprise: By assimilating and accommodating to new experiences, children develop increasingly more advanced and integrated schemes over time. From this perspective, then, it seems that children do most of the mental "work" themselves. In contrast, another early developmental theory—that of the Russian psychologist Lev Vygotsky—places much of the responsibility for a child's development on the adults in the child's society and culture. From Vygotsky's perspective, children's interactions with adults play a critical role in fostering the development of skills and thinking capabilities essential for success in the adult world. We turn now to this very different, yet equally influential, theory of cognitive development.

Vygotsky's Theory of Cognitive Development

In the "Whale Watching" case at the beginning of the chapter, a mother helps her daughter understand and interpret what might otherwise have been a very confusing event for a 6-year-old. In particular, Mother helps Kerry recall the family members who were present, attaches labels to aspects of the experience (e.g., "disaster," "seasick"), and questions Kerry's assessment of the number of whales encountered on the trip.

Vygotsky proposed that adults promote children's cognitive development by engaging them in meaningful and challenging activities, helping them perform those activities successfully, and talking with them about their experiences. Because he emphasized the importance of society and culture for promoting cognitive growth, his theory is sometimes called the **sociocultural perspective.**

Vygotsky conducted numerous studies of children's thinking from the 1920s until his premature death from tuberculosis in 1934. Western psychologists did not fully appreciate the usefulness of his work until several decades later, when his major writings were translated into English (Vygotsky, 1962, 1978, 1987, 1997). Although Vygotsky never had the chance to develop his theory fully, his ideas are clearly evident in our views of child development and classroom practice today.

Key Ideas in Vygotsky's Theory

Vygotsky acknowledged that biological factors play a role in development: Children bring certain characteristics and dispositions to the situations they encounter, and their responses to those situations vary accordingly. Furthermore, children's behaviors, which are influenced in part by inherited traits, influence the particular experiences that they have (Vygotsky, 1997). However, Vygotsky's primary focus was on the role of nurture, and especially on the ways in

sociocultural perspective
Theoretical perspective emphasizing the importance of society and culture for promoting cognitive development.

which a child's social and cultural environments foster cognitive growth. Following are central ideas and concepts in Vygotsky's theory:

■ *Complex mental processes begin as social activities; as children develop, they gradually internalize the processes they use in social contexts and begin to use them independently.* Vygotsky proposed that many thinking processes have their roots in the social interactions (conversations, arguments, etc.) that children have with other people. Children first talk about objects and events with adults and other knowledgeable individuals; in the process, they discover how the people around them think about those objects and events.

In Vygotsky's view, dialogue with others is an essential condition for promoting cognitive development. Gradually, children incorporate into their own thinking the ways that adults and others talk about and interpret the world. The process through which social activities evolve into internal mental activities is called **internalization.**

Not all mental processes emerge through children's interactions with adults, however; some processes also develop as children interact with their peers. As an example, children frequently argue with one another about a variety of matters: how best to carry out an activity, what games to play, who did what to whom, and so on. According to Vygotsky, childhood arguments help children discover that there are often several points of view about any single situation. Eventually, children can, in essence, internalize the "arguing" process, developing the ability to look at a situation from several different angles *on their own.*

■ *Thought and language become increasingly interdependent in the first few years of life.* For us as adults, thought and language are closely interconnected. We often think in terms of the specific words that our language provides; for example, when we think about household pets, our thoughts contain words such as *cat* and *dog.* In addition, we usually express our thoughts when we converse with others; as we sometimes put it, we "speak our minds."

But Vygotsky proposed that thought and language are separate functions for infants and young toddlers. In these early years, thinking occurs independently of language, and when language appears, it is first used primarily as a means of communication rather than as a mechanism of thought. But sometime around age 2, thought and language become intertwined: Children express their thoughts when they speak, and they think at least partially in terms of words (see Figure 4–8).

When thought and language merge, we begin to see **self-talk** (also known as *private speech*), whereby children talk to themselves out loud. Recall Piaget's notion of *egocentric speech,* based on his observation that young children often say things without taking into account the listener's perspective. Vygotsky proposed that such speech is better understood as talking to *oneself* than as talking to someone else. According to Vygotsky, self-talk has a specific purpose: By talking to themselves, children learn to guide and direct their own behaviors through difficult tasks and complex maneuvers in much the same way that adults have previously guided them.

Self-talk eventually evolves into **inner speech:** Children "talk" to themselves mentally rather than aloud. They continue to direct themselves verbally through tasks and activities, but others can no longer see and hear the means by which they do it.

Taken together, self-talk and inner speech illustrate the internalization process mentioned earlier: Over time, children gradually internalize the directions that they have initially received from those around them so that they are eventually giving *themselves* directions.

Recent research has supported Vygotsky's views regarding the progression and role of self-talk and inner speech. The frequency of children's audible self-talk decreases during the preschool years, but this decrease is accompanied by an increase in whispered mumbling and silent lip movements, presumably reflecting a transition to inner speech (Bivens & Berk, 1990; Owens, 1996). Furthermore, self-talk increases when children are performing more challenging tasks—tasks at which they must work harder to complete successfully (Berk, 1994; Schimmoeller, 1998).

■ *Through both informal interactions and formal schooling, adults convey to children the ways in which their culture interprets and responds to the world.* In their interactions with children, adults share with children the *meanings* that they attach to objects, events, and, more gen-

internalization
In Vygotsky's theory, the gradual evolution of external, social activities into internal, mental activities.

self-talk
Talking to oneself as a way of guiding oneself through a task.

inner speech
"Talking" to oneself mentally rather than aloud.

erally, human experience. Such meanings are conveyed through a variety of mechanisms, including language (spoken words, writing, etc.), symbols, mathematics, art, literature, and so on. Children gradually adopt their culture's interpretations of the world by internalizing the words, concepts, symbols, and other representations that people around them use.[3] In this way, all members of a community—growing children included—can share a common perspective of "how things are and should be."

Informal conversations, such as the one between Kerry and her mother, play a major role in helping children internalize their culture. No less important in Vygotsky's eyes is formal education, where teachers systematically impart the ideas, concepts, and terminology used in various academic disciplines (Vygotsky, 1962). Although Vygotsky, like Piaget, saw value in allowing children to make some discoveries themselves, he also saw value in having adults describe the discoveries of previous generations (Karpov & Haywood, 1998).

To the extent that specific cultures pass along unique conceptual tools, ideas, and belief systems, children of different cultural backgrounds will develop somewhat different knowledge, skills, and ways of thinking. Thus, Vygotsky's theory leads us to expect greater diversity among children, at least in cognitive development, than Piaget's theory does. For example, some cultures use a wide variety of maps (road maps, maps of subway systems, shopping mall layouts) and expose children to them early and frequently, whereas other cultures rarely if ever use maps (Trawick-Smith, 1997; Whiting & Edwards, 1988). In fact, cultures differ markedly in the extent to which they represent their world and experiences on paper at all (Trawick-Smith, 1997).

■ *Children can perform more challenging tasks when assisted by more advanced and competent individuals.* Vygotsky distinguished between two kinds of abilities that children are likely to have at any particular point in their development. A child's **actual developmental level** is the upper limit of tasks that he or she can perform independently, without help from anyone else. A child's **level of potential development** is the upper limit of tasks that he or she can perform with the assistance of a more competent individual. To get a true sense of children's cognitive development, Vygotsky proposed, we should assess their capabilities both when performing alone *and* when performing with assistance.

Children can typically do more difficult things in collaboration with adults than they can do on their own. For example, children may be able to read more complex prose with the assistance of a teacher or older child than they are likely to read independently. They can play more difficult piano pieces when adults help them locate some of the notes on the keyboard or provide suggestions about what fingers to use where. And notice how a student who cannot independently solve division problems with remainders begins to learn the correct procedure through an interaction with her teacher:

Teacher: [writes 6)44 on the board] 44 divided by 6. What number times 6 is close to 44?
Child: 6.
Teacher: What's 6 times 6? [writes 6]
Child: 36.
Teacher: 36. Can you get one that's any closer? [erasing the 6]
Child: 8.
Teacher: What's 6 times 8?
Child: 64 . . . 48.
Teacher: 48. Too big. Can you think of something . . .
Child: 6 times 7 is 42. (Pettito, 1985, p. 251)

[3]This process of internalizing the meanings and understandings of one's culture is sometimes called *appropriation,* a term suggested by a Russian contemporary of Vygotsky (Leont'ev, 1981).

In infancy, thought is nonverbal in nature, and language is used primarily as a means of communication.

At about 2 years of age, thought becomes verbal in nature, and language becomes a means of expressing thoughts.

With time, children begin to use *self-talk* to guide their own thoughts and behaviors.

Self-talk gradually evolves into *inner speech*, whereby children guide themselves silently (mentally) rather than aloud.

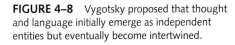

FIGURE 4–8 Vygotsky proposed that thought and language initially emerge as independent entities but eventually become intertwined.

actual developmental level
Extent to which one can successfully perform a task independently.

level of potential development
Extent to which one can successfully execute a task with the assistance of a more competent individual.

From Vygotsky's perspective, parents and teachers promote children's cognitive development in part by conveying how their culture interprets the world.

■ *Challenging tasks promote maximum cognitive growth.* The range of tasks that children cannot yet perform independently but *can* perform with the help and guidance of others is known as the **zone of proximal development (ZPD).** A child's zone of proximal development includes learning and problem-solving abilities that are just beginning to develop—abilities that are in an immature, embryonic form. Naturally, any child's ZPD will change over time; as some tasks are mastered, other, more complex ones appear on the horizon to take their place.

Vygotsky proposed that children learn very little from performing tasks they can already do independently. Instead, they develop primarily by attempting tasks they can accomplish only in collaboration with a more competent individual—that is, when they attempt tasks within their zone of proximal development. In a nutshell, it is the challenges in life—not the easy successes—that promote cognitive development.

Whereas challenging tasks are beneficial, *impossible* tasks—those that children cannot do even with considerable structure and assistance—are of no benefit whatsoever. (As a simple example, it is pointless to ask a typical kindergartner to solve for *x* in an algebraic equation.) In this way, a child's ZPD sets a limit on how quickly the child can develop cognitively.

■ *Play allows children to stretch themselves cognitively.* Recall the scenario of Jeff and Scott playing "restaurant" presented earlier in the chapter. The two boys take on several adult roles (restaurant managers, waiters, cooks) and practice a variety of adultlike behaviors: assembling the necessary materials for a restaurant, creating menus, keeping track of customers' orders, and tallying final bills. In real life, such a scenario would, of course, be impossible: Very few 5-year-old children have the cooking, reading, writing, mathematical, or organizational skills necessary to run a restaurant. Yet the element of make-believe brings the same tasks within the boys' reach (e.g., Lillard, 1993). To put this idea in Vygotsky's words:

> In play a child is always above his average age, above his daily behavior, in play it is as though he were a head taller than himself. (Vygotsky, 1978, p. 102)

In play activities, children rely on their imaginations as much as on real objects; in the process, they learn to use their thoughts to guide their behaviors. As they substitute one object for another (e.g., pretending that a cardboard box is the family car), they begin to distinguish between objects and their meanings and to respond to internal representations (e.g., the concept of *car*) as much as to external objects.

Furthermore, even when children play, their behaviors must conform to certain standards or expectations. For instance, children in preschool and the early elementary grades often act in accordance with how a "daddy," "teacher," or "waiter" would behave. In the organized group games and sports that come later, children must follow a specific set of rules. By adhering to such restrictions on their behavior, children learn to plan ahead, to think before they act, and to engage in self-restraint—skills critical for participating successfully in the adult world.

Especially within the last 20 years, many Western developmentalists have embraced and extended Vygotsky's ideas. We turn now to some modern Vygotskian perspectives about child development and educational practice.

Current Perspectives on Vygotsky's Theory

Vygotsky focused primarily on the *processes* through which children develop, rather than on the characteristics that children of particular ages are likely to exhibit. He did identify stages of development but portrayed them in only the most general terms. From our perspective, the stages are not terribly informative (we refer you to Vygotsky, 1997, pp. 214–216, if you would like to learn more about them). Largely for these reasons, Vygotsky's theory has been more difficult for researchers to test and either verify or disprove than has Piaget's theory. In fact, the most frequent criticisms of Vygotsky's ideas are his lack of precision and his inattention to details (Haenan, 1996; Hunt, 1997; Wertsch, 1984).

zone of proximal development (ZPD)
Range of tasks that one cannot yet perform independently but *can* perform with the help and guidance of others.

Despite such weaknesses, many contemporary theorists and practitioners have found Vygotsky's theory both insightful and helpful. Although they have taken Vygotsky's notions in many different directions, we can discuss much of their work within the context of several general ideas: participation in adult activities, scaffolding, apprenticeships, social construction of meaning, dynamic assessment, and the value of play.

Participation in Adult Activities Most cultures allow, and in fact often require, children to be involved in adult activities. Children's early experiences are often at the fringe of an activity—a phenomenon known as **legitimate peripheral participation** (Lave, 1991; Lave & Wenger, 1991). As the children acquire greater competence, they take an increasingly more central role in the activity until, eventually, they are full-fledged participants.

To illustrate, when our own children were preschoolers, we often let them help us bake cookies by asking them to pour the ingredients we'd measured into the mixing bowl, and we occasionally let them do some preliminary mixing as well. Similarly, when taking them to the office with us, we might have them press the appropriate buttons in the elevator, check our mailboxes, open envelopes, or deliver documents to the department secretary. In later years, we gave them increasing responsibility and independence in these arenas. For example, by the time Jeanne's son Jeff reached high school, he was baking and decorating his own cakes and cookies, and he ran errands around the community (e.g., trips to the library and post office) to help Jeanne with her book-writing efforts.

From a Vygotskian perspective, this gradual entry into adult activities increases the probability that children will engage in behaviors and thinking skills that are within their zone of proximal development. Some theorists believe that participation in everyday adult activities has an additional advantage as well. They take a **situative perspective** of cognition and cognitive development: They describe thinking as being tied to, or *situated in,* the specific tasks in which people are engaged (e.g., Light & Butterworth, 1993). They argue that children display thinking and reasoning abilities primarily within the particular contexts in which they have acquired those abilities; hence, they disagree with Piaget's view that the logical thinking abilities associated with the concrete and formal operations stages emerge independently of any single content domain. As an example, Brazilian children who work as street vendors selling gum and candy can, during their sales transactions, use mathematical operations that they seem unable to use with more traditional mathematics problems at school (Carraher, Carraher, & Schliemann, 1985). Adults' thinking can be equally context-bound; for instance, construction foremen, fishermen, and cooks more effectively use proportional reasoning when they are in their professional milieus—that is, when they are dealing with blueprints, quantities of fish, and recipes, respectively (Schliemann & Carraher, 1993). Some research findings are inconsistent with a situative perspective of cognitive abilities, however; for instance, students who learn mathematical procedures in the classroom often apply the procedures quite successfully in a wide variety of real-world contexts (Anderson, Reder, & Simon, 1997). At present, the extent to which various cognitive abilities are context-specific or context-independent is a source of considerable controversy among psychologists.

Scaffolding Theorists have given considerable thought to the kinds of assistance that can help children complete challenging tasks. The term **scaffolding** is often used here: Adults and other more competent individuals provide some form of guidance or structure that enables children to perform tasks that are in their zone of proximal development. To understand this concept, think of the scaffolding used in the construction of a new building. The *scaffold* is an external structure that provides support for the workers (e.g., a place where they can stand) until the building itself is strong enough to support them. As the building gains stability, the scaffold becomes less necessary and so is gradually removed.

In much the same way, an adult guiding a child through a new task may provide an initial scaffold to support the child's early efforts. In the teacher-student dialogue about division presented earlier, the teacher provided clues about how to proceed, such as searching for the multiple of 6 closest to, but still less than, 44. Similarly, adults provide scaffolding when they illustrate the use of particular tools or procedures, give hints about how to approach a difficult problem, or break down a complex task into smaller, easier steps (Rosenshine & Meister, 1992; Wood, Bruner, & Ross, 1976). As children become more adept at performing tasks, the scaffolding is gradually phased out, and the children are eventually performing those tasks on their own.

legitimate peripheral participation
A child's early and somewhat limited involvement in adult activities.

situative perspective
Theoretical perspective that cognitive abilities are tied to the specific contexts in which they have been acquired.

scaffolding
Support mechanism, provided by a more competent individual, that helps a child successfully perform a task within his or her zone of proximal development.

Apprenticeships In some cases, adults work with children in formal or informal **apprenticeships,** one-on-one relationships in which the adults teach the children new skills, guide their initial efforts, and present increasingly difficult tasks as proficiency improves and the zone of proximal development changes (Rogoff, 1990, 1991). Many cultures use apprenticeships as a way of gradually introducing children to the practices of the adult community. These practices might include such skills as weaving, tailoring, or midwifery (Lave & Wenger, 1991; Rogoff, 1990). Apprenticeships are also common in music instruction—for instance, in teaching a student how to play a musical instrument (Elliott, 1995).

In apprenticeships, children learn not only the behaviors but also the language of a skill or trade (Lave & Wenger, 1991). For example, when master weavers teach apprentices their art, they use such terms as *warp, weft, shuttle,* and *harness* to focus attention on a particular aspect of the process. Similarly, when teachers guide students through scientific experiments, they use words like *hypothesis, evidence,* and *theory* to help the students evaluate their procedures and results (Perkins, 1992).

Furthermore, an apprenticeship can show children how adults typically *think about* a task or activity; such a situation is sometimes called a **cognitive apprenticeship** (Brown, Collins, & Duguid, 1989; Rogoff, 1990; Roth & Bowen, 1995). For instance, a teacher and student might work together to accomplish a challenging task or solve a difficult problem (perhaps collecting data samples in biology fieldwork, solving a mathematical brainteaser, or translating a difficult passage from German to English). In the process of talking about various aspects of the task or problem, the teacher and student together analyze the situation and develop the best approach to take, and the teacher models effective ways of thinking about and mentally processing the situation.

Although apprenticeships can differ widely from one context to another, they typically have some or all of these features (Collins, Brown, & Newman, 1989):

In an apprenticeship, children learn both the skills and the language associated with a particular activity.

- *Modeling.* The adult carries out the task, simultaneously thinking aloud about the process, while the child observes and listens.
- *Coaching.* As the child performs the task, the adult gives frequent suggestions, hints, and feedback.
- *Scaffolding.* The adult provides various forms of support for the student, perhaps by simplifying the task, breaking it into smaller and more manageable components, or providing less complicated equipment.
- *Articulation.* The child explains what he or she is doing and why, allowing the adult to examine the child's knowledge, reasoning, and problem-solving strategies.
- *Reflection.* The adult asks the child to compare his or her performance with that of experts, or perhaps with an ideal model of how the task should be done.
- *Increasing complexity and diversity of tasks.* As the child gains greater proficiency, the adult presents more complex, challenging, and varied tasks to complete.
- *Exploration.* The adult encourages the child to frame questions and problems on his or her own and thereby to expand and refine acquired skills.

Social Construction of Meaning As mentioned earlier, Vygotsky proposed that, in their interactions with children, adults help children attach meaning to the objects and events around them. More recently, theorists have elaborated further on this idea. They point out that an adult such as a parent or teacher often helps a child make sense of the world through a joint discussion of a phenomenon or event they have mutually experienced (Eacott, 1999; Feuerstein, 1990; Feuerstein, Klein, & Tannenbaum, 1991; John-Steiner & Mahn, 1996). Such an interaction, sometimes called a **mediated learning experience,** encourages the child to think about the phenomenon or event in particular ways—to attach labels to it, recognize principles that underlie it, impose certain interpretations on it, and so on. For instance, in the opening case study, Kerry's mother helps Kerry better understand

apprenticeship
Situation in which a person works intensively with an expert to learn how to accomplish complex tasks.

cognitive apprenticeship
Mentorship in which a teacher and a student work together on a challenging task and the teacher suggests ways to think about the task.

mediated learning experience
Discussion between an adult and a child in which the adult helps the child make sense of an event they have mutually experienced.

the whale-watching expedition in several ways: by helping her recall the people who were present, interpreting the trip as a "disaster," describing the whales as "big," and counting the number of whales that were present. In such a conversation, the adult must, of course, consider the prior knowledge and perspectives of the child and tailor the discussion accordingly (Newson & Newson, 1975).

In addition to co-constructing meanings with adults, children often talk among themselves to derive meaning from their experiences. As we reflect back on our own childhood and adolescent years, we recall having numerous conversations with friends in joint efforts to make sense of our world, perhaps within the context of identifying the optimal food and water conditions for raising tadpoles, deciding how best to carry out an assigned school project, or figuring out why certain teenage boys were so elusive.

School is one obvious place where children and adolescents can toss around ideas about a particular issue and perhaps reach consensus about how best to interpret and understand the topic in question. As an example of how members of a classroom might work together to construct meaning, let's consider an interaction that takes place in Keisha Coleman's third-grade class (Peterson, 1992). The students are discussing how they might solve the problem $-10 + 10 = ?$. They are using a number line like this

to facilitate their discussion. Several students, including Tessa, agree that the solution is "zero" but disagree about how to use the number line to arrive at that answer. Excerpts from a discussion between Tessa and her classmate Chang (as facilitated by Ms. Coleman) follow:

Tessa:	You have to count numbers to the right. If you count numbers to the right, then you couldn't get to zero. You'd have to count to the left.
C [Ms. Coleman]:	Could you explain a little bit more about what you mean by that? I'm not quite sure I follow you. . . .
Tessa:	Because if you went that way [points to the right] then it would have to be a higher number. . . .
Chang:	I disagree with what she's trying to say. . . . Tessa says if you're counting right, then the number is—I don't really understand. She said, "If you count right, then the number has to go smaller." I don't know what she's talking about. Negative ten plus negative ten is zero. . . . What do you mean by counting to the right?
Tessa:	If you count from ten up, you can't get zero. If you count from ten left, you can get zero.
Chang:	. . . Well, negative ten is a negative number—smaller than zero.
Tessa:	I know.
Chang:	Then why do you say you can't get to zero when you're adding to negative ten, which is smaller than zero?
Tessa:	OHHHH! NOW I GET IT! This is positive. . . . You have to count right.
C:	You're saying in order to get to zero, you have to count to the right? From where, Tessa?
Tessa:	Negative 10. (Peterson, 1992, pp. 165–166)

The class continues in its efforts to pin down precisely how to use the number line to solve the problem. Eventually, Tessa offers a revised and more complete explanation. Pointing to the appropriate location on the number line, she says, "You start at negative 10. Then you add 1, 2, 3, 4, 5, 6, 7, 8, 9, 10." She moves her finger one number to the right for each number that she counts. She reaches the zero point on the number line when she counts "10" and concludes, "That equals zero."

Notice that at no time does Ms. Coleman impose her own interpretations on either the problem itself or on what Tessa and Chang have to say about the problem. Instead, she lets the two children struggle to make sense of the problem and, eventually, to agree on how best to solve it.

In recent years, many theorists have become convinced of the value of joint meaning-making discussions in helping children acquire more complex understandings of their physical, social, and academic worlds (e.g., De Corte, Greer, & Verschaffel, 1996; Hatano & Inagaki, 1993; Lampert, 1990; Sosniak & Stodolsky, 1994). This perspective, generally known as **social constructivism,** is reflected in increased advocacy for instructional practices involving student interaction—class discussions, cooperative learning activities, peer tutoring—in elementary and secondary classrooms alike.

Dynamic Assessment As noted earlier, Vygotsky believed that we can get a more complete picture of a child's cognitive development when we assess both their *actual developmental level* (the kinds of tasks they can successfully accomplish on their own) and their *level of potential development* (the kinds of tasks they can accomplish when they have the assistance of more competent individuals).

When assessing students' cognitive abilities, most school psychologists and teachers focus almost exclusively on students' *actual* developmental level: They ask students to take tests, complete assignments, and so on, without help from anyone else. To assess students' level of *potential* development, some theorists have suggested an alternative known as **dynamic assessment,** which involves (a) identifying tasks that students cannot initially do independently, (b) providing in-depth instruction and practice in behaviors and cognitive processes related to the task, and then (c) determining the extent to which each student has benefited from the instruction (Feuerstein, 1979, 1980; Kozulin & Falik, 1995; Lidz, 1997). This approach often yields more optimistic evaluations of students' cognitive capabilities than traditional measures of cognitive ability do and may be especially useful in assessing the abilities of students from diverse cultural backgrounds (Feuerstein, 1979).

Value of Play Although children's play activities may seem relatively frivolous on the surface, both Vygotsky and Piaget believed that play gives children valuable practice in adultlike behaviors. In addition, Vygotsky argued that the element of pretense in play (using a box as a car, a wooden block as a telephone, etc.) provides a means through which children begin to distinguish between objects and their meanings—a critical step in the development of thought.

Many contemporary developmentalists share Vygotsky's and Piaget's belief that play provides an arena in which youngsters can practice the skills they will need in later life. They have long been aware of the value of play for children's social development (i.e., for developing cooperation and conflict resolution skills), but increasingly they are acknowledging its importance for children's cognitive development as well. For instance, they suggest that it helps children master emerging skills, experiment with new combinations and cause-effect relationships, and (in role-playing activities) take the perspectives of people other than themselves (Chafel, 1991; Lillard, 1998; Rubin, Fein, & Vandenberg, 1983; Zervigon-Hakes, 1984). They note, too, that playful behavior is observed in many species, especially those that are relatively flexible in their behaviors (e.g., monkeys, chimpanzees, bears, dogs, cats), and so almost certainly has an adaptive purpose (Bjorklund & Green, 1992; Vandenberg, 1978).

Initially, play often takes the form of simple exploration: Infants and toddlers spend many hours manipulating toys and other objects to discover what these things can do and what effects they have. But somewhere around age 2, play takes on an element of make-believe, whereby children begin to substitute one object for another and eventually perform behaviors involving imaginary objects (e.g., "eating" imaginary food with an imaginary fork) (O'Reilly, 1995; Pederson, Rook-Green, & Elder, 1981). In the **sociodramatic play** of the preschool years, children begin to concoct elaborate scenarios in which they assume roles such as "parent," "teacher," or "doctor" (Göncü, 1993; Haight & Miller, 1993; Lyytinen, 1991). Some examples of things to look for when observing children's early play activities are presented in the Observation Guidelines table that follows.

As children reach school age, their role-playing activities gradually diminish, and other forms of play take their place. For instance, elementary school children often spend time playing cards and board games, constructing things from cardboard boxes or Legos, and engaging in team sports; many of these activities continue into adolescence as well. Although such forms of play do not mimic adult roles in as obvious a manner as "house" and "restaurant," they, too, serve a purpose. In particular, they help children and adolescents develop skills in planning, communication, cooperation, and problem solving—skills that will be important for their later success in the adult world (Bornstein, Haynes, Pascual, Painter, & Galperin, 1999; Christie & Johnsen, 1983; Sutton-Smith, 1979).

social constructivism
Theoretical perspective that focuses on people's collective efforts to impose meaning on the world.

dynamic assessment
Examining how a student's knowledge or reasoning may change as a result of learning or performing a specific task.

sociodramatic play
Play in which children take on assumed roles and act out a scenario of events.

Assessing Young Children's Play Activities

OBSERVATION GUIDELINES			
CHARACTERISTIC	**LOOK FOR**	**EXAMPLE**	**IMPLICATION**
Group Play	• Extent to which children play with one another • Extent to which children in a play group coordinate their play activities	Lamarr and Matthew are playing with trucks in the sandbox, but each boy seems to be in his own little world.	Give children opportunities to play together, and provide toys that require a cooperative effort.
Use of Symbolic Thought and Imagination	• Extent to which children use one object to stand for another • Extent to which children incorporate imaginary objects into their play	Julia tells her friend she is going to the grocery store, then opens an imaginary car door, sits on a chair inside her "car," steers an imaginary steering wheel, and says, "Beep, beep" as she blows an imaginary horn.	When equipping a play area, include objects (e.g., wooden blocks) that children can use for a variety of purposes.
Role Taking	• Extent to which children display behaviors that reflect a particular role • Extent to which children use language (e.g., tone of voice, specific words and phrases) associated with a particular person or role • Extent to which children coordinate and act out multiple roles within the context of a complex play scenario	Mark and Alisa are playing doctor. Alisa brings her teddy bear to Mark's "office" and politely says, "Good morning, Doctor. My baby has a sore throat." Mark holds a Popsicle stick against the bear's mouth and instructs the "baby" to say "aaahhh."	Provide toys and equipment associated with particular roles (e.g., toy medical kit, cooking utensils, play money).

In our discussions of Vygotsky's theory and contemporary extensions of his ideas, we have dropped numerous hints about their potential applications in the classroom. We now look more directly at educational implications.

Educational Implications of Vygotsky's Ideas

Vygotsky's work and the recent theoretical advances it has inspired yield numerous implications for classroom practice, including the following:

■ *Help students acquire the basic conceptual tools of various academic disciplines.* Through such disciplines as science, mathematics, and social studies, our culture passes along key concepts (e.g., *molecule, negative number, democracy*), symbols (e.g., H_2O, π, ∞), and visual representations (e.g., graphs, maps) that can help growing children organize and interpret the physical and social worlds in which they live. Literature, poetry, music, and fine arts help children impose meaning on the world as well—for example, by capturing the thoughts and feelings that characterize human experience.

■ *Present challenging tasks, perhaps within the context of cooperative activities.* To promote students' cognitive development, teachers should present some classroom tasks and assignments that students can perform successfully only with assistance—that is, tasks within students' zone of proximal development. To some extent, students with different zones of proximal development may need different tasks and assignments, which makes a strong case for providing as much individualized instruction as possible.

In some instances, students can accomplish challenging tasks only with the assistance of more skilled individuals, such as adults or older students. But at other times, students of equal ability can work together on difficult assignments, thereby jointly accomplishing tasks that none of them might be able to do on their own. In such situations, the students are essentially providing scaffolding for one another's efforts. Cooperative learning groups and other activities in which students work collaboratively can be highly effective in promoting both cognitive development and classroom achievement (Brown & Palincsar, 1989; Lou et al., 1996; Stevens & Slavin, 1995).

■ *Scaffold students' efforts.* When teachers provide the challenging tasks so important for cognitive development, they should also provide sufficient scaffolding to enable students to accomplish those tasks successfully. Here are some examples of how a teacher might scaffold a new and difficult task:

- Demonstrating the proper performance of the task in a way that students can easily imitate
- Dividing the task into several smaller, simpler pieces
- Providing a structure, set of steps, or guidelines for performing the task
- Asking questions that get students thinking in appropriate ways about the task
- Keeping students' attention focused on the relevant aspects of the task
- Giving frequent feedback about how students are progressing
  (Gallimore & Tharp, 1990; Good et al., 1992; Rogoff, 1990; Rosenshine & Meister, 1992; Wood et al., 1976)

As students develop increasing competence, teachers can gradually withdraw these support mechanisms and eventually allow students to perform the task independently—in other words, to stand on their own two feet.

■ *Assess students' abilities under a variety of work conditions.* Teachers need to know not only what students can and cannot do, but also under what conditions students are most likely to accomplish various tasks successfully (Calfee & Masuda, 1997). By asking students to work under varying conditions—sometimes independently, sometimes in collaboration with one or more classmates, and sometimes with teacher instruction and support—teachers get a better sense of the tasks that are in each student's zone of proximal development.

■ *Provide opportunities to engage in authentic activities.* As we've already seen, children's participation in adult activities plays a critical role in their cognitive development. Many theorists have suggested that teachers can better promote learning and cognitive development by having students engage in **authentic activities**—activities similar to those that the students may eventually encounter in the adult world—rather than in more traditional academic tasks (e.g., Hickey, 1997; Hiebert & Fisher, 1992; Lave, 1993).

Authentic activities can be identified for virtually any area of the curriculum; consider these possibilities:

Writing an editorial	Performing in a concert
Participating in a debate	Planning a family budget
Designing an electrical circuit	Conversing in a foreign language
Conducting an experiment	Making a videotape
Writing a computer program	Constructing a museum display
Creating and distributing a class newsletter	Developing a home page for the Internet

Researchers have only begun to study the effects of authentic activities on students' learning and cognitive development, but preliminary results are encouraging. For example, students may show greater improvement in writing skills when they practice by writing stories, essays, and letters to real people, rather than completing short, artificial writing exercises (Hiebert & Fisher, 1992). Likewise, students gain a more complete understanding of how to use and interpret maps when they construct their own maps than when they engage in workbook exercises involving map interpretation (Gregg & Leinhardt, 1994).

■ *Promote self-regulation by teaching children to talk themselves through difficult situations.* Through self-talk and inner speech, children begin to direct and regulate their own behaviors in much the same way that adults have previously directed them. Children who talk themselves through challenging tasks pay more attention to what they are doing and are more likely to show improvement in their performance (Berk & Spuhl, 1995).

authentic activity
Classroom activity similar to one that a student might encounter in the outside world.

Authentic activities involve tasks similar to ones that students will eventually encounter in the outside world.

Meichenbaum (1977, 1985) has successfully used five steps in teaching children how to give themselves instructions and thereby guide themselves through a new task:

1. *Cognitive modeling.* An adult model performs the desired task while verbalizing instructions that guide performance.
2. *Overt, external guidance.* The child performs the task while listening to the adult verbalize the instructions.
3. *Overt self-guidance.* The child repeats the instructions aloud (*self-talk*) while performing the task.
4. *Faded, overt self-guidance.* The child whispers the instructions while performing the task.
5. *Covert self-instruction.* The child silently thinks about the instructions (*inner speech*) while performing the task.

In this sequence of steps, depicted in Figure 4–9, the adult initially serves as a model both for the behavior itself and for the process of self-guidance. Responsibility for performing the task is soon turned over to the child; eventually, responsibility for *directing* the performance is turned over as well.

■ *Give children the chance to play.* So far, all of our suggestions—teaching concepts and symbols, presenting difficult tasks, engaging students in authentic activities, and so on—imply that facilitating children's cognitive development means giving them one or another forms of academic "work." Yet, as we have seen, informal play activities have value as well, and many theorists advocate including them in the school day, especially at the preschool level (Chafel, 1991; Hirsh-Pasek, Hyson, & Rescorla, 1990). Frost, Shin, and Jacobs (1998) have offered several suggestions for promoting preschoolers' play:

- Partition the classroom into small areas (e.g., a corner for blocks, a "housekeeping" area, an art table) that give children numerous options.
- Provide realistic toys (e.g., dolls, dress-up clothes, plastic dishes and food) that suggest certain activities and functions, as well as more versatile objects

	TASK PERFORMANCE	TASK INSTRUCTIONS
Step 1	The adult performs the task, modeling it for the child.	The adult verbalizes instructions.
Step 2	The child performs the task.	The adult verbalizes instructions.
Step 3	The child performs the task.	The child repeats the instructions aloud.
Step 4	The child performs the task.	The child whispers the instructions.
Step 5	The child performs the task.	The child thinks silently about the instructions.

FIGURE 4–9 Meichenbaum's five steps for promoting self-regulation

■ Demonstrate and encourage adultlike ways of thinking about situations.

A high school chemistry teacher places two equal-size inflated balloons into two beakers of water, one heated to 25°C and the other heated to 50°C. The students all agree that the balloon placed in the warmer water expands more. "Now *how much more* did the 50-degree balloon expand?" the teacher asks. "Let's use Charles's Law to figure it out."

■ Present some tasks that students can perform successfully only with assistance.

A fifth-grade teacher assigns students their first research paper, knowing that she will have to give them a great deal of guidance as they work on it.

■ Have students work in small groups to accomplish complex tasks.

A middle school art teacher asks his students to work in groups of four or five to design large murals that depict various ecosystems (rain forest, desert, grassland, tundra, etc.) and the kinds of species of plants and animals that live in each one. The groups then paint their murals on the walls in the school corridors.

■ Provide sufficient support (scaffolding) to enable students to perform challenging tasks successfully; gradually withdraw the support as they become more proficient.

A middle school history teacher asks students to take notes on the short lectures he presents in class. Before beginning the lecture, he gives them a detailed outline that they can use to

organize their notes, and during the lecture itself he continually reminds them about the things they should include in their notes.

■ Ask students to engage in authentic adult activities.

A third-grade teacher has her students create a class newspaper that includes news articles, a schedule of upcoming events, a couple of political cartoons, and some classified advertisements. The students assume varying roles (reporters, cartoonists, editors, proofreaders, photocopiers, and distributors) during the project.

■ Encourage students to talk themselves through difficult tasks.

As her students work on complex mathematical equations such as this one,

$$x = \frac{2(4 \times 9)^2}{6} + 3$$

a junior high school mathematics teacher gives students a mnemonic ("*Please excuse my dear Aunt Sally*") to help them remember the order in which various operations should be performed (*p*arentheses, *e*xponents, *m*ultiplication, *d*ivision, *a*ddition, *s*ubtraction).

■ Give young children numerous opportunities to practice adult roles and behaviors in play activities.

A preschool teacher equips his classroom with many household items (dress-up clothes, cooking utensils, a toy telephone, etc.) so that his students can play "house" during free-play time.

(e.g., Legos, wooden blocks, cardboard boxes) that allow children to engage in fantasy and imagination.

- Provide enough toys and equipment to minimize potential conflicts, but keep them few enough in number that children must cooperate in their use.

Comparing Piaget and Vygotsky

Together, Piaget's and Vygotsky's theories give us a more complete picture of cognitive development than either one provides alone. The Developmental Trends table that follows draws on elements of both theories to describe characteristics of children and adolescents in different age ranges.

The two theories share several common themes—themes that continue to appear in more contemporary theories of cognitive development. At the same time, they have important differences that have led modern researchers to probe more deeply into the mechanisms through which children's thinking processes develop.

Common Themes

If we look beyond the very different vocabulary Piaget and Vygotsky often used to describe the phenomena they observed, we notice three themes that their theories share: challenge, readiness, and the importance of social interaction.

Challenge We see the importance of challenge most clearly in Vygotsky's concept of the *zone of proximal development:* Children benefit most from tasks that they can perform only with the assistance of more competent individuals. Challenge appears in a more disguised form in Piaget's theory, but it plays a critical role nonetheless: Children develop more sophisticated knowledge and thought processes only when they encounter phenomena they cannot adequately understand using existing schemes—in other words, phenomena that create *disequilibrium.*

Readiness In both theories, growing children may be cognitively ready for some experiences yet not be ready for others. From Piaget's perspective, children can accommodate to new objects and events only when they can also assimilate them into existing schemes; there must be some overlap between the "new" and the "old." In addition, Piaget argued that children cannot learn from an experience until they have begun the transition into a stage that allows them to deal with and conceptualize that experience appropriately (e.g., they cannot benefit from hearing abstract ideas until they have begun the transition into formal operations).

Vygotsky, too, proposed that there are limits on the tasks that children can reasonably handle at any particular time. As children acquire some capabilities, other, slightly more advanced ones emerge in an embryonic form (they fall within the child's ZPD) and can be fostered through adult assistance and guidance.

Importance of Social Interaction In Piaget's eyes, the people in a child's life present information and arguments that create disequilibrium and foster greater perspective taking. For instance, when young children disagree with one another, they gradually begin to realize that different people may have different yet equally valid viewpoints, and so they begin to shed their preoperational egocentrism.

In Vygotsky's view, social interactions provide the very foundation for thought processes: Children internalize the processes they use when they converse with others until, ultimately, they can use them independently. Furthermore, tasks within the ZPD can, by definition, be accomplished only when others assist in children's efforts.

Theoretical Differences

Following are four questions that capture key differences between Piaget's and Vygotsky's characterizations of cognitive development.

To What Extent Is Language Essential for Cognitive Development? According to Piaget, language provides verbal labels for many of the schemes that children have previously developed; it is also the primary means through which children interact with others and so can begin to incorporate multiple perspectives into their thinking. In Piaget's view, however, much of cognitive development occurs independently of language.

For Vygotsky, language is absolutely essential for cognitive development. Children's thought processes are internalized versions of social interactions that are largely verbal in nature; for instance, through self-talk and inner speech, children begin to guide their own behaviors in ways that others have previously guided them. Furthermore, in their conversations with adults, children learn the meanings that their culture ascribes to particular events and gradually begin to interpret the world in "culturally appropriate" ways.

To what extent does cognitive development depend on language? Perhaps the truth lies somewhere between Piaget's and Vygotsky's theories. Piaget probably underestimated the importance of language: Children acquire more complex understandings of phenomena and events not only through their own interactions with the world but also (as Vygotsky suggested) by learning how others *interpret* those phenomena and events. Yet Vygotsky may have overstated the case for language: Verbal exchanges may be less important for cognitive development in some cultures than in others. For instance, in a study by Rogoff, Mistry, Göncü, and Mosier (1993), adults in four cultures—middle-class communities in the United States and Turkey, a Native American community in Guatemala, and a tribal village in India—were asked to help toddlers with the difficult tasks of getting dressed and manipulating strange new toys. Adults in the United States and Turkey provided a great deal of verbal guidance as they helped the children. The Guatemalan and Indian adults conversed less with the children; instead, much of their guidance took the form of gestures and demonstrations.

Thinking and Reasoning Skills at Different Age Levels

DEVELOPMENTAL TRENDS

AGE	WHAT YOU MIGHT OBSERVE	DIVERSITY	IMPLICATIONS
Early Childhood (2–6) 	• Rapidly developing language skills • Thinking that, by adult standards, is illogical • Limited perspective-taking ability • Frequent self-talk • Sociodramatic play • Little understanding of how adults typically interpret events	• Shyness may reduce children's willingness to talk with teachers and peers and to engage in cooperative sociodramatic play. • Adultlike logic is more likely when children have accurate information about the world (e.g., about cause-effect relationships). • Adults' interpretations of some events are culturally specific.	• Provide numerous opportunities for children to interact with one another during play and other cooperative activities. • Introduce children to a variety of real-world environments and situations through field trips and picture books. • Talk with children about their experiences and possible interpretations of them.
Middle Childhood (6–10) 	• Conservation, multiple classification, and other forms of adult logic • Limited ability to reason about abstract ideas • Emergence of group games and team sports that involve coordinating multiple perspectives • Ability to participate in many adult activities (perhaps only peripherally)	• Development of logical thinking skills is affected by the importance of those skills in a child's culture. • Formal operational reasoning may occasionally appear for simple tasks and familiar contexts, especially in 9- and 10-year-olds. • Physical maturation and psychomotor skills affect success in some games and team sports.	• Use concrete manipulatives and experiences to illustrate concepts and ideas. • Supplement verbal explanations with concrete examples, pictures, and hands-on activities. • Allow time for organized play activities. • Introduce students to various adult professions, and provide opportunities to practice authentic adult tasks.
Early Adolescence (10–14)	• Emerging ability to reason about abstract ideas • Increasing scientific reasoning abilities (e.g., separating and controlling variables, formulating and testing hypotheses) • Emerging ability to reason about mathematical proportions • Emerging idealism about political and social issues, but often without taking real-world constraints into consideration • Increasing ability to engage in adult tasks	• Students can think more abstractly when they have considerable knowledge about a topic. • Students are more likely to separate and control variables for situations with which they are familiar. • Development of formal operational reasoning skills is affected by the importance of those skills in a student's culture. • The ideals that students espouse may reflect their religious, cultural, or socioeconomic backgrounds.	• Present abstract concepts and principles central to various academic disciplines, but tie them to concrete examples. • Have students engage in scientific investigations, focusing on familiar objects and phenomena. • Assign mathematics problems that require students to use simple fractions, ratios, or decimals. • As you show students how to do a new task, also show them how you and others think about the task.
Late Adolescence (14–18)	• Abstract thought and scientific reasoning skills more prevalent, especially for topics about which students have a substantial knowledge base • Idealistic notions tempered by more realistic considerations • Ability to perform many tasks in an adultlike manner	• Abstract thinking is more common in some content areas (e.g., mathematics, science) than in others (e.g., history, geography). • Formal operational reasoning skills are less likely to appear in cultures that don't require those skills. • Students' proficiency in particular adult tasks varies considerably from student to student and from task to task.	• Study particular disciplines in depth; introduce complex and abstract explanations and theories. • Encourage classroom discussions about social, political, and ethical issues; elicit multiple perspectives regarding these issues. • Involve students in activities that are similar or identical to the things they must eventually do as adults. • Show students how experts in a field think about the tasks they perform.

Contrasting Piaget and Vygotsky

BASIC DEVELOPMENTAL ISSUES

ISSUE	PIAGET	VYGOTSKY
Nature and Nurture	Piaget believed that biological maturation probably constrains the rate at which children acquire new thinking capabilities. However, he focused on how interactions with both the physical environment (e.g., manipulation of concrete objects) and the social environment (e.g., discussions with peers) promote cognitive development.	Vygotsky acknowledged that children's inherited traits and talents affect the ways in which they deal with the environment and hence affect the experiences that they have. But his theory primarily addresses the environmental conditions (e.g., engagement in challenging activities, guidance of more competent individuals, exposure to cultural interpretations) that influence cognitive growth.
Universality and Diversity	According to Piaget, the progression of children's reasoning capabilities is similar across cultures. Once children have mastered certain reasoning processes, they can apply those processes to a wide range of tasks. Children differ somewhat in the ages at which they acquire new abilities.	From Vygotsky's perspective, the specific cognitive abilities that children acquire depend on the cultural contexts in which the children are raised and the specific activities in which they are asked and encouraged to engage.
Qualitative and Quantitative Change	Piaget proposed that children's logical reasoning skills progress through four, qualitatively different stages. Any particular reasoning capability continues to improve in a gradual (quantitative) fashion throughout the stage in which it first appears.	Vygotsky acknowledged that children undergo qualitative changes in their thinking but did not elaborate on the nature of these changes. Much of his theory points to gradual and presumably quantitative improvements in skills. For instance, a child may initially find a particular task impossible, later be able to execute it with adult assistance, and eventually perform it independently.

What Kinds of Experiences Promote Development? Piaget maintained that children's independent, self-motivated explorations of the physical world form the basis for many developing schemes, and children often construct these schemes with little guidance from others. In contrast, Vygotsky argued for exploratory activities that are facilitated and interpreted by more competent individuals. The distinction, then, is one of self-exploration versus guided exploration. Ideally, children almost certainly need both kinds of experiences—opportunities to manipulate and experiment with physical phenomena on their own *and* opportunities to draw upon the wisdom of prior generations (Karpov & Haywood, 1998).

What Kinds of Social Interactions Are Most Critical? Both theorists saw value in interacting with people of all ages. However, Piaget emphasized the benefits of interactions with peers (who could create conflict), whereas Vygotsky placed greater importance on interactions with adults and other more advanced individuals (who could support children in challenging tasks and help them make appropriate interpretations).

Some contemporary theorists have proposed that interactions with peers and interactions with adults play different roles in children's cognitive development (Damon, 1984; Rogoff, 1991; Webb & Palincsar, 1996). When children's development requires that they abandon old perspectives in favor of new, more complex ones, the sociocultural conflict that often occurs among age-mates (and the multiple perspective taking that emerges from it) may be optimal for bringing about such change. But when children's development instead requires that they learn new skills, the thoughtful, patient guidance of a competent adult is probably essential (e.g., Radziszewska & Rogoff, 1991).

How Influential Is Culture? In Piaget's mind, the nature of children's logical thinking skills and the progression of these skills over time are largely independent of the specific cultural context in which children are raised. In Vygotsky's view, however, culture is of paramount importance in determining the specific thinking skills that children acquire.

Vygotsky was probably more on target here. Earlier in the chapter, we presented evidence that children's reasoning skills do not necessarily appear at the same ages in different countries; in fact, some reasoning skills (especially those involving formal operational thought) may never appear at all.

In the Basic Developmental Issues table in this section, we contrast Piaget's and Vygotsky's theories in terms of our three general themes: nature and nurture, universality and diversity, and qualitative and quantitative changes. Keep in mind that neither of these theories is completely "right" or completely "wrong": Both have offered groundbreaking insights into the nature of children's thought processes and cognitive development, and both have guided the research of the theorists who followed them.

In fact, Piaget's and Vygotsky's theories complement each other to some extent, with the former helping us understand how children often reason on their own and the latter providing ideas about how adults can help them reason more effectively. The final case study describes how four young adolescents reason about a classic Piagetian task—the pendulum problem—and illustrates the scaffolding that a teacher can provide to help them reason in a more "formal operational" fashion.

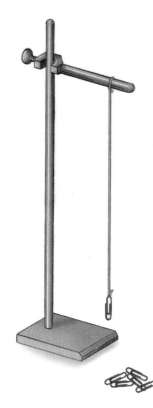

FIGURE A

CASE STUDY: ADOLESCENT SCIENTISTS

Scott Sowell has just introduced the concept of *pendulum* in his seventh-grade science class. When he asks his students to identify variables that might influence the frequency with which a pendulum swings, they suggest three possibilities: the amount of weight at the bottom, the length of the pendulum, and the "angle" from which the weight is initially dropped.

Mr. Sowell divides his students into groups of four and gives each group a pendulum composed of a long string with a paperclip attached to the bottom. He also provides extra paperclips that the students can use to increase the weight at the bottom (Figure A). He gives his students the following assignment: *Design your own experiment. Think of a way to test how each one of these affects the frequency of swing. Then carry out your experiment.*

Jon, Marina, Paige, and Wensley are coming to grips with their task as Mr. Sowell approaches their table.

Marina:	We'll time the frequency as the seconds and the . . . um . . . what? (*She looks questioningly at Mr. Sowell.*)
Mr. S.:	The frequency is the number of swings within a certain time limit.

The group agrees to count the number of swings during a 15-second period. After Jon determines the current length of the string, Wensley positions the pendulum 25 degrees from vertical. When Jon says "Go" and starts a stopwatch, Wensley releases the pendulum. Marina counts the number of swings until, 15 seconds later, Jon says, "Stop." Jon records the data from the first experiment: length = 49 cm, weight = 1 paperclip, angle = 25°, frequency = 22.

The group shortens the string and adds a second paperclip onto the bottom of the first clip. They repeat their experiment and record their data: length = 36 cm, weight = 2 paperclips, angle = 45°, frequency = 25.

Wensley:	What does the weight do to it?
Marina:	We found out that the shorter it is and the heavier it is, the faster it goes.

Mr. Sowell joins the group and reviews its results from the first two tests.

Mr. S.:	What did you change between Test 1 and Test 2?
Marina:	Number of paperclips.
Mr. S.:	OK, so you changed the weight. What else did you change?
Wensley:	The length.
Marina:	And the angle.
Mr. S.:	OK, so you changed all three between the two tests. So what caused the higher frequency?
Wensley:	The length.
Marina:	No, I think it was the weight.
Jon:	I think the weight.
Paige:	The length.

Mr. S.:	Why can't you look at your data and decide? (*The students look at him blankly.*) Take a look at the two tests. The first one had one paperclip, and the second had two. The first test had one length, and the second test had a shorter length. Why can't you come to a conclusion by looking at the two frequencies?
Marina:	All of the variables changed.

Mr. Sowell nods in agreement and then moves on to another group. The four students decide to change only the weight for the next test, so they add a third paperclip to the bottom of the second. Their pendulum now looks like Figure B. They continue to perform experiments but are careful to change only one variable at a time, or so they think. In reality, each time the group adds another paperclip, the pendulum grows longer. Mr. Sowell visits the students once again.

Mr. S.:	One thing you're testing is length, right? And another thing is weight. Look at your system. Look at how you might be making a slight mistake with weight and length. (*He takes two paperclips off and then puts one back on, hanging it, as the students have done, at the bottom of the first paperclip.*)
Marina:	It's heavier *and* longer.
Mr. S.:	Can you think of a way to redesign your experiments so that you're changing only weight? How can you do things differently so that your pendulum doesn't get longer when you add paperclips?
Jon:	Hang the second paperclip from the bottom of the string instead of from the first paperclip.

When Mr. Sowell leaves, the students add another paperclip to the pendulum, making sure that the overall length of the pendulum stays the same. They perform another test and find that the pendulum's frequency is identical to what they obtained in the preceding test. Ignoring what she has just seen, Marina concludes, "So if it's heavier, the frequency is higher."

- In what ways does Mr. Sowell scaffold the students' efforts during the lab activity?
- With which one of Piaget's stages is the students' reasoning most consistent, and why?
- Use one or more of Piaget's ideas to explain why Marina persists in her belief that weight affects a pendulum's frequency, despite evidence to the contrary.
- Drawing on post-Piagetian research findings, identify a task for which the students might be better able to separate and control variables.

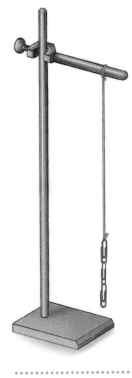

FIGURE B

SUMMARY

Piaget's Theory

Piaget portrayed children as active and motivated learners who, through numerous interactions with their physical and social environments, construct an increasingly more complex understanding of the world around them. Piaget proposed that cognitive development proceeds through four stages: (1) the sensorimotor stage (when cognitive functioning is based primarily on behaviors and perceptions); (2) the preoperational stage (when symbolic thought and language become prevalent, but reasoning is "illogical" by adult standards); (3) the concrete operations stage (when logical reasoning capabilities emerge but are limited to concrete objects and events); and (4) the formal operations stage (when thinking about abstract, hypothetical, and contrary-to-fact ideas becomes possible).

Developmental researchers have found that Piaget probably underestimated the capabilities of infants, preschoolers, and elementary school children yet overestimated the capabilities of adolescents. Researchers have found, too, that children's reasoning on particular tasks depends somewhat on their prior knowledge, experience, and formal schooling relative to those tasks. Most contemporary developmentalists doubt that cognitive development is as stagelike as Piaget proposed, but they acknowledge the value of his research methods and his views about motivation, the construction of knowledge, and the hierarchical nature of cognitive development.

Vygotsky's Theory

Vygotsky proposed that social activities are precursors to, and form the basis for, complex mental processes; as an example, the "arguing" process, first used in discussions with peers, is gradually internalized, such that children can eventually consider multiple perspectives when they think and reason. Vygotsky also proposed that children acquire more advanced ways of behaving and thinking by working on challenging tasks they can accomplish successfully only with the help of an adult or other more competent individual (i.e., tasks within their zone of proximal development). Adults promote cognitive development not only by assisting children with challenging tasks but also by passing along the meanings that their culture assigns to objects and events. Children can sometimes accomplish challenging tasks more successfully through self-talk and, eventually, inner speech.

Contemporary theorists have extended Vygotsky's theory in several directions. For instance, some recommend that adults introduce young children to authentic, adultlike tasks, initially providing the scaffolding necessary to accomplish those tasks successfully and gradually withdrawing the scaffolding as children become more proficient. Other theorists suggest that adults can help children better interpret their experiences through mediated learning experiences and cognitive apprenticeships.

Comparing Piaget and Vygotsky

Challenge, readiness, and social interaction are central to the theories of both Piaget and Vygotsky. However, the two perspectives differ on the role of language in cognitive development, the relative value of self-exploration versus guided exploration, the relative importance of interactions with peers versus adults, and the influence of culture.

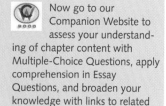

Now go to our Companion Website to assess your understanding of chapter content with Multiple-Choice Questions, apply comprehension in Essay Questions, and broaden your knowledge with links to related Developmental Psychology World Wide Web sites.

KEY CONCEPTS

cognition (p. 102)
class inclusion (p. 103)
clinical method (p. 103)
scheme (p. 104)
operation (p. 104)
adaptation (p. 104)
assimilation (p. 104)
accommodation (p. 104)
equilibrium (p. 105)
disequilibrium (p. 105)
equilibration (p. 105)
symbolic thought (p. 106)
object permanence (p. 106)
goal-directed behavior (p. 106)
preoperational egocentrism
    (p. 107)
egocentric speech (p. 107)
conservation (p. 110)

multiple classification (p. 110)
deductive reasoning (p. 110)
formal operational
    egocentrism (p. 114)
nativism (p. 115)
constructivism (p. 118)
individual constructivism
    (p. 118)
sociocognitive conflict (p. 122)
sociocultural perspective
    (p. 123)
internalization (p. 124)
self-talk (p. 124)
inner speech (p. 124)
actual developmental level
    (p. 125)
level of potential development
    (p. 125)

zone of proximal development
    (ZPD) (p. 126)
legitimate peripheral
    participation (p. 127)
situative perspective
    (p. 127)
scaffolding (p. 127)
apprenticeship (p. 128)
cognitive apprenticeship
    (p. 128)
mediated learning experience
    (p. 128)
social constructivism
    (p. 130)
dynamic assessment (p. 130)
sociodramatic play (p. 130)
authentic activity (p. 132)

Grace, age 9

Cognitive Development 2: Cognitive Processes

CASE STUDY: HOW THE UNITED STATES BECAME A COUNTRY

Our colleague Dinah Jackson once asked students in grades 2 through 8 to write essays addressing the following question: *The land we live on has been here for a very long time, but the United States has only been a country for a little more than 200 years. How did the United States become a country?* Here are some of their responses:

Second grader:

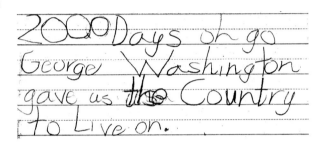

2000 Days oh go George Washington gave us the Country To Live on.

Third grader:

The pilgrams came over in 17 hundids, when they came over they bilt houses. The Idiuns tihaut they were mean. Then they came friends, and tot them stuff. Then winter came, and dlot died. Then some had babies. So thats how we got here.

Sixth grader:

The U.S.A. became a cantry by some of the British wanting to be under a different rule than of the kings. So, they sailed to the "new world" and became a new country. The only problem was that the kings from Britin still ruled the "new world." Then they had the revolutionary war. They beat Britin, and became an independent country.

Eighth grader:

We became a country through different processes. Technology around the world finally caught up with the British. There were boats to travel with, navigating tools, and the hearts of men had a desire to expand. Many men had gone on expeditions across the sea. A very famous journey was that of Christopher Columbus. He discovered this land that we live. More and more people poured in, expecting instant wealth, freedom, and a right to share their opinions. Some immigrants were satisfied, others were displeased. Problems in other countries forced people to move on to this New World, such as potato famins and no freedom of religions. Stories that drifted through people grew about this country. Stories of golden roads and free land coaxed other families who were living in the slums. Unfortunately, there were slums in America. The people helped this country grow in industry, cultures, religions, and government. Inventions and books were now better than the Europeans. Dime-novels were invented, and the young people could read about heroes of this time. May the curiosity and eagerness of the children continue.

Responses courtesy of Dinah Jackson.

THESE FOUR COMPOSITIONS ILLUSTRATE several changes in children's knowing and thinking as they grow older. Not surprising, of course, is an increase in knowledge: The sixth and eighth graders know considerably more—not only about the origins of their country but also about correct spelling and rules of punctuation and capitalization—than the second and third graders do. Furthermore, whereas the third grader describes the nation's history as a list of seemingly unrelated facts, the sixth and eighth graders have pulled what they have learned into an integrated whole that "hangs together." In addition, the younger children's descriptions reflect very simplistic and concrete understandings (e.g., the country was a gift from George Washington, the Pilgrims came over and built houses); in contrast, the eighth grader uses abstract concepts (e.g., technological progress, freedom of religion, overly optimistic expectations for wealth) to explain immigration to the United States.

In this chapter, we look at contemporary theories of cognition and cognitive development—theories that focus not only on changes in the nature of children's knowledge but also on changes in children's thinking and learning processes. We begin by looking at *information processing theory,* a perspective that underlies much of the current research in cognitive development. We follow up with an in-depth examination of *metacognition* and *cognitive strategies,* processes through which growing children become increasingly able to control and regulate their own thinking and learning processes. Later, we introduce *theory theory,* a perspective that describes how children construct increasingly complex, but not always accurate, understandings (theories) of their physical and mental worlds. We then build on both Piaget's theory and information processing concepts to explore *neo-Piagetian* approaches to cognitive development. Finally, we consider *exceptionalities in information processing,* including learning disabilities, attention-deficit hyperactivity disorder, and autism.

Information Processing Theory

Do children become better able to pay attention as they grow older? Do they learn and remember things more effectively as they move through the grade levels? How does the nature of their knowledge change over time? Such questions reflect the approach of **information processing theory,** a collection of theories that focus on how children receive, think about, mentally modify, and remember information, and on how such cognitive processes change over the course of development.

Information processing theory emerged in the late 1950s and early 1960s and has continued to evolve in the decades that have followed. Initially, many information processing theorists believed that human beings might think in ways similar to how computers operate, and they borrowed computer terminology to describe human thought processes. For example, they described people as *storing* (i.e., putting) information in memory and then *retrieving* it from memory (i.e., finding it) when they needed it at a later time.

In recent years, however, theorists have found that people often think in distinctly *non*-computer-like ways. Much of information processing theory now has a *constructivist* flavor similar to that of Piaget's theory (Derry, 1996; Mayer, 1996). In other words, human beings construct their own unique understandings of the world; they don't simply receive and absorb knowledge from the outside world in the relatively "mindless" way that a computer does. As an example of such construction, consider once again the second grader's explanation in the opening case study:

> 2000 Days oh go George Washington gave us the Country to Live on.

Almost certainly, no one ever told her that Washington *gave* us the United States. Instead, she uses something she *has* been told (i.e., that Washington was a key figure in the country's early history) to concoct what is, to her, a reasonable explanation of her country's origin. Similarly, the student has probably never seen the word *ago* spelled as "oh go," yet she uses two words she *has* seen to construct a reasonable (albeit incorrect) spelling.

Key Ideas in Information Processing Theory

Information processing theorists don't always agree about the specific mechanisms involved in learning and remembering information. Nevertheless, many of them agree on several key concepts and ideas:

■ *Input from the environment provides the raw material for cognitive processing.* People receive input from the environment through the senses (sight, hearing, smell, taste, and touch) and subsequently translate that raw input into more meaningful information. The first part of this process, detecting stimuli in the environment, is **sensation;** the second part, interpreting those stimuli, is **perception.**

Because even the simplest interpretation of an environmental event takes time, many theorists believe that human memory includes a mechanism that allows people to remember raw sensory data for a very short time (perhaps 2 to 3 seconds for auditory information, and probably less than a second for visual information). We will refer to this mechanism as the **sensory register,** but theorists actually use a variety of labels (e.g., *brief sensory store, sensory buffer, iconic memory, echoic memory*) when they talk about it.

■ *In addition to a sensory register, human memory includes two other storage mechanisms: working memory and long-term memory.* **Working memory** is the component of memory where people first

information processing theory
Theoretical perspective that focuses on the specific ways in which people mentally think about ("process") the information they receive.

sensation
Physiological detection of stimuli in the environment.

perception
Cognitive interpretation of stimuli that the body has sensed.

sensory register
Component of memory that holds incoming information in an unanalyzed form for a very brief time (2–3 seconds or less).

working memory
Component of memory that enables people to actively think about and process a small amount of information.

hold new information while they mentally process it. Working memory is where most thinking, or cognitive processing, occurs; for instance, it is where people try to solve a problem or make sense of a textbook passage. **Long-term memory** is the component that allows people to keep the many things they learn from their experiences over the years, including such knowledge as when they graduated from high school and how much 2 and 2 equal, as well as such skills as how to ride a bicycle and how to use a microscope.

Working memory keeps information for only a very short time (perhaps 20 to 30 seconds unless the individual continues to think about and actively process it); hence, it is sometimes called *short-term memory*. Working memory also appears to have a limited capacity: It has only a small amount of "space" in which people can hold and think about events or ideas. As an illustration, try computing the following division problem in your head:

$$59\overline{)49,383}$$

Did you find yourself having trouble remembering some parts of the problem while you were dealing with other parts? Did you ever arrive at the correct answer of 837? Most people cannot solve a division problem with this many numbers unless they can write the problem on paper. There simply isn't "room" in working memory to hold all the numbers you need to remember to solve the problem in your head.

In contrast to working memory, long-term memory lasts an indefinitely long time. Some theorists propose that anything stored in long-term memory remains there for a lifetime, but others believe that information may slowly fade away over time, especially if its owner doesn't use it after initially storing it. Long-term memory is assumed to have an unlimited capacity: It can "hold" as much information as its owner wants to save.

To think about information previously stored in long-term memory, people must retrieve it and examine it in working memory. Thus, although people's capacity to *store* information in long-term memory may be boundless, their ability to *think about* what they've stored is limited to whatever they can hold in working memory at any one time.

■ *Attention is essential to the learning process.* Most information processing theorists believe that attention plays a key role in the interpretation of information and its storage in memory. Attention is the primary process, and perhaps the *only* process, through which information moves from the sensory register into working memory. Many theorists argue that when people *don't* pay attention to something, they essentially lose it from memory and so cannot possibly remember it later on.

■ *A variety of cognitive processes are involved in moving information from working memory to long-term memory.* Whereas attention is instrumental in moving information from the sensory register to working memory, other, more complex processes are needed if people are to remember information for longer than a minute or so. Some theorists suggest that repeating information over and over (*rehearsing* it) is sufficient for its long-term storage. Others propose that people store information effectively only when they connect it to concepts and ideas that already exist in long-term memory—for instance, when they use what they already know to *organize* or expand (i.e., *elaborate*) on the new information. The three processes just listed—rehearsal, organization, and elaboration—are examples of the *executive functions* described in Chapter 3. We will look at their development more closely later in the chapter.

■ *People control how they process information.* Some sort of cognitive "supervisor" is almost certainly necessary to ensure that a person's learning and memory processes work effectively. This mechanism, sometimes called the **central executive**, oversees the flow of information throughout the memory system. Although it is perhaps the most critical, and certainly the most "intelligent," aspect of human cognition, information processing theorists haven't yet pinned down its exact nature.

Figure 5–1 presents a model of how the mechanisms and processes just described fit together into an overall human information processing system.

■ *Cognitive development involves gradual changes in various components of the information processing system.* Information processing theorists reject Piaget's notion of discrete developmental stages. Instead, they believe that children's cognitive processes and abilities develop through

long-term memory
Component of memory that holds knowledge and skills for a relatively long time.

central executive
Component of the human information processing system that oversees the flow of information throughout the system.

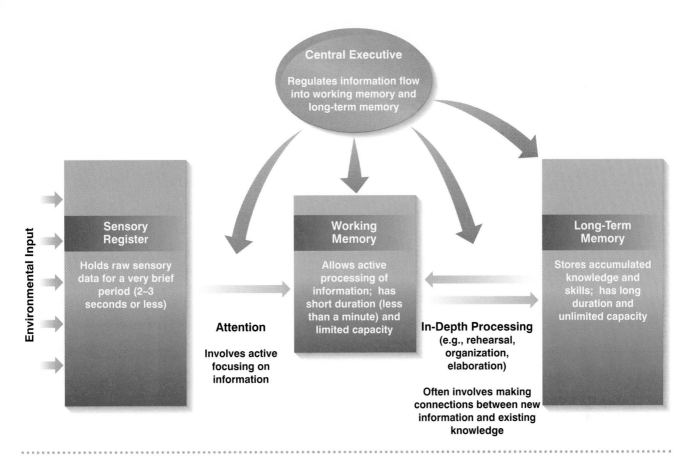

FIGURE 5–1 A model of the human information processing system

more steady and gradual *trends*. In the following sections, we look at developmental trends in sensation and perception, attention, working memory, and long-term memory.

Sensation and Perception

Many sensory capabilities are present at birth; for example, newborns can discriminate among different tastes, smells, sounds, and sound sequences (Bijeljac-Babic, Bertoncini, & Mehler, 1993; Rosenstein & Oster, 1988; Steiner, 1979). Some elements of perception (the *interpretation* of sensed stimuli) appear early as well; for instance, 1-week-old infants seem to understand that objects maintain the same shape and size even when they are rotated or moved farther away and so *look* different (Slater, Mattock, & Brown, 1990; Slater & Morison, 1985). But other sensory and perceptual capabilities, such as visual focusing, color discrimination, and the ability to locate the source of sounds, continue to develop during the first few months of life (Adams, 1987; Aslin, 1993; Hillier, Hewitt, & Morrongiello, 1992). In fact, visual perception is probably not fully developed until the preschool years, when the visual cortex of the brain reaches an adultlike form (Hickey & Peduzzi, 1987).

Experience plays a role in the development of sensation and perception. For instance, infants are more likely to show fear of heights if they have had a lot of crawling experience (Bertenthal & Campos, 1987). Furthermore, research with cats indicates the possible existence of sensitive periods in the development of visual sensation: Kittens deprived of normal sight during only the first 2 to 3 months of life have limited sensitivity to light later on (Bruer, 1999; Wiesel & Hubel, 1965).

How much can young children *remember* of what they sense and perceive? The sensory registers of 5-year-olds can apparently hold almost as much raw sensory data as those of adults (Sheingold, 1973). The significant memory differences we see between school-age children and adults, according to information processing theorists, seem to lie further along in the memory system—perhaps in attentional processes, working memory, or long-term memory.

Attention

As children grow older, their ability to pay attention changes in the following ways:

■ *Distractibility decreases; thus, sustained attention increases.* Young children's attention often moves quickly from one thing to another, and it is easily drawn to objects, events, and thoughts unrelated to whatever the children are "supposed" to be doing (Dempster & Corkill, 1999; Ruff & Lawson, 1990). Preschool and kindergarten children in free-play situations typically spend only a few minutes engaged in one activity before they move on to another (Stodolsky, 1974).

Over time, children become better able to focus their attention on a particular task and keep it there, and they are less distracted by irrelevant occurrences (Higgins & Turnure, 1984; Lane & Pearson, 1982; Ruff & Lawson, 1990). For example, in one experiment (Higgins & Turnure, 1984), children in three age groups (preschool, second grade, and sixth grade) were given age-appropriate visual discrimination tasks. Some children worked on the tasks in a quiet room, others worked in a room with a little background noise, and still others worked with a great deal of background noise. Preschool and second-grade children performed most effectively under the quiet conditions and least effectively under the very noisy conditions. But the sixth graders performed just as well in a noisy room as in a quiet room. Apparently the older children could ignore the noise, whereas the younger children could not.

As children grow older, they become better able to focus their attention on a particular task and keep it there.

■ *Attention becomes increasingly purposeful.* During the elementary school years, children become better at identifying the information most relevant to the task at hand and paying attention accordingly (Pick & Frankel, 1974; Strutt, Anderson, & Well, 1975). As a result, their learning becomes increasingly a function of what they are *asked* to learn (Hagen & Stanovich, 1977). To illustrate, imagine that you have six cards in front of you on a table. Each card has a different background color and a picture of a different object, much like the cards in Figure 5–2. You are told to remember only the *colors* of those cards. Now the cards are flipped over, and you are asked where the green card is, where the orange card is, and so on. You are then asked to name the picture that appeared on each card. Do you think you would remember the colors of the cards (the information that you intended to learn)? Do you think you would remember the objects (information that you did *not* intend to learn)?

In a study by Maccoby and Hagen (1965), children in grades 1 through 7 were asked to perform a series of tasks similar to the one just described. The older children remembered the background colors more accurately than the younger children did. Yet the older children were no better than younger ones at remembering the objects pictured on the cards; in fact, the oldest group in the study remembered the *fewest* number of objects. Older children, then, are better at paying attention to and learning the things they *intend* to learn; they are not necessarily better at learning irrelevant information.

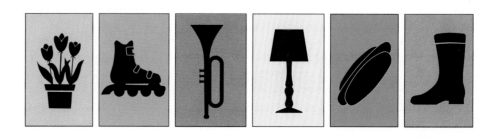

FIGURE 5–2 Imagine that you are told to remember the colors of each of these cards. After the cards are flipped over, do you think you would remember where each color appeared? Would you also remember what object appeared on each card, even though you were *not* asked to remember the objects?
Modeled after stimuli used by Maccoby & Hagen, 1965.

Working Memory

As you should recall, working memory is the component of the human information processing system where active, conscious thinking occurs. As children grow older, they become capable of thinking about a greater number of things at once and performing more complex cognitive tasks (Flavell et al., 1993; Gathercole & Hitch, 1993). This developmental trend is probably the combined result of three more specific trends related to working memory:

■ *Processing speed increases.* Children execute many cognitive processes more quickly and efficiently as they get older (Fry & Hale, 1996; Gathercole & Hitch, 1993; Siegler, 1991). For example, older children can make comparisons among similar stimuli, retrieve information from long-term memory, and solve simple problems more quickly than younger children (Cerella & Hale, 1994). Processing speed continues to increase, and thus the time to execute many mental tasks continues to *decrease*, until early adulthood (Kail, 1993).

With time and practice, some of the things that children know and can do become **automatized:** Children can perform certain mental tasks very quickly and with little or no conscious effort. Once mental activities become automatized, they take up very little "space" in working memory; as a result, children can devote more working memory capacity to other, potentially more complex tasks and problems.

As one simple example of such automatization, consider how children's reading ability improves over time. When children first begin to read, they often devote considerable mental effort to identifying the words on the page—remembering what the letter configuration FRIEND spells, sounding out an unfamiliar word such as *elementary*, and so on—and so may remember little of the content. But with increasing exposure to a variety of reading materials, word identification gradually becomes an automatized process, such that children recognize most of the words they encounter almost immediately. At this point, children can concentrate on (i.e., devote most of their working memory capacity to) what is ultimately the most important part of the reading process—understanding the ideas that an author is trying to communicate. (This is *not* to say, however, that teachers should postpone teaching reading comprehension until word recognition is automatized; we will return to this point in Chapter 8.)

Automatization increases the likelihood that a child will respond to a particular situation in a particular way. In many instances, the child will have practiced and automatized the *best* response for that situation—"best," at least, for that child's environment and culture. But different environments and cultures sometimes require very different responses, and children need to learn the most effective ways of responding within the contexts in which they are growing up. Thus, the *non*automatized cognitive processes of young children may, to some degree, be a blessing rather than a curse, in that children can practice and automatize the processes that are most likely to serve them well in their own circumstances (Bjorklund & Green, 1992).[1]

■ *Children acquire more effective cognitive processes.* Not only do children process information more quickly, but they also acquire new and better cognitive strategies as they grow older (Kail & Park, 1994). For example, when preschoolers are asked to add 3 blocks and 5 more blocks, they are likely to count all the blocks to arrive at the answer "8." In contrast, third graders given the same problem are likely to retrieve the number fact "3 + 5 = 8" from long-term memory—a strategy that involves considerably less working memory capacity. Later in the chapter, we describe some of the learning and problem-solving strategies that emerge over time.

■ *The physical capacity of working memory may increase somewhat.* Much of the apparent increase in working memory capacity is probably due to the increased speed and efficiency in children's cognitive processes, rather than to an increase in memory "space" per se (Fry & Hale,

---

[1]In Chapter 3, we considered the same idea from the standpoint of brain physiology. In the early years, many new synapses among neurons spring up (the process of *synaptogenesis*), allowing the possibility of adapting to a variety of environmental conditions. Soon after, the frequently used synapses are strengthened and the little-used synapses wither away (the process of *synaptic pruning*), resulting in a system that is especially suited for a particular environment.

automatization
Process of becoming able to respond quickly and efficiently while mentally processing or physically performing certain tasks.

1996; Gathercole & Hitch, 1993; Siegler, 1991). Theorists disagree as to whether the actual "hardware" of working memory increases and becomes more efficient with development, but some evidence suggests that it does. For instance, older children perform cognitive tasks more quickly than younger children, and adults perform them even *more* quickly, even when all groups have had extensive practice on those tasks and so presumably have automatized them (Kail, 1993).

Long-Term Memory

While working memory is an active processing center, long-term memory is more of a repository for the information and skills that people gather over the years. Some of this knowledge is almost certainly universal; for instance, children all over the globe soon learn that people typically have two legs but cats and dogs have four. Other knowledge is, of course, more dependent on children's unique experiences and on the cultural contexts in which they grow up. For example, in the four children's compositions in the opening case study, we consistently see a European American perspective of the early days of the United States: The focus is on immigration and early European colonization. Were we to ask Native American children how the United States came into being, we might get a very different perspective, perhaps one with elements of invasion, confiscation, or demolition.

As children grow older, several developmental changes in long-term memory converge to enhance their ability to understand and respond to their world:

■ *The amount of knowledge stored in long-term memory increases many times over.* This trend is an obvious one, and the four essays in the opening case study illustrate it clearly. Yet the obviousness of the trend should not negate its importance in cognitive development. Long-term memory is the repository for children's accumulating body of information and skills; thus, it provides the **knowledge base** from which children draw as they encounter, interpret, and respond to new experiences. As this knowledge base grows, then, children can interpret new experiences with increasing sophistication and respond to them with increasing effectiveness (Flavell et al., 1993).

■ *Knowledge becomes increasingly symbolic in nature.* As you should recall from Chapter 4, Piaget proposed that infants' and toddlers' schemes are predominantly sensorimotor in nature; that is, they are based on behaviors and perceptions. Near the end of the sensorimotor stage (at about 18 months, Piaget suggested), children begin to think in terms of **symbols,** mental entities (such as words) that do not necessarily reflect the perceptual and behavioral qualities of the objects or events they represent.

Piaget was probably correct in his idea that sensorimotor representations of objects and events precede symbolic representations. However, the shift from one to the other is apparently more gradual than Piaget believed. Long before children reach school age, they begin to use such symbols as words, numbers, pictures, and miniature models to represent and think about real-life objects and events (DeLoache, Miller, & Rosengren, 1997; Flavell et al., 1993). Symbolic thought is also reflected in their pretend play, such as when they use a doll as a real baby or a banana as a telephone receiver (Fein, 1979). Early symbol use is not entirely dependable, however. For example, when 3-year-old and 5-year-old children are asked to recall what happened during a recent visit to the pediatrician's office, they can do so more completely when they *act out* the visit than when they verbally describe it (Greenhoot, Ornstein, Gordon, & Baker-Ward, 1999). Furthermore, as children make the transition to more advanced forms of reasoning about Piagetian tasks, they often show such reasoning in their *gestures* before they show it in their speech (Goldin-Meadow, 1997). The following scenario illustrates:

> [A] 6-year-old child [is] attempting to justify her belief that the amount of water changed when it was poured from a tall, skinny glass into a short, wide dish. The child says, "It's different because this one's tall and that one's short," thus making it clear that she has focused on the heights of the two containers. However, in the very same utterance, the child indicates with her hand shaped like a C first the diameter of the glass and then, with a wider C, the larger diameter of the dish. The child speaks about the heights but has also noticed—not necessarily consciously—that the containers differ in width as well. (Goldin-Meadow, 1997, p. 13)

knowledge base
One's knowledge about specific topics and the world in general.

symbol
Mental entity that represents an external object or event, often without reflecting its perceptual and behavioral qualities.

Once children begin elementary school, they come face to face with a wide variety of symbols and may initially have limited success in dealing with them. For instance, elementary school teachers often use blocks and other concrete objects to represent numbers or mathematical operations, but not all kindergartners and first graders make the connection between the objects and the concepts they stand for (DeLoache et al., 1997; Uttal et al., 1998). Maps, too, are largely symbolic in nature, and as noted in the preceding chapter, children in the early grades often interpret them too literally—for instance, by thinking that a road that is red on a map is actually painted red (Liben & Downs, 1989). But as children grow older, their use of symbols to think, remember, and solve problems grows in frequency and sophistication.

■ *Children's knowledge about the world becomes increasingly integrated.* Although young children certainly know how certain aspects of their world fit together, their knowledge base consists largely of separate, isolated facts. In contrast, older children's knowledge includes many associations and interrelationships among concepts and ideas (Bjorklund, 1987; Flavell et al., 1993). This developmental change is undoubtedly one reason why older children can think more logically and draw inferences more readily: They have a more cohesive understanding of the world around them.

As an example, let's return once again to the essays in the opening case study. Notice how the third grader presents a chronological list of events without any attempt at tying them together:

> The Idiuns thout they were mean. Then they came friends, and tot them stuff. Then winter came, and alot died. Then some had babies.

In contrast, the eighth grader frequently identifies cause-effect relationships among events:

> More and more people poured in, expecting instant wealth, freedom, and a right to share their opinions. Some immigrants were satisfied, others were displeased. Problems in other countries forced peobo move on to this New World, such as potato famins and no freedom of religions. Stories that drifted through people grew about this country. Stories of golden roads and free land coaxed other families who were living in the slums.

Another example of increasing integration is seen in children's knowledge of their local communities (Forbes, Ormrod, Bernardi, Taylor, & Jackson, 1999). In Figure 5–3 we present maps that three children drew of their hometown. The first grader's "map" includes only the few features of her town (her house, her school, nearby mountains) that she knows well, and the spatial relationships among the features are inaccurate. The third grader's map shows many features of his immediate neighborhood and their proximity to one another. The seventh grader's map encompasses numerous town landmarks and their relative locations on major streets; it also makes greater use of symbols (e.g., single lines for roads, squares for buildings, and a distinctive "M" to indicate a McDonald's restaurant).

Children and adults alike sometimes organize their knowledge into what psychologists call *schemas* and *scripts*. **Schemas** (similar, but not identical, to Piaget's *schemes*) are tightly organized bodies of information about specific objects or situations; for example, you might have a schema for what a typical horse looks like (it's a certain height, and it has an elongated head, a mane, four legs, etc.) and a schema for what a typical office contains (it probably has a desk, chair, bookshelves, books, manila folders, etc.). **Scripts** encompass knowledge about the predictable sequence of events related to particular activities; for example, you probably have scripts related to how church weddings typically proceed and about what usually happens when you go to a fast-food restaurant. Schemas and scripts help children to make sense of their experiences more readily and to predict what is likely to happen in familiar contexts on future occasions.

Schemas and scripts increase in both number and complexity as children grow older (Farrar & Goodman, 1992; Flavell et al., 1993). Like Piaget's schemes, children's earliest schemas and scripts may be behavioral and perceptual in nature; for instance, toddlers can act out typical scenarios (scripts) with toys long before they have the verbal skills to describe what they are doing (Bauer & Dow, 1994). With development, these mental structures presumably loosen their ties to physical actions and perceptual qualities.

schema
Organized and internalized body of knowledge about a specific topic.

script
Schema that involves a predictable sequence of events related to a common activity.

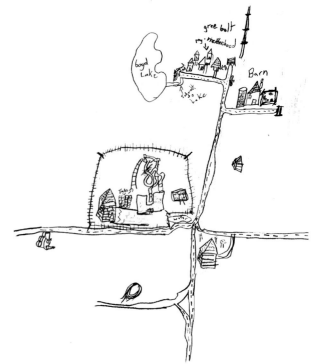

FIGURE 5–3 Three maps of Loveland, Colorado, drawn by a first grader (above), a third grader (right), and a seventh grader (below).

Maps courtesy of Dinah Jackson.

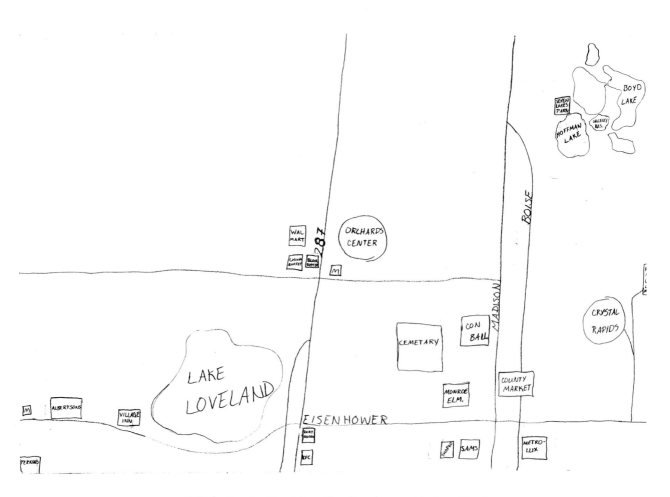

Schemas and scripts often differ somewhat from one culture to another, and such cultural differences may influence the ease with which children can understand and remember the information they encounter (Lipson, 1983; Pritchard, 1990; Reynolds, Taylor, Steffensen, Shirey, & Anderson, 1982). For example, in one study (Lipson, 1983), elementary school children read stories called "First Communion" and "Bar Mitzvah," which described coming-of-age celebrations within the Catholic and Jewish religions respectively. Children with Catholic backgrounds remembered more from "First Communion," whereas children with Jewish backgrounds remembered more from "Bar Mitzvah." In another study (Reynolds et al., 1982), eighth graders read a letter written by a young teenager, Sam, to his friend Joe. In it, Sam describes an incident in the school cafeteria earlier that day:

As these children play "store," they show that they already have a well-developed script for what typically happens at the grocery check-out counter.

> I got in line behind Bubba. As usual the line was moving pretty slow and we were all getting pretty restless. For a little action Bubba turned around and said, "Hey Sam! What you doin' man? You so ugly that when the doctor delivered you he slapped your face!" Everyone laughed, but they laughed even harder when I shot back, "Oh yeah? Well, you so ugly the doctor turned around and slapped your momma!" It got even wilder when Bubba said, "Well man, at least my daddy ain't no girl scout!" We really got into it then. After a while more people got involved—4, 5, then 6. It was a riot! People helping out anyone who seemed to be getting the worst of the deal. All of a sudden Mr. Reynolds the gym teacher came over to try to quiet things down. The next thing we knew we were all in the office. The principal made us stay after school for a week; he's so straight! On top of that, he sent word home that he wanted to talk to our folks in his office Monday afternoon. Boy! Did I get it when I got home. That's the third notice I've gotten this semester. As we were leaving the principal's office, I ran into Bubba again. We decided we'd finish where we left off, but this time we would wait until we were off the school grounds. (Reynolds et al., 1982, p. 358, italics omitted)

Many European American students incorrectly interpreted the story as one that described physical aggression, but African American students saw it for what it really was—a story about **sounding,** a friendly exchange of insults common among male youth in some African American communities.

■ *Children's growing knowledge base facilitates more effective learning.* As a general rule, older children and adults learn new information and skills more easily than younger children. A key reason for their facility is that they have more existing knowledge (including more schemas and scripts) that they can use to help them understand and organize what they learn (Eacott, 1999; Halford, 1989; Kail, 1990). When the tables are turned—for instance, when children know more about a particular topic than adults do—then children are often the more effective learners (Chi, 1978; Rabinowitz & Glaser, 1985). For example, when Jeanne's son Alex was about 5 or 6, the two of them used to read books about lizards together. Alex always remembered more from the books than Jeanne did, because he was a self-proclaimed "lizard expert," and Jeanne knew very little about reptiles of any sort.

Educational Implications of Information Processing Theory

Our discussion of information processing theory thus far leads to several implications for classroom practice:

■ *Keep distracting stimuli to a minimum.* As you have seen, students must pay attention if they are to learn and remember information and skills related to classroom subject matter. Yet many students, young ones especially, are easily distracted by the sights and sounds around them. They can more readily concentrate on the task at hand if attractive objects remain out of view, small-group activities take place as far from one another as possible, and conversations among others in the room are relatively quiet.

Despite such precautions, students can't keep their minds on a single classroom task forever—not even highly motivated high school students. Furthermore, some students (perhaps because of a seemingly boundless supply of physical energy or perhaps because of a cognitive,

sounding
Friendly, playful exchange of insults.

APPLYING INFORMATION PROCESSING THEORY

■ Minimize distractions, especially when working with young children.

As his class begins a writing assignment, a first-grade teacher asks his students to put all objects except pencil and paper inside their desks.

■ Help students automatize essential basic skills.

Students in a fourth-grade class always have a high-interest, age-appropriate children's novel tucked in their desks. Their teacher encourages them to pull out their novels whenever they have free time (e.g., when they've finished an assignment early), partly as a way of helping them automatize their ability to recognize the printed forms of many English words.

■ Begin at a level consistent with students' existing knowledge base.

At the beginning of the school year, a ninth-grade mathematics teachers gives her students a pretest covering the mathematical concepts and operations they studied the year before. She finds that many students still have difficulty computing the perimeter and area of a rectangle. She reviews these procedures and gives students additional practice with them before beginning a unit on computing the volume of objects with rectangular sides.

■ Take students' cultural backgrounds into account when considering what they probably do and do not know.

A middle school social studies class includes students who have recently immigrated from either Mexico or the Far East. When the teacher begins a lesson on courtship and wedding traditions around the world, he asks students from various ethnic backgrounds to describe the typical dating practices and wedding ceremonies in their homelands.

■ Ask students to apply classroom material to familiar contexts.

A third-grade teacher asks her students to write word problems that shows how they might use addition in their own lives. Noah writes a problem involving himself and his sister:

> Noah Had 20 Pennes. ANd She A Had 15 Pennes. Haow Mech Wad that Mack. 35.

emotional, or behavioral disability) have a more difficult time paying attention than others. With these facts in mind, teachers should give their students regular breaks from any intensive sedentary activities that they plan (Pellegrini & Bjorklund, 1997). Some breaks are built into the daily school schedule in such forms as recess, passing periods, and lunch. Teachers may want to give students additional mental "breathers" as well—perhaps by alternating relatively sedentary cognitive activities with more physical, active ones.

■ *Remember that students can think about only a small amount of information at any one time.* Although working memory capacity increases somewhat during childhood and adolescence, students of all ages (college students included!) can mentally manipulate only a very limited amount of material in their heads at once. Thus, teachers should pace any presentation of new information slowly enough that students have time to "process" it all. Teachers should also consider writing complex problems on the chalkboard or asking students to write them on paper. And they can teach students more effective strategies for learning and solving problems (more about such strategies shortly).

■ *Give students ongoing practice in using basic information and skills.* Some information and skills are so fundamental that students should be able to retrieve and use them quickly and effortlessly. To read well, students must be able to recognize most of the words on the page without having to sound them out or look them up in the dictionary. To solve mathematical word problems, students should have such number facts as "2 + 4 = 6" and "5 × 7 = 35" on the tips of their tongues. And to write well, students should be able to form letters and words without having to stop and think about how to make an uppercase *G* or spell the word *the*.

Ultimately, students can automatize basic information and skills only through using and practicing them repeatedly (Anderson, 1983; Schneider & Shiffrin, 1977). This is definitely *not* to say that teachers should fill each school day with endless drill-and-practice exercises involving isolated facts and procedures. Teachers can promote automatization just as effectively by embedding the basics in a variety of stimulating, challenging (and perhaps authentic) activities throughout the school year.

■ *Consider not only what students say, but also what they do, when determining what they know or are ready to learn.* Earlier we described a 6-year-old who said that a tall, thin glass had more water than a short, wide dish because of the height difference between the two containers. At the same time, she showed through her gestures that the tall container had a smaller diameter than the short one. Such discrepancies in what children say and do suggest a possible readiness for developing new ideas and logical reasoning skills—for instance, a readiness for acquiring conservation of liquid (Goldin-Meadow, 1997).

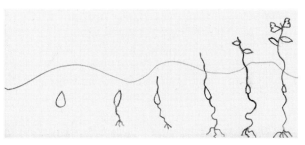

FIGURE 5–4 Noah's picture of how a seed becomes a plant

Teachers might also assess students' current knowledge by asking them to *draw* rather than describe what they have learned. For example, Figure 5–4 shows 8-year-old Noah's knowledge of how a seed becomes a plant. His picture clearly reflects his understanding that roots typically go down before a stalk grows up and that leaves gradually increase in size and number.

■ *Relate new information to students' existing knowledge base.* Numerous research studies support the idea that students learn new information more effectively when they can relate it to what they already know (e.g., Dole, Duffy, Roehler, & Pearson, 1991; McKeown & Beck, 1994). Yet students don't always make such connections on their own; for instance, they may not realize that subtraction is simply the reverse of addition or that Shakespeare's *Romeo and Juliet* has similarities to modern-day racism in the United States and to ethnic clashes in Eastern Europe. By pointing out such connections, teachers can foster not only more effective learning but also the development of a more integrated knowledge base.

The following Developmental Trends table summarizes the information processing capabilities of children and adolescents at various age levels. Up to this point, however, we have said very little about the *central executive,* the cognitive supervisor of the information processing system. Although theorists have not carefully formulated the nature of the central executive, they have learned a great deal about two of its manifestations: metacognition and cognitive strategies.

Development of Metacognition and Cognitive Strategies

As an adult with many years of formal education behind you, you have probably learned a great deal about how you think and learn. For example, you may have learned that you cannot absorb everything in a textbook the first time you read it. You may also have learned that you remember information better when you try to make sense of it based on what you already know rather than when you simply repeat it over and over again in a rote, meaningless fashion. The term **metacognition** refers both to the knowledge that people have about their own cognitive processes and to the intentional use of certain cognitive processes to improve learning and memory.

As children develop, the mental processes they use to learn information and solve problems—their **cognitive strategies**—become increasingly sophisticated and effective. Their awareness of their own thought, their beliefs about the nature of knowing and learning, and their ability to direct and regulate their own learning also change in significant ways. In the following sections we describe development in each of these areas; we then identify additional implications for instructional practice.

Learning Strategies

As children get older, they develop increasingly effective methods of learning and remembering information. Toddlers and preschoolers often recognize the need to remember something but seem to have little idea of how to go about learning it, apart from looking or pointing at it (DeLoache, Cassidy, & Brown, 1985; Kail, 1990; Wellman, 1988). But as they progress through the elementary and secondary grades, children and adolescents develop several

metacognition
Knowledge and beliefs about one's own cognitive processes, as well as efforts to regulate those cognitive processes to maximize learning and memory.

cognitive strategy
Specific mental process that people use to acquire or manipulate information.

Basic Information Processing Abilities at Different Age Levels

DEVELOPMENTAL TRENDS

AGE	WHAT YOU MIGHT OBSERVE	DIVERSITY	IMPLICATIONS
Early Childhood (2–6) 	• Short attention span • Distractibility • Emerging understanding and use of symbols • Very limited knowledge base with which to interpret new experiences	• Pronounced disabilities in information processing (e.g., ADHD, dyslexia) begin to reveal themselves in children's behavior. • Children's prior knowledge differs markedly depending on their cultural and socioeconomic backgrounds.	• Change activities often. • Keep unnecessary distractions to a minimum. • Provide a variety of experiences (field trips to the library, fire department, etc.) that enrich students' knowledge base.
Middle Childhood (6–10) 	• Increasing ability to attend to important stimuli and ignore irrelevant stimuli • Increasingly symbolic nature of thought and knowledge • Gradual automatization of basic skills • Increasing exposure to environments beyond the home and family, leading to an expanding knowledge base • Knowledge of academic subject matter relatively unintegrated, especially in science and social studies	• Mild disabilities may not become evident until the middle or upper elementary grades. • Many children with learning disabilities or ADHD have short attention spans and are easily distracted. • Some children with learning disabilities have a smaller working memory capacity than their classmates.	• Intersperse sedentary activities with more physically active ones, as a way of helping children maintain attention on classroom tasks. • Give students many opportunities to practice basic knowledge and skills (e.g., number facts, word recognition), often through authentic, motivating, and challenging tasks. • Begin to explore hierarchies, cause and effect, and other interrelationships among ideas in science, history, geography, and other subject areas • Consult experts when you suspect that learning or behavior problems might reflect a cognitive disability.
Early Adolescence (10–14) 	• Ability to attend to a single task for an hour or more • Basic skills in reading, writing, and mathematics (e.g., word identification, common word spellings, basic math facts) largely automatized • Growing (though not necessarily well-organized) knowledge base in various academic disciplines	• Many students with information processing difficulties have trouble paying attention for an entire class period. • Many students with sensory or physical disabilities (e.g., students who are blind or in a wheelchair) have a more limited knowledge base than their classmates, due to fewer opportunities to explore the local community.	• Provide variety in classroom tasks as a way of keeping students' attention. • Frequently point out how concepts and ideas are related to one another, both within and across academic disciplines. • Provide extra guidance and support for students with diagnosed or suspected information processing difficulties.
Late Adolescence (14–18) 	• Ability to attend to a single task for lengthy periods • Extensive and somewhat integrated knowledge about some content domains	• High school students have choices in course selection, leading to differences in the extent of their knowledge base in various content domains.	• Occasionally give assignments that require students to focus on a particular task for a long period. • Consistently encourage students to think about the "hows" and "whys" of what they are learning. • Assess students' learning in ways that require them to depict relationships among ideas.

learning strategies—specific methods of learning information—that help them learn more effectively. Here we describe three learning strategies that appear during the school years: rehearsal, organization, and elaboration.

Rehearsal   What do you do if you need to remember a telephone number for a few minutes? Do you repeat it to yourself over and over as a way of keeping it in your working memory until you can dial it? This process of **rehearsal** is rare in preschoolers but increases in frequency and effectiveness throughout the elementary school years (Bjorklund & Coyle, 1995; Gathercole & Hitch, 1993; Kail, 1990).

Rehearsal takes different forms at different ages; following are some examples:

- When preschoolers are asked to remember a particular set of toys, they tend to look at, name, and handle the toys more than they would otherwise; however, such actions have little effect on their memory for the toys (Baker-Ward, Ornstein, & Holden, 1984).
- At age 6, children can be trained to repeat a list of items as a way of helping them remember those items, but even after such training they rarely use rehearsal unless specifically told to do so (Keeney, Canizzo, & Flavell, 1967).
- By age 7 or 8, children often rehearse information spontaneously, as evidenced by lip movements and whispering during a learning task. However, they tend to repeat each item they need to remember in isolation from the others (Gathercole & Hitch, 1993; Kunzinger, 1985).
- By age 9 or 10, children combine items into a single list as they rehearse (Gathercole & Hitch, 1993; Kunzinger, 1985). As an example, if they hear the list "cat . . . dog . . . horse," they will repeat "cat" after the first item, say "cat, dog" after the second, and say "cat, dog, horse" after the third. Combining the separate items during rehearsal helps children remember them more effectively.

Keep in mind, of course, that the ages we've just presented are *averages;* some children develop various forms of rehearsal sooner than others.

Organization   Take a minute to study the following 12 words; then cover them up and try to recall as many as you can.

shirt	table	hat
carrot	bed	squash
pants	potato	stool
chair	shoe	bean

In what order did you remember the words? Did you recall them in their original order, or did you rearrange them somehow? If you are like most people, then you grouped the words into three semantic categories—clothing, furniture, and vegetables—and recalled them category by category. In other words, you used **organization** to help you learn and remember the information. Research consistently shows that organized information is learned more easily and remembered more completely than unorganized information.

Even preschoolers organize information under certain circumstances. For instance, imagine that an experimenter shows you 12 identical containers, several candies, and several wooden pegs (see Figure 5–5). The experimenter places either a piece of candy or a wooden peg in each one and then closes it so that you cannot see its contents. How can you remember what each container holds? An easy yet effective strategy is to divide the containers into two groups, one with candy and one with pegs, as the experimenter fills them. Many 4-year-old children spontaneously use this strategy (DeLoache & Todd, 1988).

Yet in the preschool and early elementary years, children often have little awareness that they're organizing what they're trying to remember, and the categories they form are based on appearance, function, or common associates (e.g., table–chair, dog–cat). As children move through the late elementary, middle school, and secondary grades, however, they increasingly organize information to help them learn it, and they often do so intentionally. Furthermore, their organizational patterns become more sophisticated, reflecting semantic, and often fairly abstract, categories (e.g., furniture, animals) (Bjorklund & Jacobs, 1985; Bjorklund, Schneider, Cassel, & Ashley, 1994; DeLoache & Todd, 1988; Plumert, 1994).

learning strategy
Specific mental process used in acquiring new information.

rehearsal
Attempt to learn and remember information by repeating it over and over.

organization
Finding interrelationships among pieces of information as a way of learning them more effectively.

FIGURE 5–5

While you watch, an experimenter randomly places either a candy or a wooden peg into each of 12 containers and closes its lid. What simple strategy could you use to help you remember which containers hold candy?

Modeled after DeLoache & Todd, 1988.

Elaboration   If we tell you that we've both spent many years living in Colorado, you will probably conclude that we either live or have lived in or near the Rocky Mountains. You might also infer that we have, perhaps, done a lot of skiing, hiking, or camping. In this situation, you are learning more than the information we actually gave you; you are also learning some information that you, yourself, supplied. This process of **elaboration**—adding additional ideas to new information based on what you already know—clearly facilitates learning and memory, sometimes quite dramatically.

Children begin to elaborate on their experiences as early as the preschool years (Fivush, Haden, & Adam, 1995). As a strategy that students *intentionally* use to help them learn, however, elaboration appears relatively late in child development (usually around puberty) and gradually increases throughout the teenage years (Flavell et al., 1993; Schneider & Pressley, 1989; Siegler, 1991). Even in high school, it is primarily students with high academic achievement who use their existing knowledge to help them learn new information. Low-achieving high school students are much less likely to use elaboration strategies as an aid to learning, and many students of all ability levels resort to rehearsal for difficult, hard-to-understand material (Pressley, 1982; Wood, Motz, & Willoughby, 1997; Wood, Willoughby, Reilley, Elliott, & DuCharme, 1994). In general, students are unlikely to engage in elaboration when they are traveling in unfamiliar waters—when they have *no* prior knowledge to which they can relate what they are studying.

Environmental and Cultural Influences on Learning Strategy Development
Environment appears to play a major role in the kinds of strategies children develop. For example, children are more likely to use effective learning strategies when teachers and other adults teach and encourage their use (Flavell et al., 1993; Ryan, Ledger, & Weed, 1987). Culture, too, makes a difference. Children in African schools have better strategies for remembering orally transmitted stories than children in American schools (Dube, 1982). Children in China and Japan rely more heavily on rehearsal than their counterparts in Western schools, perhaps because their schools place a greater emphasis on rote memorization and drill-and-practice (Ho, 1994; Purdie & Hattie, 1996). Children in typical Western schools appear to have better strategies for learning lists of words (e.g., rehearsal, organization) than unschooled children in developing nations, probably because list-learning tasks are more common in school settings (Cole & Schribner, 1977; Flavell et al., 1993).

This is not to say that schooling aids the development of *all* learning strategies, however. For instance, in a study by Kearins (1981), unschooled children in Australian aborigine

elaboration
Using prior knowledge to expand on new information and thereby learn it more effectively.

communities more effectively remembered the spatial arrangements of objects than children who attended Australian schools. The aborigine children lived in a harsh desert environment with little rainfall, and so their families moved frequently from place to place in search of new food sources. With each move, the children had to quickly learn the spatial arrangements of subtle landmarks in the local vicinity so that they could find their way home from any direction (Kearins, 1981).

Problem-Solving Strategies

As children develop, they acquire increasingly more powerful and effective ways of solving problems (e.g., Siegler, 1981, 1991). Consider the following problem: *If I have 2 apples and you give me 4 more apples, how many apples do I have altogether?* Young children can often solve such problems even if they have not yet had specific instruction in addition at school. A strategy that emerges early in development is simply to put up two fingers and then four additional fingers and count all the fingers to reach the solution of "6 apples." Somewhat later, children may begin to use a *min* strategy, whereby they start with the larger number (for the apple problem, they would start with 4) and then add on, one by one, the smaller number (e.g., counting "four apples . . . then five, six . . . six apples altogether") (Siegler & Jenkins, 1989). Still later, of course, children learn the basic addition facts (e.g., "2 + 4 = 6") that enable them to bypass the relatively inefficient counting strategies they've used earlier.

Children's problem solving sometimes involves applying certain *rules* to a particular type of problem, with more complex and effective rules evolving over time. As an example, consider the balancing task depicted in Figure 5–6. The first picture in the figure shows a wooden beam resting on a fulcrum; because the fulcrum is located at the exact middle of the beam, the beam balances, with neither side falling down. Imagine that, while holding the beam horizontal, we hang a 6-pound weight on the fourth peg to the right of the fulcrum and a 3-pound weight on the ninth peg to the left of the fulcrum. Will the beam continue to be balanced when we let go of it, or will one side fall?

Robert Siegler (1976, 1978, 1991) has found that children acquire a series of increasingly more complex rules to solve such a problem. Initially (perhaps at age 5), they consider only the amount of weight on each side of the beam; comparing 6 pounds to 3 pounds, they would predict that the right side of the beam will fall. Later (perhaps at age 9), they begin to consider distance as well as weight, recognizing that weights located farther from the fulcrum have a greater effect, but their reasoning is not precise enough to ensure correct solutions; in the balance problem in Figure 5–6, they would merely guess at how greater distance compensates

The equipment: Balance and weights

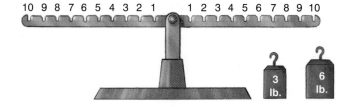

The problem:

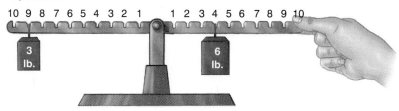

FIGURE 5–6 A beam without weights balances on a fulcrum located at its center. After weights are hung from the beam in the manner shown here, will the beam continue to balance? If not, which side of the beam will drop?

for greater weight. Eventually (perhaps in high school), they may develop a rule that reflects a multiplicative relationship between weight and distance:

For the beam to balance, the product of weight and distance on one side must equal the product of weight and distance on the other side. In cases where the two products are unequal, the side with the larger product will fall.

Applying this rule to the problem in Figure 5–6, a student would determine that the product on the left side (3 × 9 = 27) is greater than the product on the right side (6 × 4 = 24) and so would correctly predict that the left side will fall.

Strategy Development as "Overlapping Waves"

Information processing theorists have found that a cognitive strategy doesn't necessarily appear all at once; instead, it emerges gradually over time. For instance, children first use learning strategies (e.g., organization and elaboration) somewhat accidentally; only later do they recognize the effectiveness of these strategies and intentionally use them to remember new information (DeLoache & Todd, 1988; Flavell et al., 1993). Children also use newly acquired strategies infrequently, and often ineffectively, at the beginning. With time and practice, they become more adept at applying their strategies successfully, efficiently, and flexibly as they tackle challenging tasks (Alexander, Graham, & Harris, 1998; Flavell et al., 1993; Siegler, 1991).

Once children reach elementary school, they often have several strategies to choose from when dealing with a particular learning or problem-solving task, and so they may vary from one day to the next in their use of these strategies (Siegler & Ellis, 1996). Some strategies may be developmentally more advanced than others, yet because children initially have trouble using them effectively, they may resort to less efficient but more dependable "backup" strategies. For example, when children first learn basic number facts, they cannot always retrieve those facts quickly and easily and so may instead count on their fingers—a strategy that they *know* will yield a correct answer—when dealing with simple math problems. Eventually, however, they acquire sufficient proficiency with their new strategies that they can comfortably leave the earlier ones behind (Siegler, 1989; Siegler & Jenkins, 1989).

From an information processing perspective, then, strategic development does *not* occur in stages, one step at a time. Instead, each strategy emerges slowly and increases in frequency and effectiveness over a lengthy period, perhaps over several months or several years. As children gain competence and confidence with more sophisticated strategies, they slowly shed their less efficient ones (Alexander et al., 1998; Flavell et al., 1993; Siegler & Jenkins, 1989). Siegler (1996b) has used the analogy of *overlapping waves,* depicted in Figure 5–7, to describe this process.

Just as there is variability in the strategies that each child uses from one occasion to the next, so, too, is there variability in the strategies that different children of the same age use for any particular situation (Siegler & Jenkins, 1989). For instance, in any high school classroom, some students may use organization and elaboration to study for a test whereas others resort to rote rehearsal. Such individual differences are due, in part, to the fact that some children and adolescents acquire competence with particular strategies sooner than others do. Other factors make a difference as well: Familiarity with the subject matter fosters more advanced strategies, as does personal interest in the task at hand (Alexander et al., 1998; Bergin, 1996; Folds, Footo, Guttentag, & Ornstein, 1990; Woody-Ramsey & Miller, 1988).

Metacognitive Awareness

In addition to acquiring new cognitive strategies, children acquire increasingly sophisticated knowledge about the nature of thinking. Such **metacognitive awareness** includes (a) awareness of the existence of thought and then, later, awareness about (b) one's own thought processes, (c) the limitations of memory, and (d) effective learning and memory strategies.

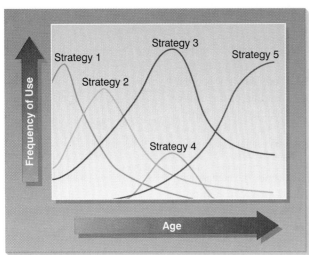

FIGURE 5–7 Strategic development as overlapping waves: Students gradually replace simple cognitive strategies with more advanced and effective ones. Here we see how five different strategies for dealing with the same task might change in frequency over time.

From *Children's Thinking* (3rd ed., p. 92), by R. Siegler, 1998, Upper Saddle River, NJ: Prentice Hall. Copyright 1998 by Prentice Hall. Adapted with permission.

metacognitive awareness
Extent to which one is able to reflect on the nature of one's own thinking processes.

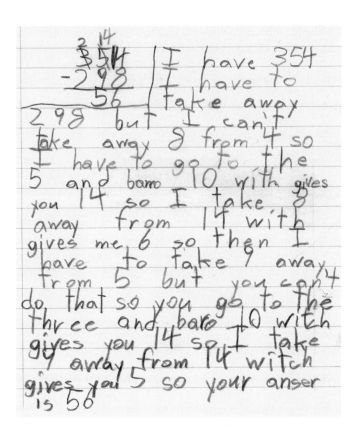

Awareness of the Existence of Thought By the time children reach the age of 3, they are aware of thinking as an entity in its own right (Flavell, Green, & Flavell, 1995). Their initial understanding of thought is quite simplistic, however. They are likely to say that a person is "thinking" only when he or she is actively engaged in a challenging task and has a thoughtful or puzzled facial expression. They also view thought and learning as relatively passive activities (e.g., the mind acquires and holds information but doesn't do much with it), rather than as the active, constructive processes that they really are (Flavell et al., 1995; Wellman, 1990).

Awareness of One's Own Thought Processes Although many preschoolers have the words *know, remember,* and *forget* in their vocabularies, they don't fully grasp the nature of knowing, remembering, and forgetting. For instance, 3-year-olds use the term *forget* simply to mean "not knowing" something, regardless of whether they knew the information at an earlier time (Lyon & Flavell, 1994). When 4- and 5-year-old children are taught a new piece of information, they may say that they've known it for quite some time (Taylor, Esbensen, & Bennett, 1994).

During the elementary and secondary school years, children and adolescents become better able to reflect on their own thought processes and so are increasingly aware of the nature of their thinking and learning (Flavell et al., 1993; Wellman & Hickling, 1994). To some extent, teachers and other adults may foster such development by talking about the mind's activities—for instance, when they speak about someone "thinking a lot" or about someone's mind "wandering," and when they encourage children to "think harder" or "keep your mind on what you're doing" (Berk, 1997). Possibly beneficial, too, is specifically *asking* children to reflect on what they're thinking. As an example, Figure 5–8 shows 8-year-old Noah's explanation of how he solved the problem 354 − 298.

Awareness of Memory Limitations Young children tend to be overly optimistic about how much they can remember. As they grow older and encounter a greater variety of learning tasks, they discover that some things are more difficult to learn than others (Bjorklund & Green, 1992; Flavell et al., 1993). They also begin to realize that their memories are not perfect—that they cannot possibly remember everything they see or hear. As an example of the latter trend, let's consider an experiment with elementary school children (Flavell, Friedrichs, & Hoyt, 1970).

Children in four age groups (ranging from preschool to fourth grade) were shown strips of paper with pictures of 1 to 10 objects. The children were asked to predict how many of the objects they could remember over a short period of time. The average predictions of each age group, and the average number of objects the children actually *did* remember, were as follows:

Age Group	Predicted Number	Actual Number
Preschool	7.2	3.5
Kindergarten	8.0	3.6
Grade 2	6.0	4.4
Grade 4	6.1	5.5

Notice how all four age groups predicted that they would remember more objects than they actually could. But the older children were more realistic about the limitations of their memories than the younger ones. The kindergartners predicted they would remember eight objects, when they actually remembered fewer than four!

Children's overly optimistic assessment of their own learning and memory capabilities may actually be beneficial for their cognitive development. In particular, it may give them the confidence to try new and difficult tasks—the challenges that, from Vygotsky's perspective, promote cognitive growth—that they would probably avoid if they were more realistic about their abilities (Bjorklund & Green, 1992). Too often we have seen older children and adolescents *not* take on challenging tasks simply because they were aware of their own limitations and so had doubts that they could succeed.

Knowledge About Effective Learning and Memory Strategies   Imagine this: It is January, and you live in a cold climate. Just before you go to bed, some friends ask you to go ice skating with them right after class tomorrow. What might you do to be sure that you remember to take your ice skates to class with you?

Older children typically generate more strategies than younger children for remembering to take a pair of skates to school. Yet even kindergartners can often identify one or more effective strategies. In a classic study, Kreutzer, Leonard, & Flavell (1975) found that children in the elementary grades tend to depend on external reminders rather than on internal, mental strategies. For instance, some children said that they might write a note to themselves, and others thought that they might ask a parent to remind them. One ingenious child suggested that sleeping with his skates on would be a sure-fire way of remembering them the following morning.

As mentioned earlier, children show greater use of such internal learning and memory strategies as rehearsal, organization, and elaboration as they grow older. With experience, they also become increasingly aware of what strategies are effective in different situations (Lovett & Flavell, 1990; Short, Schatschneider, & Friebert, 1993; Wellman, 1985). For example, consider the simple idea that, when you don't learn something the first time you try, you need to study it again. This is a strategy that 8-year-olds use, but 6-year-olds do not (Masur, McIntyre, & Flavell, 1973). In a similar way, 10th graders are more aware than 8th graders of the advantages of using elaboration to learn new information (Waters, 1982). Even so, many students of all ages seem relatively uninformed about which learning strategies work most effectively in different situations (Ormrod & Jenkins, 1989; Thomas, 1993; Waters, 1982).

Two aspects of self-regulation are planning effective use of study time and evaluating knowledge gained from a learning activity. This student planned to read one chapter during study hour and ask himself questions about it afterward.

self-regulated learning
Directing and regulating one's own cognitive processes in order to learn successfully.

Self-Regulated Learning

As children and adolescents grow more aware of their own learning and memory processes, they also become more capable of directing and regulating their learning. To engage in such **self-regulated learning**, learners must have acquired capabilities such as the following (Schunk & Zimmerman, 1997; Winne, 1995a):

- Setting goals for a learning activity
- Planning an effective use of learning and study time
- Maintaining attention on the subject matter to be learned
- Identifying and using appropriate learning strategies
- Monitoring progress toward goals, evaluating the effectiveness of learning strategies, and adjusting goals or learning strategies as necessary
- Evaluating the final knowledge gained from the learning activity

As you can see, self-regulated learning is a complex, multifaceted process. In its "mature" form, it is virtually nonexistent in elementary school students. Even at the secondary level, few students can effectively regulate their own learning; those who *are* self-regulating tend to be the most academically successful (Bronson, 2000; Schunk & Zimmerman, 1997; Zimmerman & Risemberg, 1997).

Three theoretical perspectives have contributed to developmentalists' current understanding of self-regulated learning. First, of course, is information processing theorists' work regarding the nature of learning and memory. Second is social cognitive theorists' research on self-regulated behavior (more on this topic in Chapter 11). Third is Vygotsky's proposal that, through such mechanisms as self-talk and inner speech, growing children gradually transform social interactions into mental processes.

Here we look briefly at three aspects of self-regulated learning: attention control, monitoring progress toward goals, and evaluating the effectiveness of learning strategies. We then consider how the process of *co-regulation* can foster the development of self-regulation.

Attention Control   As a college student, you probably do several things to keep your attention focused on the subject matter you want to learn. Perhaps you identify a time when you know you will be alert and ready to concentrate, locate a quiet place to read, and then, as you study, try to keep your mind clear of irrelevant thoughts. Such efforts to control your own attentional processes are critical to effective self-regulated learning (Rothbart & Ahadi, 1994).

As noted earlier, many children, younger ones especially, are easily distracted by the sights and sounds around them and so have difficulty paying attention for any length of time. Yet children can learn to better control their attention through self-talk, perhaps through the five steps presented in Chapter 4 (see Figure 4–9). Through these five steps, impulsive and distractible elementary school children can effectively learn to slow themselves down and think through what they are doing (Meichenbaum & Goodman, 1971). For example, notice how one formerly impulsive student was able to talk his way through a matching task in which he needed to find two identical pictures among several very similar ones:

> I have to remember to go slowly to get it right. Look carefully at this one, now look at these carefully. Is this one different? Yes, it has an extra leaf. Good, I can eliminate this one. Now, let's look at this one. I think it's this one, but let me first check the others. Good, I'm going slow and carefully. Okay, I think it's this one. (Meichenbaum & Goodman, 1971, p. 121)

Monitoring Progress Toward Goals   When you study, what do you do to make sure you're learning the subject matter? Perhaps you think about how various ideas are either consistent or inconsistent with things you already know. Perhaps you ask yourself questions about the material and then try to answer them. Perhaps you study with friends, reviewing the material as a group and identifying possible differences of opinion about what a particular author is trying to communicate. Such activities are examples of **comprehension monitoring**, the process of checking one's understanding regularly while learning.

Children's ability to monitor their own comprehension improves throughout the school years, and so children and adolescents become increasingly aware of when they actually know something. Young children (e.g., those in the early elementary grades) often think they know or understand something before they actually do. As a result, they don't study classroom material as much as they should, and they often don't ask questions when they receive incomplete or confusing information (Markman, 1977; McDevitt, Spivey, Sheehan, Lennon, & Story, 1990). Even high school and college students sometimes have difficulty assessing their own knowledge accurately; for example, they often overestimate how well they will perform on an exam (Horgan, 1990; Ormrod & Wagner, 1987).

Evaluating the Effectiveness of Learning Strategies   Not only do children and adolescents often misjudge the degree to which they have learned something, but they may also fail to evaluate the effectiveness of the learning strategies they are using. As a result, they don't always choose the most effective learning strategies (Pressley, Levin, & Ghatala, 1984; Pressley, Ross, Levin, & Ghatala, 1984).

For example, in one study (Pressley, Ross, et al., 1984), 10- to 13-year-olds learned the definitions of new vocabulary words (e.g., *handsel* means "a small payment") using two different techniques. For some words, they used a strategy they had used in their classes many times

comprehension monitoring
Process of checking oneself to make sure one understands what one is learning.

before: Construct a sentence that contains the new vocabulary word. For other words, they were taught a new strategy: Identify a common word (*keyword*) that sounds like the vocabulary word and then construct a sentence that incorporates both the keyword and the vocabulary word's meaning. To illustrate, a keyword for *handsel* might be *hand;* thus, one could construct the sentence "She carried a *small payment* in her *hand* (Pressley, Ross, et al., 1994, p. 492). The children remembered vocabulary words' meanings much more easily using the keyword method. However, when later asked to learn additional vocabulary words, the majority of students rejected the keyword method in favor of the less effective but more familiar use-the-word-in-a-sentence method. Only when the experimenter specifically asked them to consider how they had performed previously after using each of the two methods did they spontaneously choose to use the keyword method in vocabulary learning tasks.

Co-Regulation as a Facilitator of Self-Regulation   Using Vygotsky's perspective, we might reasonably suspect that self-regulated learning has its roots in, and so must be preceded by, socially regulated learning, in the following fashion: Initially, other people (e.g., parents, teachers) help children learn by setting goals for a learning activity, keeping their attention focused on the learning task, suggesting effective learning strategies, monitoring learning progress, and so on. Over time, children assume increasing responsibility for these processes; that is, they begin to set their *own* learning goals, stay on task with little prodding from others, identify potentially effective strategies, and evaluate their own learning.

Developmentally speaking, a reasonable bridge between other-regulated learning and self-regulated learning is **co-regulated learning**, in which a teacher and students share responsibility for directing the various aspects of the learning process (McCaslin & Good, 1996). For instance, the teacher and students might mutually agree on the specific goals of a learning endeavor, or the teacher might describe the criteria that indicate successful learning and then have students evaluate their own performance in light of those criteria. Initially, the teacher might provide considerable structure, or scaffolding, for the students' learning efforts; in a true Vygotskian fashion, such scaffolding is gradually removed as students become more effectively self-regulating.

Epistemological Beliefs

As people who learn new things every day, we all have ideas about what "knowledge" and "learning" are—ideas that are collectively known as **epistemological beliefs.** Included in people's epistemological beliefs are their views about

- The certainty of knowledge
- The simplicity and structure of knowledge
- The source of knowledge
- The speed of learning
- The nature of learning ability

As children and adolescents develop, many (though not all) of them change their beliefs in each of these areas; typical changes are shown in Table 5–1. For example, children in the elementary grades typically believe in the certainty of knowledge; they think that the absolute truth about any topic is somewhere "out there" waiting to be discovered (Astington & Pelletier, 1996). As they reach the high school and college years, some begin to realize that knowledge is a subjective entity and that different perspectives on a topic may be equally valid (Perry, 1968; Schommer, 1994b, 1997). Additional changes may also occur in high school; for example, students in 12th grade are more likely than 9th graders to believe that knowledge consists of complex interrelationships (rather than discrete facts), that learning happens slowly (rather than quickly), and that learning ability can improve with practice (rather than being fixed at birth) (Schommer, 1997).

Students' epistemological beliefs influence the ways in which they study and learn (Hofer & Pintrich, 1997; Purdie, Hattie, & Douglas, 1996; Schommer, 1997). For example, when students believe that knowledge is black-and-white (ideas are indisputably either right or wrong), that one either has that knowledge or doesn't, and that learning is a relatively rapid process, they give up quickly if they find themselves struggling to understand classroom material. In contrast, when students believe that knowledge is a complex body of information that is learned gradu-

co-regulated learning
Process through which a teacher and learner share responsibility for directing various aspects of the learning process.

epistemological beliefs
Beliefs regarding the nature of knowledge and knowledge acquisition.

TABLE 5–1 Developmental Changes in Epistemological Beliefs

WITH REGARD TO . . .	CHILDREN INITIALLY BELIEVE THAT . . .	AS THEY DEVELOP, THEY MAY EVENTUALLY BEGIN TO REALIZE THAT . . .
The certainty of knowledge	Knowledge about a topic is a fixed, unchanging, absolute "truth."	Knowledge about a topic (even that of experts) is a tentative, dynamic entity that continues to evolve as ongoing inquiry and research add new insights and ideas.
The simplicity and structure of knowledge	Knowledge is a collection of discrete and isolated facts.	Knowledge is a set of complex and interrelated ideas.
The source of knowledge	Knowledge comes from outside the learner; that is, it comes from a teacher or "authority" of some kind.	Knowledge is derived and constructed by learners themselves.
The speed of learning	Knowledge is acquired quickly, and in an all-or-none fashion, or else not at all. As a result, people either know something or they don't.	Knowledge is acquired gradually over time. Thus, people can have greater or lesser degrees of knowledge about a topic.
The nature of learning ability	People's ability to learn is fixed at birth (it is inherited).	People's ability to learn can improve over time with practice and the use of better strategies.

Sources: Astington & Pelletier, 1996; Hammer, 1994; Hofer & Pintrich, 1997; Hogan, 1997; Linn, Songer, & Eylon, 1996; Perry, 1968; Schommer, 1994a, 1994b, 1997.

ally with time and effort, they are likely to use a wide variety of learning strategies, and they persist until they have made sense of the ideas they are studying (Butler & Winne, 1995; Kardash & Howell, 1996; Schommer, 1994a, 1994b). Not surprisingly, then, students with more advanced epistemological beliefs achieve at higher levels in the classroom (Schommer, 1994a).

Furthermore, more advanced levels of academic achievement may, in turn, bring about more advanced views about knowledge and learning (Schommer, 1994b; Strike & Posner, 1992). The more that students get beyond the "basics" and explore the far reaches of the disciplines—whether science, mathematics, history, literature, or something else—the more they discover that learning involves acquiring an integrated and cohesive set of ideas, that even the experts don't know everything about a topic, and that truly complete and accurate "knowledge" of how the world operates may ultimately be an unattainable goal.

We speculate, however, that less sophisticated epistemological beliefs probably have some benefits for young children. Children may initially be more motivated to learn about a topic if they think there are absolute, unchanging facts (and sometimes there are!) that they can easily learn and remember. And it is often very efficient to rely on parents, teachers, and the library as authoritative sources for desired information.

Interdependence of Cognitive and Metacognitive Processes

Developmental changes in the various areas we've described—attention, memory, knowledge base, cognitive strategies, metacognitive awareness, self-regulated learning, and epistemological beliefs—are clearly interdependent. For instance, children's improving ability to pay attention and their increasing self-regulatory efforts to *control* their attention enable them to learn more from classroom activities. Their growing knowledge base, in turn, enhances their ability to use such learning strategies as organization and elaboration while reading and studying. As learning and problem-solving strategies become more effective and efficient, these strategies require less working memory capacity and so enable children to deal with more complex tasks and problems.

As adolescents' beliefs about the nature of knowledge become more sophisticated, so, too, are their learning strategies likely to change in light of those beliefs. For example, if high school students conceptualize "knowledge" about a topic as a unified body of facts and inter-relations, they are more likely to use such strategies as organization and elaboration, rather than simple rehearsal, to master that topic. Furthermore, their growing comprehension-monitoring abilities give them feedback about what they are and are not learning and so may enhance their awareness of which learning strategies are effective and which are not.

Educational Implications of Metacognitive and Strategic Development

Theories and research on the development of metacognition and cognitive strategies yield several implications for instruction:

■ *Teach, model, and encourage effective learning and problem-solving strategies.* Cognitive strategies make such a difference in students' classroom achievement that teachers shouldn't leave the development of these strategies to chance. As teachers ask students to study and learn classroom subject matter, they should also give students suggestions about *how* to study and learn it. Such an approach is consistent not only with information processing theory but also with Vygotsky's proposal that adults can better promote children's cognitive development by talking about how they themselves think about challenging tasks.

A rapidly growing body of research indicates that children and adolescents *can* be taught to use more effective cognitive strategies. For instance, even 4- and 5-year-olds can be taught to organize objects into categories as a way of helping them remember the objects (Carr & Schneider, 1991; Lange & Pierce, 1992). As children encounter increasingly challenging learning tasks, organization alone is, of course, not enough. By the time they reach high school, adolescents will need to learn—and should be explicitly taught—many additional learning strategies, such as elaboration, comprehension monitoring, goal setting, note taking, and time management. Explicit instruction about how to use such strategies fosters better learning and higher classroom achievement (Hattie, Biggs, & Purdie, 1996). It is most effective when

- Strategies are taught within the context of specific academic subject matter, rather than in isolation from actual classroom tasks.
- Students learn many different strategies and the situations in which each one is appropriate.
- Students practice new strategies frequently and with a wide variety of learning and problem-solving tasks.
  (Hattie et al., 1996; Pressley, El-Dinary, Marks, Brown, & Stein, 1992)

Small-group learning activities, especially when structured in particular ways, can also promote more sophisticated cognitive strategies. One approach is to teach students to ask one another thought-provoking questions about the material they are studying. This technique, sometimes called **elaborative interrogation,** appears to promote both better recall for facts and increased integration of ideas (Kahl & Woloshyn, 1994; King, 1994; Wood et al., 1999). Following is a dialogue between two seventh graders who have been taught to use elaborative interrogation:

Jon:	How does the muscular system work, Kyle?
Kyle:	Well . . . it retracts and contracts when you move.
Jon:	Can you tell me more?
Kyle:	Um . . . well . . .
Jon:	Um, why are muscles important, Kyle?
Kyle:	They are important because if we didn't have them we couldn't move around.
Jon:	But . . . how do muscles work? Explain it more.
Kyle:	Um, muscles have tendons. Some muscles are called skeletal muscles. They are in the muscles that—like—in your arms—that have tendons that hold your muscles to your bones—to make them move and go back and forth. So you can walk and stuff.
Jon:	Good. All right! How are the skeletal muscles and the cardiac muscles the same?
Kyle:	Uhh—the cardiac and the smooth muscles?
Jon:	The cardiac and the skeletal.
Kyle:	Well, they're both a muscle. And they're both pretty strong. And they hold things. I don't really think they have much in common.
Jon:	Okay. Why don't you think they have much in common?

elaborative interrogation
Study strategy in which students develop and answer questions designed to promote elaboration of new material.

PROMOTING METACOGNITIVE AND STRATEGIC DEVELOPMENT

■ Encourage learning strategies appropriate for the age group.

An elementary teacher encourages his students to study their spelling words by repeating the letters of each word over and over to themselves. In contrast, a high school teacher asks her students to think about why certain historical events may have happened as they did; for example, she encourages them to speculate about the personal motives, economic circumstances, and political and social issues that may have influenced people's decision making at the time.

■ Model effective learning and problem-solving strategies and encourage students to use such strategies themselves.

A high school chemistry teacher tells her students, "Learning the symbols for all the elements is going to take some time. Some, like H for hydrogen and O for oxygen, are easy. But others, like K for potassium and Na for sodium, are more challenging. Let's take five new symbols each day and develop a strategy that can help you remember each one."

■ Identify situations in which various strategies are likely to be useful.

A fifth-grade teacher says to his class, "We've studied several features of the nine planets in our solar system—size, color, composition, distance from the sun, and duration of revolution around the sun. This sounds like a situation where a two-dimensional chart might help us organize the information."

■ Give students opportunities to practice learning with little or no help from their teacher; provide the scaffolding necessary to ensure their success.

A middle school social studies teacher distributes various magazine articles related to current events in the Middle East, making sure that each student receives an article appropriate for his or her reading level. She asks her students to read their articles over the weekend and prepare a one-paragraph summary to share with other class members. She also provides guidelines about what information students should include in their summaries.

■ Give students numerous opportunities to assess their own learning efforts and thereby to find out what they do and don't know.

A health teacher has students read a textbook chapter at home and then gives them a nongraded quiz to help them identify parts of the chapter that they may need to read again.

■ Encourage students to assess their own learning, perhaps by suggesting that they ask themselves questions both as they study and at some time later.

An elementary teacher instructs his students to study their spelling words as soon as they get home from school, then to make sure they can still remember how to spell the words after they have eaten dinner. "You might also want to ask a family member to test you on the words," he suggests.

■ Talk with students about the nature of knowledge and learning in various disciplines.

A history teacher has students read three different accounts of a particular historical event as a way of helping them discover that history is not necessarily all clear-cut facts—that there are sometimes varying perspectives on what occurred and why.

Kyle: Because the smooth muscle is—I mean the skeletal muscle is voluntary and the cardiac muscle is involuntary. Okay, I'll ask now. What do you think would happen if we didn't have smooth muscles?

Jon: We would have to be chewing harder. And so it would take a long time to digest food. We would have to think about digesting because the smooth muscles—like the intestines and stomach—are *involuntary.*

Kyle: Have you really thought about it?

Jon: Yeah.

Kyle: Yeah, well—um—but, do you think it would *hurt* you if you didn't have smooth muscles?

Jon: Well, yeah—because you wouldn't have muscles to push the food along—in the stomach and intestines—you'd get plugged up! Maybe you'd hafta drink liquid— just liquid stuff. Yuk. (King, Staffieri, & Adelgais, 1998, p. 141)

Elaborative interrogation is probably effective, at least in part, because it encourages students to use sophisticated learning processes (e.g., organization, elaboration) rather than rote rehearsal. Furthermore, in a Vygotskian fashion, students may eventually internalize such mutual question asking, so that they eventually ask *themselves,* and then answer, equally challenging questions as they study.

These students are asking each other thought-provoking questions about the chapter they are studying. This technique, sometimes called *elaborative interrogation,* promotes better recall for facts and increased integration of ideas.

■ *Give students frequent feedback about their learning progress.* When teachers give frequent feedback, they not only promote students' learning and classroom achievement but foster metacognitive development as well. Students who get regular and specific feedback about what they are and are not learning are likely to discover that their memories are, at best, only imperfect records of their experiences and that learning tends to be a slow, gradual process rather than a rapid, all-or-none occurrence.

Teachers can also use feedback to encourage the development of more effective learning strategies. In particular, they might ask students to study similar sets of information in two different ways—perhaps to study one using rehearsal and another using elaboration. They can then assess students' recollection of both sets of information: Presumably the more effective strategy will have promoted better learning and memory. With repeated, concrete comparisons of the effectiveness of different strategies, students will gradually discard the less effective ones for those that will serve them well as they encounter more challenging learning tasks in the years to come.

■ *Provide opportunities for students to evaluate their own learning, and help them develop mechanisms for doing so effectively.* As noted earlier, self-regulated learners monitor their progress throughout a learning task and then evaluate their ultimate success in mastering the material they have been studying. Theorists have offered several recommendations for promoting self-monitoring and self-evaluation in students:

- Teach students to ask themselves, and then answer, questions about the material they are reading and studying (Rosenshine, Meiser, & Chapman, 1996).
- Have students set specific goals for each study session and then describe their achievements relative to those objectives (Morgan, 1985).
- Provide specific criteria that students can use to judge their performance (Winne, 1995b).
- On some occasions, delay teacher feedback, so that students first have the opportunity to evaluate their own performance (Butler & Winne, 1995; Schroth, 1992).
- Encourage students to evaluate their performance realistically, and then reinforce them (e.g., with praise or extra-credit points) when their evaluations match the teacher's evaluation or some other external standard (McCaslin & Good, 1996; Schraw, Potenza, & Nebelsick-Gullet, 1993; Zuckerman, 1994).
- Have students compile **portfolios** that include samples of their work, along with a written reflection on the quality and significance of each sample (Paris & Ayres, 1994; Perry, 1998; Silver & Kenney, 1995).

portfolio
Systematic collection of a student's work over a lengthy period of time.

By engaging regularly in self-monitoring and self-evaluation of classroom assignments, students should eventually develop appropriate standards for their performance and apply those standards regularly to their accomplishments—true hallmarks of a self-regulated learner.

■ *Expect and encourage more independent learning over time.* As you have seen, self-regulated learning is a complex endeavor that involves many abilities (goal setting, attention control, flexible use of cognitive strategies, comprehension monitoring, etc.) and takes many years to master. Throughout the elementary and secondary school years, teachers must encourage and scaffold it in age-appropriate ways. For instance, they might provide examples of questions that students can use to monitor their comprehension as they read (e.g., "Explain how . . . ," "What is a new example of . . . ?"). They might provide a general organizational framework that students can follow while taking notes. They might provide guidance about how to develop a good summary (e.g., "Identify or invent a topic sentence," "Find supporting information for each main idea"). Such **metacognitive scaffolding** is most likely to be helpful when students are studying subject matter they find difficult to comprehend yet *can* comprehend if they apply appropriate metacognitive strategies (Pressley et al., 1992). In other words, metacognitive scaffolding is most beneficial when the subject matter is within students' zone of proximal development.

As students develop increasing proficiency with each self-regulating strategy, teachers can gradually withdraw the scaffolds they have previously provided. Ideally, by the time students finish high school, they should have sufficient metacognitive skills to pursue further academic education or career training programs with little or no assistance from others.

■ *Promote more sophisticated epistemological beliefs.* Teachers must communicate to students, not only in what they say but also in what they *do* (e.g., what activities they assign, how they assess students' learning), that knowledge is not a cut-and-dried set of facts and that effective learning is not simply a process of repeating those facts over and over again. For maximal learning and achievement, especially in the secondary and post-secondary school years, students must learn that

- Learning involves active construction of knowledge, rather than just a passive "reception" of it.
- Knowledge involves knowing the interrelationships among ideas as well as the ideas themselves.
- Knowledge does not always mean having clear-cut answers to difficult, complex issues.
- Understanding a body of information and ideas often requires persistence and hard work. (Hofer & Pintrich, 1997; Schommer, 1994b)

One possible way to change students' epistemological beliefs is to talk specifically about the nature of knowledge and learning—for example, to describe learning as an active, ongoing process of finding interconnections among ideas and eventually constructing one's own understanding of the world (Schommer, 1994b). But probably an even more effective approach is to provide classroom experiences that lead students to discover that knowledge is dynamic, rather than static, and to realize that successful learning sometimes occurs only through effort and persistence. For example, teachers can give their students complex problems that have no clear-cut right or wrong answers (Schommer, 1994b). They can have students read conflicting accounts and interpretations of historical events (Britt, Rouet, Georgi, & Perfetti, 1994; Leinhardt, 1994). They can ask students to compare several, possibly equally valid explanations of a particular phenomenon or event (Linn et al., 1996). And they can show students, perhaps by presenting puzzling phenomena, that their own current understandings, and sometimes even those of experts in the field, do not yet adequately explain all of human experience (Chan, Burtis, & Bereiter, 1997; Vosniadou, 1991).

Having students interact with one another may also influence their views of the nature of knowledge and learning. Heated discussions about controversial topics (e.g., pros and cons of capital punishment, interpretation of classic works of literature, or theoretical explanations of scientific phenomena) should help students gain an increased understanding that there is not always a simple "right" answer to a question or issue. Furthermore, by wrestling and struggling as a group with difficult subject matter, students may begin to understand that one's knowledge about a topic is likely to evolve and improve gradually over time. Finally, teachers must remember that group methods of inquiry are a critical feature of how the adult world tackles

metacognitive scaffolding
Supportive technique that guides students in their use of metacognitive strategies.

challenging issues and problems (Good et al., 1992; Greeno, 1997; Pogrow & Londer, 1994). By providing opportunities for students to formulate questions and problems, discuss and critique one another's explanations and analyses, and compare and evaluate potential solutions, teachers give students practice in these all-important adult strategies.

As a brief aside, we should note that, although some children have frequent opportunities to exchange ideas with adults at home (e.g., at the family dinner table), other children, including many who are at risk for academic failure and dropping out of school, rarely have opportunities to discuss academic subject matter at home. Class discussions about puzzling phenomena or controversial topics may fill a significant void in the cognitive experiences of these children (Pogrow & Londer, 1994).

Children's Construction of Theories

Growing human beings develop beliefs not only about the nature of knowledge and learning but about many other aspects of their world as well. Some psychologists have proposed that children eventually combine their beliefs into integrated belief systems, or *theories,* about particular topics (Hatano & Inagaki, 1996; Keil, 1989; Keil & Silberstein, 1996). This perspective, sometimes called **theory theory,**[2] is illustrated by the following dialogue in Keil (1989) between an experimenter (E) and child (C):

[E:]	These fruits are red and shiny, and they're used to make pies and cider, and everybody calls these things apples. But some scientists went into an orchard where some of these grow and they decided to study them really carefully. They looked way deep inside them with microscopes and found out these weren't like most apples. These things had the inside parts of pears. They had all the cells of pears and everything like that, and when they looked to see where they came from they found that these came off of pear trees. And, when the seeds from this fruit were planted, pear trees grew. So what are these: apples or pears? (pp. 305–306)
C:	Pears.
E:	How do you know?
C:	Because the seeds, when you plant the seeds a pear tree would grow, and if it were an apple, an apple tree would grow. They've got the insides of a pear and an apple wouldn't have the insides of a pear if it wasn't a pear.
E:	Then how come it looks like this?
C:	It's been sitting out for a long time and it turned red.
E:	And it doesn't have a pear shape? . . . How did that happen?
C:	(Shrug) (p. 171)

This child, like many elementary school children, clearly recognizes that the essential nature of living things is determined by their internal makeup (e.g., their cells) rather than by their outward appearance. Yet children apply a very different principle to nonliving things, as another dialogue from Keil (1989) illustrates:

[E]:	These things are used for holding hot liquids like coffee and tea and cocoa or milk to drink, and everybody calls these things cups. Some scientists went to the factory where some of these are made . . . to study them. They looked way deep inside with microscopes and found out these weren't like most cups. The ones made at this factory had the inside parts of bowling balls. And when they looked to see how they were made, they found out that bowling balls were ground up to make them. So what do you think these things really are: cups or bowling balls? (p. 306)
C:	They're used for the same purpose as cups and they look like cups and you can drink from them and you can't bowl with them, they're definitely cups!
E:	Can they still be cups if they're made out of the same stuff as bowling balls?
C:	Yeah . . . and if you could melt down a glass and make it into a bowling ball without breaking it to bits, it would still be a bowling ball and not a cup. (p. 174)

theory theory
Theoretical perspective proposing that children construct increasingly integrated and complex understandings of physical and mental phenomena.

---

[2]No, you're not seeing double. Although the term *theory theory* may seem rather odd, to us it suggests that many psychologists, "dry" as their academic writings might sometimes be, do indeed have a sense of humor.

In this situation, the internal makeup of cups and bowling balls is irrelevant; instead, the *function* of the object is paramount.

Children as young as 8 or 9 seem to make a basic distinction between biological entities (e.g., apples, pears) and human-made objects (e.g., cups, bowling balls). Furthermore, they seem to conceptualize the two categories in fundamentally different ways (Keil, 1987, 1989). Biological entities are defined primarily by their origins (e.g., their DNA, the parents who brought them into being). Even preschoolers will tell you that you can't change a yellow finch into a bluebird by giving it a coat of blue paint or dressing it in a "bluebird" costume (Keil, 1989). In contrast, human-made objects are defined largely by the functions they serve (e.g., holding coffee, knocking down bowling pins). Thus, if cups are melted and reshaped into bowling balls, their function changes, and so they become entirely different entities.

By the time they reach school age, most children have developed preliminary beliefs and theories about the physical world, the biological world, and, to some extent, even the mental world (Flavell et al., 1993; Wellman & Gelman, 1992). What do such theories entail? We look now at one example: children's theory of mind.

Children's Theory of Mind

As children grow older, they acquire increasingly sophisticated beliefs about the nature of the mind and the nature of thinking. John Flavell has proposed that such beliefs—their **theory of mind**—evolve over time to include five postulates (Flavell et al., 1993):

1. *The mind exists.* Children's awareness that people are thinking, feeling beings probably emerges gradually during the first 2 to 3 years of life. Although infants may not consciously know that people have thoughts and emotions, they quickly learn that human beings are different from other entities in their environment; for instance, they discover that their parents respond to their needs in ways that inanimate objects do not. Eventually, too, they learn that they can predict other people's behaviors and, in fact, can influence others by hurting, teasing, or comforting them (Flavell et al., 1993). By age 3, children refer to a variety of mental states when describing themselves and others; for instance, they use such words and phrases as *think, know,* and *feel bad* (Astington & Pelletier, 1996; Bretherton & Beeghly, 1982).

2. *The mind has connections to the physical world.* Preschoolers realize that people's mental states (e.g., their perceptions, desires, and emotions) influence their behaviors (Astington & Pelletier, 1996; Flavell et al., 1993; Wellman, 1988). For instance, a 2½-year-old is likely to predict that a child who wants a cookie may try to get one. Furthermore, preschoolers can infer people's mental states from their behaviors and other events (Flavell et al., 1993; Wellman & Woolley, 1990). For example, they reasonably conclude that a person who cannot find a lost item feels sad and will probably continue looking for it.

3. *The mind is distinct from the physical world.* By the time children are 3, they know that thoughts are not physical entities (Flavell et al., 1993; Wellman & Estes, 1986). They know, too, that they can fantasize about things—ghosts, monsters, and so on—that don't exist in reality (Wellman & Estes, 1986).

4. *The mind can represent objects and events accurately or inaccurately.* By about age 4 or 5, children realize that people's perceptions of the world do not necessarily reflect reality (Astington & Pelletier, 1996; Lillard, 1999). In one study (Wimmer & Perner, 1983), preschoolers were told a story about a boy who puts chocolate in a particular place in the kitchen; later, while he's gone, his mother moves it to a different spot. The children were asked where the boy would think the chocolate was located once he returned home. Five-year-olds understood that the boy would think it was where he had left it. In contrast, 3-year-olds mistakenly believed that the boy would know the chocolate was in its new location.

By the time they are 5, children understand not only that people sometimes have inaccurate beliefs about the world but also that people's beliefs and misbeliefs influence what they do and say (Astington & Pelletier, 1996). They know, too, that people's behaviors do not always reflect their mental states—for instance, that people who *appear* to be happy may actually feel sad (Flavell et al., 1993).

5. *The mind actively thinks about the interpretation of reality and the emotion experienced.* By the time children are 6 or 7, they can reflect on the nature of cognition—that is, they can *think*

theory of mind
Child's integrated beliefs about the existence and nature of thought.

about thinking to some degree. At this point, they understand that people interpret what they see and hear, rather than just "record" it verbatim, and so realize that people may occasionally misconstrue an event they have witnessed (Chandler & Boyes, 1982; Flavell et al., 1993). They also realize that people who have false beliefs about the world may think that their beliefs are actually correct (Astington & Pelletier, 1996).

Within this context, we find another possible explanation of the *egocentric speech* that Piaget described. As you should recall from Chapter 4, young children often tell stories without providing the details necessary for their listeners to understand. Piaget proposed that such egocentric speech reflects *preoperational egocentrism,* an inability to view a situation from another person's perspective. A theory-of-mind framework puts a different spin on this idea: Egocentric speech may reflect young children's ignorance about how the mind works; in particular, they don't yet realize that people can make sense of new information only to the extent that they have sufficient knowledge to do so (Perner, 1991).

A child's theory of mind continues to evolve throughout the elementary and secondary school years. For instance, between the ages of 5 and 10, children gain an increasing understanding that people think actively only when they are conscious, that little or no thinking occurs during deep, dreamless sleep (Flavell, Green, Flavell, & Lin, 1999). And, as noted earlier in the chapter, epistemological beliefs about the nature of learning change even during the high school years. The following Developmental Trends table summarizes what researchers have learned about the development of children's cognitive strategies, metacognitive awareness, and theory of mind.

Factors Promoting Development of a Theory of Mind Theorists have offered several hypotheses about conditions that may promote the development of children's theories of mind. Discussions with adults about thoughts, feelings, motives, needs, and so forth almost certainly promote greater awareness about the existence of mental events as entities separate from physical reality. Parents who openly consider differing points of view during family discussions may help children realize that different points of view can legitimately exist (Astington & Pelletier, 1996). Pretend play activities, in which children assume the roles of parents, teachers, doctors, and so on, can help children to imagine what people probably think and feel in different contexts (Harris, 1989; Lillard, 1998).

Culture probably makes a difference as well. Whereas some cultures frequently explain people's behaviors in terms of people's states of mind, others are more likely to interpret behaviors in terms of situational circumstances, *without* reference to people's thoughts or feelings per se (Lillard, 1999). In the United States, children who live in urban areas often refer to people's psychological states when explaining good and bad behaviors; for example, a child might say, "He helped me to catch bugs, because he and I like to catch bugs." In contrast, children who live in rural areas are more likely to attribute people's behaviors to situational factors; for example, a child might say, "She helped me pick up my books, because if she didn't I would have missed the bus." The latter approach is evident not only in rural American cultures but also in many Asian cultures (Lillard, 1999).

How Accurate Are Children's Theories?

Up to this point, we have been discussing children's developing theories as if they are accurate (albeit incomplete) reflections of the domains they represent. But especially in the early years, children's theories develop with little or no direct instruction from other, more knowledgeable individuals. As a result, they often include naive beliefs and misconceptions[3] about how the world operates. Consider the following conversation with a 7-year-old whom we'll call Rob:

Adult: How were the mountains made?
Rob: Some dirt was taken from outside and it was put on the mountain and then mountains were made with it.
Adult: Who did that?

---

[3]Theorists use a variety of terms when referring to such beliefs, including *naive beliefs, misconceptions, alternative frameworks, lay conceptions,* and *children's science* (Duit, 1991; Magnusson, Boyle, & Templin, 1994).

Cognitive Strategies and Metacognitive Awareness at Different Age Levels

DEVELOPMENTAL TRENDS

AGE	WHAT YOU MIGHT OBSERVE	DIVERSITY	IMPLICATIONS
Early Childhood (2–6) 	• General absence of intentional learning and problem-solving strategies • Belief that learning is a relatively passive activity • Overestimation of how much a person can typically remember • Growing realization that the mind does not always represent events accurately	• Children's awareness of the mind and mental events varies to the extent that the adults in their lives talk with them about thinking processes.	• Model strategies for simple memory tasks (e.g., pinning permission slips on jackets to remind children to get their parents' signatures). • Talk about thoughts and feelings as a way of helping children become more aware of their own mental life and develop a theory of mind.
Middle Childhood (6–10) 	• Use of rehearsal as the primary learning strategy • Gradual emergence of organization as a learning strategy • Emerging ability to reflect on the nature of one's own thought processes • Frequent overestimation of one's own memory capabilities • Little if any self-regulated learning	• Chinese and Japanese children rely more heavily on rehearsal than their peers in Western schools; this difference continues into adolescence. • Children with information processing difficulties are less likely to organize material as they learn it. • A few high-achieving students are capable of sustained self-regulated learning, particularly in the upper elementary grades.	• Encourage students to repeat and practice the things they need to learn. • Ask students to study information that is easy to categorize, as a way of promoting organization as a learning strategy (Best & Ornstein, 1986). • Ask students to engage in simple, self-regulated learning tasks (e.g., small-group learning tasks); give them suggestions about how to accomplish those tasks successfully.
Early Adolescence (10–14)	• Emergence of elaboration as an intentional learning strategy • Few and relatively ineffective study strategies (e.g., poor note-taking skills, little if any comprehension monitoring) • Increasing flexibility in the use of learning strategies • Emerging ability to regulate one's own learning • Belief that "knowledge" about a topic is merely a collection of discrete facts	• Students differ considerably in their use of effective learning strategies (e.g., organization, elaboration). • Some students, including many with information processing difficulties, have insufficient strategies for engaging in self-regulated learning.	• Ask questions that encourage students to elaborate on new information. • Teach and model effective strategies within the context of various subject areas. • Assign homework and other tasks that require independent learning tasks; provide sufficient structure to guide students in their efforts. • Give students frequent opportunities to assess their own learning.
Late Adolescence (14–18)	• Increase in elaboration • Growing awareness of what cognitive strategies are most effective in different situations • Increasing self-regulatory learning strategies (e.g., comprehension monitoring) • Increasing recognition that knowledge involves understanding interrelationships among ideas	• Only high-achieving students use sophisticated learning strategies (e.g., elaboration); others resort to simpler, less effective strategies (e.g., rehearsal). • Many students with information processing difficulties have insufficient reading skills to learn successfully from typical high school textbooks; furthermore, their study skills tend to be unsophisticated and relatively ineffective.	• Continue to teach and model effective learning strategies across the curriculum. • Assign more complex independent learning tasks, giving the necessary guidance to students who are not yet self-regulated learners. • Present academic disciplines as dynamic entities that continue to evolve with new discoveries, information, and ideas.

Rob:	It takes a lot of men to make mountains, there must have been at least four. They gave them the dirt and then they made themselves all alone. [*sic*]
Adult:	But if they wanted to make another mountain?
Rob:	They pull one mountain down and then they could make a prettier one. (dialogue from Piaget, 1929, p. 348)

Construction workers apparently play a major role in Rob's theory about the origins of the physical world.

Children and adolescents typically have many erroneous beliefs about the world around them; for instance, they may believe that the sun revolves around the earth, that the Great Lakes contain salt water, and that rivers can run from north to south but *not* from south to north. Sometimes such beliefs result from how things *appear* to be (Byrnes, 1996; diSessa, 1996; Duit, 1991); for example, from our perspective living here on the earth's surface, the sun looks as if it moves around the earth, rather than vice versa. Sometimes misconceptions are encouraged by common expressions in language; for instance, we often talk about the sun "rising" and "setting" (Duit, 1991; Mintzes, Trowbridge, Arnaudin, & Wandersee, 1991). Sometimes children infer incorrect cause-effect relationships between two events simply because those events often occur at the same time (Byrnes, 1996; Keil, 1991); such thinking reflects the *transductive reasoning* of which Piaget spoke. Perhaps even fairy tales and television cartoon shows play a role in promoting misconceptions (Glynn, Yeany, & Britton, 1991); as an example, after cartoon "bad guys" run off the edge of a cliff, they usually remain suspended in air until they realize that there's nothing solid holding them up. Sometimes children acquire erroneous ideas from others; in some instances, teachers or textbooks even provide such misinformation (Begg, Anas, & Farinacci, 1992; Duit, 1991).

Earlier in the chapter, we presented the principle that *children's growing knowledge base facilitates more effective learning.* This principle holds true only when that knowledge is an accurate representation of reality. When children's "knowledge" is inaccurate, it often has a counterproductive effect, in that *children's erroneous beliefs about a topic interfere with their understanding of new information related to that topic.* For example, many children in the early elementary grades believe that the earth is flat rather than round. When their teachers tell them that the earth is actually round, they may interpret that information within the context of what they already "know" and so think of the earth as being both flat *and* round—in other words, shaped like a pancake (Vosniadou, 1994).

Educational Implications of Theory Theory

Children's theories about mental events, the biological world, and the physical world have several implications for classroom practice:

■ *Remember that young children have limited ability to understand and reflect on the nature of their own and others' thoughts and feelings.* Children in the primary grades have difficulty taking other people's knowledge and thought processes into account during social interactions. And many preschoolers do not yet understand that people's perceptions of the world are sometimes inaccurate and that people's facial expressions may belie their true emotions. Such limitations must inevitably hamper young children's communication and perspective-taking skills, as you will discover in our discussions of language development and interpersonal relationships in later chapters.

■ *When introducing a new topic, determine what students already know and believe about the topic.* Teachers can more successfully address students' misconceptions when they know what those misconceptions are (Roth & Anderson, 1988; Smith, Maclin, Grosslight, & Davis, 1997; Vosniadou & Brewer, 1987). Thus, teachers should probably begin any new topic by assessing students' current beliefs about the topic, perhaps simply by asking a few informal questions that probe what students know and *misknow.*

■ *When students have misbeliefs about a topic, work actively to help them acquire more accurate understandings.* When children encounter more accurate and adultlike perspectives about the world, their existing misconceptions do not necessarily disappear. In fact, because early "knowledge" influences the interpretation of subsequent experiences, misconceptions are often quite resistant to change even in the face of blatantly contradictory information (Chambliss, 1994; Chinn & Brewer, 1993; Shuell, 1996). Thus, teachers must make a concerted effort to help students modify their early, inaccurate theories to incorporate more accurate and productive world views—in other words, to undergo **conceptual change**. Theorists and researchers have offered several strategies for promoting conceptual change in children and adolescents:

- Asking questions that challenge students' current beliefs
- Presenting phenomena that students cannot adequately explain within their existing perspectives
- Engaging students in discussions of the pros and cons of various explanations
- Pointing out, explicitly, what the differences between students' beliefs and "reality" are
- Showing how the correct explanation of an event or phenomenon is more plausible (i.e., makes more sense) than anything students themselves can offer
 (Chan et al., 1997; Chinn & Brewer, 1993; Posner, Strike, Hewson, & Gertzog, 1982; Prawat, 1989; Roth, 1990; Slusher & Anderson, 1996; Vosniadou & Brewer, 1987)

In our discussions thus far, we have drawn often from Piaget's theory and research to better understand the nature and development of children's cognitive processes; for instance, the interview with Rob about where mountains come from was conducted in Piaget's laboratory. Some contemporary theories of cognitive development rely even more heavily on Piaget's work. We turn to these *neo-Piagetian* approaches now.

Neo-Piagetian Approaches to Cognitive Development

For reasons we considered in the preceding chapter, many contemporary developmentalists have largely abandoned Piaget's early notions regarding children's cognitive development. Yet some psychologists believe that, by rejecting Piaget's theory, we may be throwing the baby out with the bath water. These psychologists have combined some of Piaget's ideas with concepts from information processing theory to construct **neo-Piagetian theories** of how children's learning and reasoning capabilities change over time (e.g., Case, 1985; Case & Okamoto, 1996; Fischer, Knight, & Van Parys, 1993).

Key Ideas in Neo-Piagetian Theories

Neo-Piagetian theorists do not always agree about the exact nature of children's thinking at different age levels or about the exact mechanisms that promote cognitive development. Nevertheless, several ideas are central to neo-Piagetian approaches:

■ *Children acquire general structures that pervade their thinking in particular content domains.* Piaget proposed that over time, children develop increasingly integrated systems of mental processes (operations) that they can apply with equal effectiveness to a wide variety of tasks and content domains. However, as noted in Chapter 4, recent research indicates that children's ability to think logically depends considerably on their specific knowledge, experiences, and instruction related to the task at hand. Thus, the sophistication of children's reasoning is far more variable from one situation to the next than Piaget predicted (Case & Edelstein, 1993; Case & Okamoto, 1996).

To address such variability, neo-Piagetians propose that children do not develop a single system of logical operations; instead, they develop more specific systems, or **structures**,[4] of concepts and thinking skills that influence thinking and reasoning capabilities within particular content domains. Accordingly, neo-Piagetian approaches are sometimes referred to as *structuralism* or *neo-structuralism* (e.g., Case & Edelstein, 1993).

■ *Cognitive development is constrained by the maturation of information processing mechanisms.* As noted earlier, children's working memory capacity increases over time; accordingly, children acquire an increasing ability to think about several things simultaneously. Neo-Piagetians

conceptual change
Revising one's knowledge and understanding of a topic in response to new information about the topic.

neo-Piagetian theory
Theoretical perspective that combines elements of both Piaget's theory and information processing theory and portrays cognitive development as involving a series of distinct stages.

structure
In neo-Piagetian theory, a specific system of concepts and thinking skills that influence thinking and reasoning in a particular content domain.

---

[4]One neo-Piagetian, Kurt Fischer, instead uses the term *skill* (e.g., Fischer & Bidell, 1991; Fischer et al., 1993).

believe that the changing capacity of working memory is, in large part, a function of neurological maturation. They further propose that children's limited working memory capacity at younger ages restricts their ability to acquire complex thinking and reasoning skills; in a sense, it places a "ceiling" on what they can accomplish at any particular age (Case & Okamoto, 1996; Fischer & Bidell, 1991; Lautrey, 1993).

■ *Formal schooling has a greater influence on cognitive development than Piaget believed.* Within the limits set by neurological maturation, formal schooling plays a critical role in children's cognitive development. For instance, Robbie Case has proposed that cognitive development results from both active attempts at learning (e.g., paying attention, thinking about how ideas are interrelated) and subconscious "associative" learning (e.g., learning gradually and unintentionally that certain stimuli are often encountered together in one's experiences). In Case's view, both forms of learning can promote the acquisition of knowledge about specific situations *and* the development of more general cognitive structures. Subsequently, specific knowledge and general structures each contribute to the development of the other in a reciprocal fashion (Case & Okamoto, 1996).

■ *Development in specific content domains can be characterized as a series of stages.* Although neo-Piagetians reject Piaget's notion that a single series of stages characterize *all* of cognitive development, they speculate that cognitive development in *specific* content domains may have a stagelike nature (e.g., Case, 1985; Case & Okamoto, 1996; Fischer & Bidell, 1991). Children's entry into a particular stage is marked by the acquisition of new abilities, which they practice and gradually master over time. Eventually, they integrate these abilities into more complex structures that mark their entry into a subsequent stage.

Recently, however, Kurt Fischer has suggested that even in a particular content domain, cognitive development is not necessarily a single series of stages through which children progress as if they were climbing rungs on a ladder. Instead, it might be better characterized as progression along "multiple strands" of skills that interconnect in a weblike fashion (Fischer et al., 1993). From this perspective, children may acquire more advanced levels of competence in a particular area through any one of several pathways. For instance, as children become increasingly proficient in reading, they may gradually develop their word decoding skills, their comprehension skills, and so on, but the relative rates at which they master each of these skills will vary from one child to the next.

To give you a better understanding of the nature of cognitive development from a neo-Piagetian perspective, we now look at a theory proposed by Robbie Case, a researcher at the University of Toronto until his untimely death in 2000.

Development of Central Conceptual Structures: Case's Theory

Case proposed that integrated networks of concepts and cognitive processes—**central conceptual structures**—form the basis for much of children's thinking, reasoning, and learning in specific content domains (Case & Okamoto, 1996; Case, Okamoto, Henderson, & McKeough, 1993). Over time, these structures undergo several major transformations, each of which marks a child's entry to the next higher stage of development.

Case speculated about the nature of children's central conceptual structures in three specific areas: social thought, spatial relationships, and number. A central conceptual structure related to *social thought* underlies children's reasoning about interpersonal relationships, their knowledge of common scripts related to human interaction, and their comprehension of short stories and other works of fiction; this structure includes children's general beliefs about human beings' mental states, intentions, and behaviors. A central conceptual structure related to *spatial relationships* underlies children's performance in such areas as drawing, construction and use of maps, replication of geometric patterns, and psychomotor activities (e.g., writing in cursive, hitting a ball with a racket); this structure enables children to align objects in space in accordance with one or more reference points (e.g., the x- and y-axes used in graphing). A central conceptual structure related to *number* underlies children's ability to reason about and manipulate mathematical quantities; this structure reflects an integrated understanding of how such mathematical concepts and operations as numbers, counting, addition, and subtraction are interrelated (Case & Okamoto, 1996).

central conceptual structure Integrated network of concepts and cognitive processes that forms the basis for much of one's thinking, reasoning, and learning in specific content domains.

From Robbie Case's neo-Piagetian perspective, children develop central conceptual structures in social thought, spatial relationships, and number (and perhaps in other areas as well). These structures affect children's reasoning and performance on a variety of relevant tasks.

Case proposed that, from ages 4 to 10, parallel changes occur in children's central conceptual structures in each of the three areas, with such changes reflecting increasing integration and multidimensional reasoning over time (Case & Okamoto, 1996). We describe the development of children's understanding of number as an example.

Development of a Central Conceptual Structure for Number   Case and his colleagues (Case & Okamoto, 1996; Case et al., 1993; Griffin, Case, & Siegler, 1994) developed a relatively precise model of the nature of children's knowledge about quantities and numbers during the preschool and elementary years. At age 4, children understand the difference between "a little" and "a lot" and recognize that addition leads to *more* objects and subtraction leads to *less*; such knowledge might take the form depicted in the top half of Figure 5–9. Furthermore, 4-year-olds can accurately count a small set of objects and conclude that the final number they reach equals the total number of objects in the set; this process is depicted in the bottom half of Figure 5–9. For example, 4-year-olds can visually compare a group of 5 objects with a group of 6 objects and tell you that the latter group contains more. They can also count accurately to either 5 or 6. Yet they *cannot* answer a question such as, "Which is more, 5 or 6?"—a question that involves knowledge of both more-versus-less and counting. It appears that they have not yet integrated their two understandings of number into a single conceptual framework.

By the time children are 6, they can easily answer simple "Which is more?" questions. Case proposed that at the age of 6, the two structures in Figure 5–9 have become integrated into the more comprehensive structure depicted in Figure 5–10. As illustrated in the figure, children's knowledge and reasoning about numbers now includes several key elements:

- Children recognize the written numerals 1, 2, 3, etc.
- They understand and can say the verbal numbers "one," "two," "three," etc.
- They have a systematic process for counting objects: They say each successive number as they touch each successive object in a group. Eventually, children count by mentally "tagging" (rather than physically touching) each object.
- They understand that movement from one number to the next is equivalent to either adding one unit to the set or subtracting one unit from it, depending on the direction of movement.
- They realize that any change in one dimension (e.g., from 3 to 4) must be accompanied by an equivalent change along other dimensions (e.g., from "three" to "four," and from ••• to ••••).
- They equate movement toward higher numbers with such concepts as "a lot," "more," and "bigger." Similarly, they equate movement toward lower numbers with such concepts as "a little," "less," and "smaller."

Neo-Piagetian Approaches to Cognitive Development | **177**

FIGURE 5–9 Hypothetical numerical structures at age 4

From "The Role of Central Conceptual Structures in the Development of Children's Thought" by R. Case, Y. Okamoto, in collaboration with S. Griffin, A. McKeough, C. Bleiker, B. Henderson, & K. M. Stephenson, 1996, *Monographs of the Society for Research in Child Development, 61*(1, Serial No. 246), p. 6. Copyright 1996 by the Society for Research in Child Development. Adapted with permission from the Society for Research in Child Development.

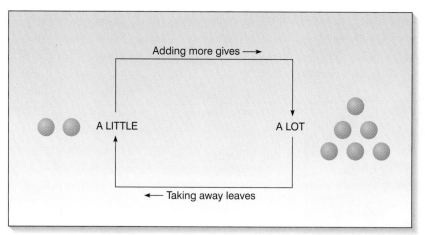

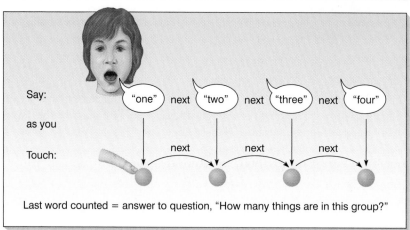

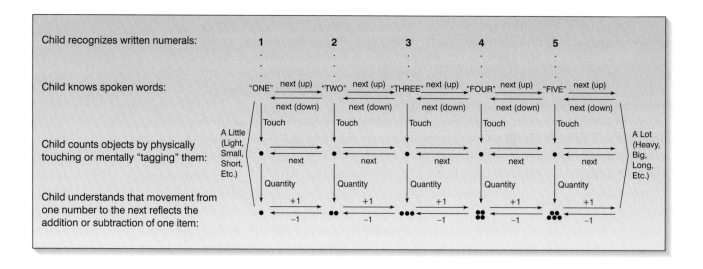

FIGURE 5–10 Hypothetical central conceptual structure at age 6

From "The Role of Central Conceptual Structures in the Development of Children's Thought" by R. Case, Y. Okamoto, in collaboration with S. Griffin, A. McKeough, C. Bleiker, B. Henderson, & K. M. Stephenson, 1996, *Monographs of the Society for Research in Child Development, 61*(1, Serial No. 246), p. 7. Copyright 1996 by the Society for Research in Child Development. Adapted with permission from the Society for Research in Child Development.

In essence, such a structure forms a mental "number line" that children can use to facilitate their understanding and execution of such processes as addition, subtraction, and comparisons of various quantities.

At age 8, Case proposed, children have sufficiently mastered this structure that they can begin using two number lines simultaneously to solve mathematical problems. For instance, they can now answer such questions as, "Which number is bigger, 32 or 28?" and "Which number is closer to 25, 21 or 18?" Such questions require them to compare digits in both the 1s column and 10s column, with each comparison taking place along a separate number line. In addition, 8-year-olds presumably have a better understanding of operations that require transformations across columns, such as "carrying 1" to the 10s column during addition or "borrowing 1" from the 10s column during subtraction.

Finally, at about age 10, children become capable of generalizing the relationships of two number lines to the entire number system. They now understand how the various columns (1s, 10s, 100s, etc.) relate to one another and can expertly move back and forth among the columns. They can also treat the answers to mathematical problems as mental entities in and of themselves and so can answer such questions as "Which number is bigger, the difference between 6 and 9 or the difference between 8 and 3?"

Case tracked the development of children's central conceptual structure for number only until age 10. He acknowledged, however, that children's understanding of numbers continues to develop well into adolescence. For instance, he pointed out that teenagers often have trouble with questions such as "What is a half of a third?" and suggested that their difficulty results from an incomplete conceptual understanding of division and the results (i.e., fractions) that it yields.

Effects of Instruction and Culture on Central Conceptual Structures Whereas Piaget downplayed the importance of education in the development of children's logical reasoning capabilities, Case believed that, within the limits of children's neurological maturation and working memory capacity, formal instruction can definitely promote the development of children's central conceptual structures (Case & Okamoto, 1996; Case et al., 1993; Griffin, Case, & Capodilupo, 1995). For instance, explicit training in such activities as counting, connecting specific number words (e.g., "three," "five") with specific quantities of objects, and making judgments about relative number (e.g., "Since this set [•••] has more than this set [••], we can say that 'three' has more than 'two' ") leads to improved performance not only in these tasks but in other quantitative tasks as well (Case & Okamoto, 1996; Griffin et al., 1995).

In several studies of children from diverse cultural backgrounds, Case found *no* significant cross-cultural differences in abilities that Case proposed are related to children's central conceptual structures for number, social thought, and spatial relations. For instance, when the drawings of Chinese and Japanese children (who receive a great deal of training in drawing skills beginning in preschool) are compared with those of Canadian and American children (who are given numerous opportunities to draw but little if any explicit instruction in how to draw), differences are found in the content and complexity of the pictures but not in the spatial relationships among the figures that the drawings contain. Similarly, Japanese and American children differ in the content of the stories they tell (reflecting cultural differences in the events they experience) but not in their storytelling skills per se (reflecting similar abilities in social thought) (Case & Okamoto, 1996). Such findings suggest that the conceptual structures Case described may develop within the context of a wide variety of educational and cultural experiences.

Educational Implications of Neo-Piagetian Theories

Neo-Piagetian theories lead to some of the same implications that we have derived from other theories. For example, like information processing theory and theory-theory approaches, neo-Piagetian approaches lead to the conclusions that teachers should relate new information to students' existing knowledge base and that they should accommodate children's limited working memory capacities. But these theories have two additional implications as well:

■ *Don't predict students' performance in one domain based on their performance in a very different domain.* From a neo-Piagetian perspective, students may develop at different rates in different content areas; for example, some students may be more advanced in social reasoning than in spatial relations, whereas the reverse may be true for other students. In the next chapter, we will see a similar idea reflected in Gardner's theory of multiple intelligences.

■ *Identify and teach concepts and skills central to students' understanding of a particular content area.* Some classroom subject matter may be information that is highly situation-specific and therefore has little relevance to students' learning in other areas. For instance, although knowing the capital city of one's home state or province is probably important, such knowledge is unlikely to impact students' overall cognitive development. But other subject matter may provide the foundation on which a great deal of subsequent learning depends; for instance, knowledge and skills related to counting, interpretation of people's motives and actions, and the ability to locate objects accurately in two-dimensional space fall into this category. If Case and his colleagues are correct, then training in such essential knowledge skills should be high on a teacher's list of instructional objectives.

Critique of Information Processing, Theory Theory, and Neo-Piagetian Approaches

The following Basic Developmental Issues table contrasts information processing theory, theory theory, and neo-Piagetian theory with respect to the three themes: nature versus nurture, universality versus diversity, and qualitative versus quantitative changes.

As you have probably realized, much work remains to be done on the nature and course of cognitive development. For instance, we do not yet have closure on the question of whether we can better characterize cognitive development in terms of stages or trends. Whereas Case has proposed that the integration of knowledge central to children's thinking in certain content domains (mathematics, social reasoning, spatial relations) occurs in a series of discrete stages, many other theorists (e.g., Keating, 1996; Siegler, 1996a) remain unconvinced.

Nor have developmentalists completely resolved the issue of general versus domain-specific changes. General changes do seem to occur in attention, working memory capacity, learning strategies, and metacognitive awareness, and such changes probably influence children's thinking and learning across a broad range of contexts and subject areas. But to what extent do children acquire general knowledge structures (e.g., *theories* or *central conceptual structures*) that underlie much of their thinking and reasoning in particular content domains? Researchers have only recently begun to study this critical developmental question, and so a firm answer is probably many years away.

Nevertheless, contemporary theories have extended our understanding of cognitive development far beyond Piaget's and Vygotsky's early ideas. Information processing theory has made significant inroads into the question of how human beings mentally process and learn new information and how cognitive processes change over the course of childhood and adolescence. Theory theory helps us understand why children's naive beliefs (e.g., "The world is flat") may persist even in the face of contradictory evidence. The neo-Piagetian perspective has provided food for thought about the precise nature of children's knowledge in certain content areas. All three approaches have led to the conclusion that cognitive development involves more gradual changes, and the evolution of children's reasoning capabilities is more domain-specific, than Piaget suggested. And developmentalists now agree almost without exception that children's knowledge becomes increasingly integrated over time; such integration may, depending on one's theoretical perspective, take the form of *schemas, scripts, theories,* or *central conceptual structures.*

What we have learned about cognitive development helps us understand not only how children typically develop but also how some children may process information very differently from their age-mates. We turn now to exceptionalities in information processing.

Contrasting Three Theories of Cognitive Development

	BASIC DEVELOPMENTAL ISSUES		
ISSUE	INFORMATION PROCESSING THEORY	THEORY THEORY	NEO-PIAGETIAN THEORY
Nature and Nurture	Focus is on how environmental input is interpreted, stored, integrated, and remembered and on how formal instruction can best facilitate more effective learning and cognitive development. Information processing difficulties (learning disabilities, ADHD, autism) often have biological origins.	From interactions with their physical and social environments, children construct integrated understandings and beliefs about various physical and mental phenomena.	Both informal experiences and formal schooling promote cognitive development. However, biological maturation places an upper limit on the complexity of knowledge and skills that children can acquire at a particular age level.
Universality and Diversity	The components of the information processing system (e.g., working memory, long-term memory, central executive) are universal. However, some people use their information processing capabilities more effectively than others. People's prior knowledge and their mastery of various cognitive strategies influence the degree to which they can learn new information and skills effectively.	The specific theories that children construct are influenced by informal experiences, formal schooling, and cultural practices and beliefs.	Children develop systems of integrated concepts and thinking skills (structures) that influence much of their thinking and learning within particular content domains. In the preschool and elementary years, these structures are likely to be similar across diverse cultures; in the secondary years, they become more culture-specific.
Qualitative and Quantitative Change	With development, children and adolescents acquire numerous cognitive strategies that are qualitatively different from one another. Each strategy evolves gradually over a lengthy period and becomes increasingly flexible, efficient, and effective. Theorists disagree about whether the physical capacity of working memory increases with age.	As children gain more information about their world, they may add to and embellish upon their theories; such changes reflect quantitative increases. Under certain conditions, however, new and compelling experiences spur children to overhaul their theories in a way that reflects qualitative change.	Structures increase in complexity in a stagelike fashion; at each successive stage, they become more complex and integrated and so are qualitatively different from preceding stages. Within each stage, children develop increasing proficiency in using newly acquired concepts and skills.

Exceptionalities in Information Processing

All human beings learn and process information in a somewhat unique, idiosyncratic manner. Because growing children have had varying experiences, their knowledge bases are somewhat different, and so the ways in which they make sense of and elaborate on new information must also be different. There are individual differences, too, in children's ability to pay attention, working memory capacity, learning and problem-solving strategies, and metacognitive awareness.

The information processing capabilities of some children are different enough as to require the use of specially adapted instructional practices and materials. Here we consider three groups of students with exceptionalities in information processing: those with learning disabilities, attention-deficit hyperactivity disorder, and autism.

Learning Disabilities

Children and adolescents with **learning disabilities** comprise the largest single category of students in need of special educational services (U.S. Department of Education, 1996). Educators have not reached complete agreement about how best to define this category.

learning disability
Significant deficit in one or more cognitive processes, to the point where special educational services are required.

Perceptual difficulty. Students may have difficulty understanding or remembering the information they receive through a particular sensory modality.

Memory difficulty. Students have less capacity to remember the information they receive, either over the short or long run; more specifically, they may have problems with either working memory or long-term memory.

Metacognitive difficulty. Students may have difficulty using effective learning strategies, monitoring their own comprehension, and in other ways regulating their own learning.

Difficulty processing oral language. Students may have trouble understanding spoken language or remembering what they have been told.

Reading difficulty. Students may have trouble recognizing printed words or comprehending what they read. An extreme form of this condition is known as *dyslexia*.

Written language difficulty. Students may have problems in handwriting, spelling, or expressing themselves coherently on paper.

Mathematical difficulty. Students may have trouble thinking about or remembering information involving numbers. For example, they may have a poor sense of time or direction or they may have difficulty learning basic number facts. An extreme form of this condition is known as *dyscalculia*.

Difficulty with social perception. Students may have trouble interpreting the social cues and signals that others give them (e.g., they may have difficulty perceiving another person's feelings or reactions to a situation) and so may respond inappropriately in social situations.

Sources: Conte, 1991; Eden, Stein, & Wood, 1995; Landau & McAninch, 1993; Lerner, 1985; Mercer, 1997; Swanson, 1993; Swanson & Cooney, 1991; Turnbull, Turnbull, Shank, & Leal, 1999; Wong, 1991.

FIGURE 5–11 Examples of information processing deficiencies in students with learning disabilities

Nevertheless, most apply the following criteria when classifying a child as having a learning disability (Mercer, Jordan, Allsopp, & Mercer, 1996; National Joint Committee on Learning Disabilities, 1994):

- *The child has significant difficulties in one or more specific cognitive processes.* For instance, the child may have difficulties in certain aspects of perception, language, memory, or metacognition. Such difficulties are typically present throughout the individual's life and are assumed to result from a specific, possibly inherited neurological dysfunction (Light & Defries, 1995; Manis, 1996). Figure 5–11 lists several forms that a student's learning disability may take.

- *The child's difficulties cannot be attributed to other disabilities, such as mental retardation, an emotional or behavioral disorder, hearing loss, or a visual impairment.* Many children with learning disabilities have average or above-average intelligence. For example, they may obtain average scores on an intelligence test, or at least on many of its subtests.

- *The child's difficulties interfere with academic achievement to such a degree that special educational services are warranted.* Students with learning disabilities invariably show poor performance in one or more specific areas of the academic curriculum; their achievement in those areas is much lower than would be expected based on their overall intelligence level. At the same time, they may exhibit achievement consistent with their intelligence in other subjects.

Several lines of research converge to indicate that learning disabilities often have a biological basis. Some children with learning abilities have slight abnormalities in parts of the brain involved in language processing (Manis, 1996). Some are apparently prone to "interference" from signals in the brain that are irrelevant to the task at hand (Dempster & Corkill, 1999). Furthermore, learning disabilities often run in families (Light & Defries, 1995; Oliver, Cole, & Hollingsworth, 1991).

Children identified as having a learning disability are a particularly heterogeneous group: They are far more different than they are similar (Bassett et al., 1996; Chalfant, 1989; National

Joint Committee on Learning Disabilities, 1994). Yet teachers are likely to see several characteristics in many of them. Students with learning disabilities may take a "passive" approach to learning rather than actively involving themselves in a learning task; for instance, they may stare at a textbook without thinking about the meaning of the words printed on the page. They are less likely to be aware of and use effective learning and problem-solving strategies. Some of them appear to have less working memory capacity than their age-mates, and so they have difficulty engaging in several cognitive processes simultaneously (Brownell, Mellard, & Deshler, 1993; Mercer, 1997; Swanson, 1993; Turnbull et al., 1999; Wong, 1991).

Learning disabilities may manifest themselves somewhat differently in elementary and secondary school (J. W. Lerner, 1985). At the elementary level, students with learning disabilities are likely to exhibit poor attention and motor skills and often have trouble acquiring one or more basic skills. As they reach the upper elementary grades, they may also begin to show emotional problems, due at least partly to frustration about their repeated academic failures. In the secondary school grades, difficulties with attention and motor skills may diminish. But at this level, students with learning disabilities may be particularly susceptible to emotional problems. On top of dealing with the usual emotional issues of adolescence (e.g., dating, peer pressure), they must also deal with the more stringent demands of the junior high and high school curriculum. Learning in secondary schools is highly dependent on reading and learning from relatively sophisticated textbooks, yet the average high school student with a learning disability reads at a third- to fifth-grade level and has acquired few if any effective study strategies (Alley & Deshler, 1979; Ellis & Friend, 1991; Heward, 1996). Perhaps for these reasons, adolescents with learning disabilities are often among those students most at risk for failure and dropping out of school (Barga, 1996).

Students with learning disabilities typically have less effective learning and memory skills than their classmates and so may need extra structure and guidance to help them study effectively.

Attention-Deficit Hyperactivity Disorder

Children with **attention-deficit hyperactivity disorder (ADHD)** have either or both of the following characteristics (American Psychiatric Association, 1994; Landau & McAninch, 1993):

- *Inattention.* Children with ADHD may have considerable difficulty focusing and maintaining attention on the task before them; they are easily distracted either by external stimuli or by internal thought processes. Such inattentiveness may manifest itself in behaviors such as daydreaming, difficulty listening to and following directions, frequent and careless mistakes, and an inability to persist at tasks that require sustained mental effort.
- *Hyperactivity and impulsivity.* Children with ADHD may seem to have an excess amount of energy; for instance, they are likely to be fidgety, move around the classroom at inappropriate times, talk excessively, and have difficulty working or playing quietly. In addition, they may show such impulsive behaviors as blurting out answers, interrupting others, and acting without thinking about the potential consequences of behaviors. Such impulsivity may reflect a general inability to inhibit responses to external stimuli (Barkley, 1998).

In addition to inattentiveness, hyperactivity, and impulsivity, students identified as having ADHD may have difficulties with cognitive processing, interpersonal skills, or appropriate classroom behavior (Claude & Firestone, 1995; Gresham & MacMillan, 1997; Grodzinsky & Diamond, 1992; Lorch et al., 1999). Regardless of the specific nature of a child's difficulties, a deficit in executive functioning (the elusive *central executive* that we spoke of earlier) may be at the heart of ADHD (Barkley, 1998).

ADHD is assumed to have a biological and possibly genetic origin (Barkley, 1998; Landau & McAninch, 1993). It seems to run in families, is three times as likely to be identified in boys as in girls, and is more frequently shared by identical twins than by fraternal twins (Conte, 1991; Faraone et al., 1995; Gillis, Gilger, Pennington, & DeFries, 1992). The characteristics associated with ADHD typically last throughout the school years and into adulthood (Claude & Firestone, 1995); perhaps as a result of the difficulties that such characteristics may create in

attention-deficit hyperactivity disorder (ADHD)
Disability (probably biological in origin) characterized by inattention and/or hyperactivity and impulsive behavior.

school, students with ADHD are at greater than average risk for dropping out (Barkley, 1998). But once children are identified as having ADHD, many of them can be helped to control their symptoms through a combination of medication (e.g., Ritalin) and specific instruction to promote more appropriate behavior (Barkley, 1998; Carlson, Pelham, Milich, & Dixon, 1992).

Autism

On the surface, **autism** appears to be more of a disability in social and emotional functioning than in cognitive processing. Probably its most central characteristic is a marked impairment in social interaction: Many children with autism form weak if any emotional attachments to other people and prefer to be alone (Denkla, 1986; Schreibman, 1988). Several other characteristics are also common, including communication impairments (e.g., absent or delayed speech), repetitive behaviors (e.g., continually rocking or waving fingers in front of one's face), narrowly focused and odd interests (e.g., an unusual fascination with watches), and a strong need for a predictable environment (American Psychiatric Association, 1994; Carr et al., 1994; Dalrymple, 1995; Turnbull et al., 1999).

Yet an information processing abnormality may be at the root of autism; in particular, many children with autism appear to have either an undersensitivity or an oversensitivity to sensory stimulation (Sullivan, 1994; Williams, 1996). Temple Grandin, a woman who has gained international prominence as a designer of livestock facilities, reflects on her childhood experiences with autism:

> From as far back as I can remember, I always hated to be hugged. I wanted to experience the good feeling of being hugged, but it was just too overwhelming. It was like a great, all-engulfing tidal wave of stimulation, and I reacted like a wild animal. . . .
>
> Shampooing actually hurt my scalp. It was as if the fingers rubbing my head had sewing thimbles on them. Scratchy petticoats were like sandpaper scraping away at raw nerve endings. . . .
>
> When I was little, loud noises were also a problem, often feeling like a dentist's drill hitting a nerve. They actually caused pain. I was scared to death of balloons popping, because the sound was like an explosion in my ear. Minor noises that most people can tune out drove me to distraction. (Grandin, 1995, pp. 63, 66, 67)

Thus, the abnormal behaviors so commonly associated with autism may reflect a child's attempts to make the environment more tolerable (Carr et al., 1994; Grandin, 1995). Social withdrawal and the desire for a predictable environment both help keep environmental stimulation at a comfortable level. Rocking behaviors, too, can help moderate stimulation, as Grandin explains:

> Rocking made me feel calm. It was like taking an addictive drug. The more I did it, the more I wanted to do it. (Grandin, 1995, p. 45)

Autism is a condition that is almost certainly caused by a brain abnormality (Gillberg & Coleman, 1996). Its origins are often genetic, and it is more commonly seen in males than females (Bristol et al., 1996; Bryson, 1997).

Children and adolescents with autism often show great variability in their cognitive abilities (American Psychiatric Association, 1994). Some have exceptional strengths in visual-spatial skills (Grandin, 1995; Williams, 1996). In a few instances, a child with autism possesses an extraordinary ability (such as exceptional musical talent) that is quite remarkable in contrast to other aspects of mental functioning (Cheatham, Smith, Rucker, Polloway, & Lewis, 1995; Treffert, 1989).

Helping Students with Information Processing Difficulties

Instructional practices and materials for students with learning disabilities, attention-deficit hyperactivity disorder, and autism should, of course, be individualized in accordance with each student's strengths and weaknesses. Yet several strategies are applicable to students with a variety of information processing difficulties:

■ *Help students keep their attention on classroom subject matter.* Many students with information processing difficulties are easily distracted. Therefore, teachers should minimize the presence of other stimuli likely to compete for students' attention, perhaps by making sure

autism
Disability (probably biological in origin) characterized by infrequent social interaction, communication impairments, repetitive behaviors, narrowly focused interests, and a strong need for a predictable environment.

ACCOMMODATING INFORMATION PROCESSING DIFFICULTIES

■ Minimize the presence of distracting stimuli.

A teacher has a student with attention-deficit hyperactivity disorder sit near her desk, away from distractions that classmates may provide; she also encourages the student to keep his desk clear of all objects and materials except those with which he is presently working (Buchoff, 1990).

■ Give students the extra structure they may need to succeed on academic tasks.

A teacher provides a particular format for writing an expository paragraph: one sentence expressing the main idea, followed by three sentences that support the idea and a final, concluding sentence.

■ Look at students' errors for clues about possible processing difficulties.

When a seventh grader spells *refrigerator* as "refegter" and *hippopotamus* as "hep-opoms," her teacher hypothesizes that she has difficulty relating written words to the phonetic sounds they represent.

■ When reading difficulties are evident, minimize dependence on reading materials or provide materials written at a lower-level.

For two high school students reading well below grade level, a teacher finds some supplementary reading materials related to the topics the class is studying; although written for adults, these materials use simpler language than the class textbook. The teacher also meets with the students once a week for verbal explanations of class material and a hands-on exploration of scientific principles.

■ Give students explicit guidance about how to study.

A teacher tells a student, "When you study a new spelling word, it helps if you repeat the letters out loud while you practice writing the word. Let's try it with *house*, the word you are learning this morning. Watch how I repeat the letters—H...O...U...S...E—as I write the word. Now you try doing what I just did."

---

that the classroom is fairly quiet during tasks requiring considerable concentration or by pulling down window shades when other students are playing in the schoolyard. Teachers can also teach their students strategies—keeping one's eyes focused on whoever is speaking, moving to a new location if the current one presents too many distracting sights and sounds, and so on—for maintaining attention on classroom tasks (Buchoff, 1990).

■ *Teach strategies for controlling hyperactivity and impulsivity.* All students, but especially those with information processing difficulties, need regular opportunities to release pent-up energy, such as recess, physical education, and hands-on classroom activities (e.g., Panksepp, 1998). In addition, teachers might give students a "settling-in" time after recess or lunch before asking them to engage in a sedentary activity (Pellegrini & Horvat, 1995); as an example, many elementary teachers begin the afternoon by reading a chapter from a high-interest storybook. Teachers can also teach students to use self-talk as a way of helping them resist the tendency to respond too quickly and impulsively to questions and problems (Meichenbaum & Goodman, 1971).

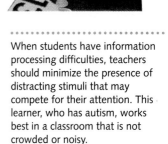

■ *Analyze students' errors for clues about their processing difficulties.* Students with information processing difficulties are, like anyone else, apt to make errors in responding to questions, problems, and other academic tasks. Rather than think of certain responses simply as being wrong, teachers should scrutinize students' errors for clues about the specific difficulties students are having (J. W. Lerner, 1985). For example, a student who solves a subtraction problem this way

$$\begin{array}{r} 83 \\ -27 \\ \hline 64 \end{array}$$

may be applying an inappropriate strategy (*always subtract the smaller number from the larger one*) to subtraction.

When students have information processing difficulties, teachers should minimize the presence of distracting stimuli that may compete for their attention. This learner, who has autism, works best in a classroom that is not crowded or noisy.

Assessing Students' Information Processing and Metacognitive Skills

CHARACTERISTIC	LOOK FOR	EXAMPLE	IMPLICATION
Attention span	• Ability to stay on task for an age-appropriate period • On-task behavior when distracting stimuli are present	In a fifth-grade "literature circle," a teacher aide and five students discuss Wilson Rawls's *Where the Red Fern Grows.* Four students are attentive throughout the 30-minute discussion, but Ben continually fidgets and looks at what other groups in the classroom are doing.	Monitor students' ability to pay attention in an age-appropriate fashion. If students have exceptional difficulty staying on task, minimize distractions and teach them strategies for focusing their attention more effectively.
Automatization of basic skills	• Retrieval of simple facts in a rapid, effortless fashion • Ability to use simple problem-solving strategies quickly and efficiently	Elena easily solves the problem $$\frac{4}{12} = \frac{x}{36}$$ because she immediately reduces $\frac{4}{12}$ to $\frac{1}{3}$.	Give students numerous opportunities to use and practice essential facts and skills; do so within the context of interesting and motivating activities.
Choice of learning strategies	• Use of rehearsal in the elementary grades • Use of more integrative strategies (e.g., organization, elaboration) in the secondary grades • Flexible use of strategies for different learning tasks	Terry studies each new concept in her high school physics class by repeating the textbook definition aloud three or four times in a row. Later, she can barely remember the definitions she has studied, and she is unable to apply the concepts when trying to solve physics problems.	Show students that their learning difficulties may be due to ineffective strategies, and teach them strategies that can help them learn more successfully.
Self-regulated learning capabilities	• Intentional efforts to keep attention focused on an assigned task • Effective planning and time management • Realistic appraisal of what has and has not been learned	When John has trouble hearing the video that his teacher is showing, he moves to a vacant seat closer to the video screen.	When students fail to complete independent assignments in a timely or thorough manner, provide more structure for subsequent assignments. Gradually remove the structure over time as students become better able to regulate their own learning.
Beliefs about knowledge and learning	• Optimism that knowledge and ability improve with practice and persistence • Striving to understand interrelationships among ideas • Comparing and evaluating various perspectives and theories	Several students are studying for a test on westward migration in North America during the 1800s. Some students focus on interrelationships among events (e.g., demands in Europe for beaverskin hats led to increased fur-trapping along the Platte River). Others make a list of facts from the textbook (e.g., many wagon trains began their trips at St. Louis) and study them in a piecemeal fashion.	Convey the message that mastering a topic is an ongoing, lifelong enterprise that requires effort and persistence. Especially in the secondary grades, convey the message that knowledge about a topic includes an understanding of how different ideas interrelate and a recognition that competing perspectives are not necessarily right or wrong.

Ideally, teachers should look closely at how *all* their students process information. Suggestions about what to look for are presented in the Observation Guidelines table above.

■ *Teach learning and memory strategies.* In comparison with their classmates, students with information processing difficulties use relatively ineffective learning strategies and study skills (Wong, 1991). Thus, teachers must often provide explicit instruction in how students can best learn and study classroom subject matter. For instance, teachers might give students suggestions on how to take notes and then periodically monitor students' notes for accuracy and completeness (Wood & Rosbe, 1985). Teachers might also teach students certain **mnemonics,** or "memory tricks," to help them learn new information (Mastropieri & Scruggs, 1992); for instance, they might suggest *ROY G. BIV* as a way of remembering the colors of the spectrum (red, orange, yellow, green, blue, indigo, violet) or *HOMES* for recalling the five Great Lakes (Huron, Ontario, Michigan, Erie, Superior).

■ *Provide study aids.* In addition to teaching more effective learning strategies, teachers can provide scaffolding that facilitates the sometimes overwhelming task of studying classroom material. For instance, they can distribute study guides that help students identify important ideas (Mastropieri & Scruggs, 1992). They can show how material is organized, perhaps with outlines that enumerate major and subordinate ideas or with graphics that show how key concepts are interrelated (Brigham & Scruggs, 1995; Wood & Rosbe, 1985). They can let students copy the notes of a classmate who is a particularly good note taker (Turnbull et al., 1999).

■ *Keep the classroom schedule and environment relatively predictable.* Some novelty in classroom activities does wonders for maintaining students' interest in academic subject matter (Renninger, Hidi, & Krapp, 1992). But a school day that has surprises around every corner may arouse excessive anxiety in some students, and such anxiety interferes with effective information processing (Eysenck, 1992; Lazarus, 1991). Furthermore, many students with autism find comfort and security in the predictability of their environment. To maintain some sense of predictability in the classroom, teachers might schedule certain activities at the same time each day or on a particular day of each week (Dalrymple, 1995). When there is a change in the schedule (perhaps because of a fire drill or school assembly), they should give students advance warning of the change and indicate when the schedule will be back to normal again (Dalrymple, 1995). And if the class includes one or more students with autism, teachers should change the physical arrangement of their classrooms infrequently if at all.

Students with learning disabilities, ADHD, and autism are not the only ones who have trouble processing and learning information. As a general rule, *children and adolescents process information less effectively than adults do.* Teachers must remember, then, that their students will not always learn classroom material as quickly or effectively as they themselves would. The final case study is a clear example.

CASE STUDY: THE LIBRARY PROJECT

As Jeanne writes this book, she is also supervising several interns who, in the final year of their college teacher education program, are teaching in partnership with experienced middle school teachers. One intern, who is teaching eighth-grade social studies, has assigned her students a month-long group project that involves considerable library research. Midway through the project, she writes the following entry in her journal:

> Within each group, one student is studying culture of the region, one has religion, one has economy, and one government. The point is for the students to become "experts" on their topic in their region. There are a lot of requirements to this assignment. I'm collecting things as we go along because I think a project this long will be difficult for them to organize. . . .
>
> So we spent all week in the library. I collected a minimum of two pages of notes yesterday, which will be a small part of their grade. The one thing that surprised me in our work in the library was their lack of skills. They had such difficulty researching, finding the information they needed, deciding what was important, and organizing and taking notes. As they worked, I walked around helping and was shocked. The librarian had already gotten out all of the appropriate resources. Even after they had the books in front of them, most did not know what to do. For instance, if they were assigned "economy," most looked in the index for that particular word. If they didn't find it, they gave up on the book. After realizing this, I had to start the next day with a brief lesson on researching and cross-referencing. I explained how they could look up *commerce, imports, exports,* and how these would all help them. I was also shocked at how poor their note-taking skills were. I saw a few kids copying paragraphs word for word. Almost none of them understood that notes don't need to be in full sentences. So, it was a long week at the library.

mnemonics
Special memory aid or trick designed to help students learn and remember a particular piece of information.

Next week is devoted to group work and time to help them work on their rough drafts. With the difficulty they had researching, I can imagine the problems that will arise out of turning their notes into papers. (courtesy of Jessica Jensen)

- Initially, the intern realizes that her students will need some structure to complete the project successfully. In what ways do she and the librarian structure the assignment for the students?
- What specific strategies do the students use as they engage in their library research? How are their strategies less effective than an adult's might be?
- How does the students' prior knowledge (or lack thereof) influence the effectiveness of their strategies?

SUMMARY

Information Processing Theory

Information processing theory focuses on how children receive, think about, mentally modify, and remember information, and on how such cognitive processes change over the course of development. Information processing theorists propose that cognitive capabilities improve with age and experience; such improvements take the form of gradual trends rather than discrete stages. In general, children are less efficient learners than adults are; they have shorter attention spans, a smaller working memory capacity, and a smaller and less integrated knowledge base to which they can relate new information.

Development of Metacognition and Cognitive Strategies

The term *metacognition* refers both to the knowledge that people have about their own cognitive processes and to their intentional use of certain cognitive processes to facilitate learning and memory. Children's metacognitive knowledge and intentional cognitive strategies improve throughout the school years. For instance, children become more proficient in such learning strategies as rehearsal, organization, and elaboration, and they acquire increasingly powerful and effective ways of solving problems. With age, they become more aware of the nature of thinking, learning, and knowledge, and they develop strategies for regulating their own learning.

Theory Theory

Some psychologists propose that growing children gradually construct integrated belief systems (theories) about the biological world, the physical world, and mental events; for instance, they develop a *theory of mind* that encompasses beliefs about how human beings think, feel, and reason. Such theories are not always accurate; to the extent that they include misunderstandings about the world, they may interfere with children's ability to acquire scientifically more sophisticated understandings.

Neo-Piagetian Theories

Neo-Piagetian theories combine elements of Piaget's theory with concepts from information processing theory. Neo-Piagetians reject Piaget's proposal that children acquire a single system of logical operations. Instead, they suggest that children acquire several more specific systems of concepts and thinking skills relevant to particular content domains (e.g., Robbie Case proposed that specific systems develop for social thought, spatial relationships, and number). Neo-Piagetians further suggest that these systems develop in a stagelike manner, with slowly maturing information processing mechanisms (e.g., working memory capacity) setting an upper limit on the complexity of thinking and reasoning skills that can emerge during infancy and childhood.

Now go to our Companion Website to assess your understanding of chapter content with Multiple-Choice Questions, apply comprehension in Essay Questions, and broaden your knowledge with links to related Developmental Psychology World Wide Web sites.

Exceptionalities in Information Processing

The information processing capabilities of some children are different enough as to require the use of specially adapted instructional practices and materials. Children with learning disabilities have significant difficulties in one or more specific cognitive processes. Children with attention-deficit hyperactivity disorder (ADHD) have difficulty focusing attention on assigned tasks and/or are unusually hyperactive and impulsive for their age group. Children with autism exhibit a marked impairment in social interaction; oftentimes, their behaviors result from an extreme undersensitivity or oversensitivity to sensory stimulation.

KEY CONCEPTS

information processing theory (p. 145)
sensation (p. 145)
perception (p. 145)
sensory register (p. 145)
working memory (p. 145)
long-term memory (p. 146)
central executive (p. 146)
automatization (p. 149)
knowledge base (p. 150)
symbol (p. 150)
schema (p. 151)
script (p. 151)
sounding (p. 153)
metacognition (p. 155)

cognitive strategy (p. 155)
learning strategy (p. 157)
rehearsal (p. 157)
organization (p. 157)
elaboration (p. 158)
metacognitive awareness (p. 160)
self-regulated learning (p. 162)
comprehension monitoring (p. 163)
co-regulated learning (p. 164)
epistemological beliefs (p. 164)
elaborative interrogation (p. 166)
portfolio (p. 168)

metacognitive scaffolding (p. 169)
theory theory (p. 170)
theory of mind (p. 171)
conceptual change (p. 175)
neo-Piagetian theory (p. 175)
structure (in neo-Piagetian theory) (p. 175)
central conceptual structure (p. 176)
learning disability (p. 181)
attention-deficit hyperactivity disorder (ADHD) (p. 183)
autism (p. 184)
mnemonics (p. 187)

Shea, age 9

Personal and Emotional Development

CASE STUDY: MARY

In 1954, Dr. Emmy Werner and her colleagues began a longitudinal study of children born on the island of Kauai, Hawaii. Children in the study faced numerous problems in their early years: They lived in poverty, had parents with mental health problems, received inadequate care, and so on. Despite exposure to numerous risk factors, the majority of these children had *no* serious learning or behavior problems during childhood or adolescence.

Mary was one of these resilient children. Her father was a plantation laborer with only 4 years of formal education. Her mother was seriously overweight and suffered from a variety of medical problems while pregnant with Mary. Nevertheless, Mary's parents were happy about her birth and gave her good care.

At 12 months of age, Mary was described as "easy to deal with," "very active," and a "healthy, alert child who is apparently given much attention." At 22 months, she was an "active, cheerful, energetic, and determined child who showed independence, perseverance, and feminine characteristics, but who also seemed somewhat excitable, distractible, and nervous" (Werner & Smith, 1982, p. 141).

As Mary entered middle childhood, her family environment deteriorated. Her mother had mood swings, suffered from several major illnesses, and was hospitalized twice for emotional disturbance. Mary, too, had her troubles. Her mother reported that, at age 10, Mary had "crying spells and headaches, temper tantrums, and stubborn, contrary behavior" (Werner & Smith, 1982, p. 142).

Later, Mary showed some understanding of her mother's behavior:

> . . . very grumpy—well, she's going through change of life early—every little thing bothers her. She's lonely. My father leaves her a lot and we have our own life. When they're that age, they do get lonely. . . . I used to be blamed for every little thing that my sister did when my parents went out, and when my father went to work, my mother used to hit me and beat me. That's how come I'm not very close to my mother. In a way I used to hate her, but as I got older I understood her better, how she was going through that change of life—but we're not really close. (Werner & Smith, 1982, p. 142)

Her description of her father was more positive and affectionate:

> . . . soft-hearted, very soft-hearted—he cares for our happiness and has always been like that. He's generous, not selfish. I feel very close to him. (Werner & Smith, 1982, p. 142)

As an adolescent, Mary was outgoing, sociable, and concerned with how others perceived her. She believed that she controlled her own destiny—she was not at the mercy of forces beyond her control—and she approached new situations cautiously, typically seeking information before acting. She disliked tension in her interpersonal relationships and avoided conflict whenever possible:

> Me, I don't start fights too much. My mother, she'll go around the house grumbling, until I finally get up to a point where I can't stand it. I can't stand to see a family fighting. Parents shouldn't fight, they should be able to talk things out. (Werner & Smith, 1982, p. 143)

Mary was a good student who scored in the top 25% on achievement tests in high school. Thus, while her family life was often troubled, school was an arena in which she could succeed.

When Mary met with the researchers for the last time, she was 18 and planning to enroll in a community college to prepare for a career in medical or legal secretarial work. She described herself this way:

> If I say how I am, it sounds like bragging—I have a good personality and people like me. I'm not the greedy type—I'm jealous a lot of times, yes. And I don't like it when people think they can run my own life—I like to be my own judge. I know right and wrong, but I feel I have a lot more to learn and go through. Generally, I hope I can make it—I hope. (Werner & Smith, 1982, p. 140)

MARY'S CASE UNDERSCORES THE significance of children's emotional ties to their caregivers. As an adolescent, Mary felt very close to her father but had mixed feelings for her mother. During her infancy, and before her mother's emotional breakdowns, observers found both parents affectionate. It seems likely, then, that Mary initially formed a close emotional bond with her mother but later learned to keep her distance as she encountered instability, irritability, and criticism. In this chapter, we learn about the early attachments children form with their parents, siblings, and other caregivers. We find that these social bonds, when warm and nurturing, give children a secure base from which to explore the world and form later relationships with other people. However, we will also see that healthy social bonds do not ensure good outcomes, nor do weak social bonds guarantee bad ones; intervening social experiences steer the trajectory of later social adjustment.

A second theme in this case, and throughout the chapter as well, is the centrality of emotions in defining experience. Emotions saturate the lives of children, adolescents, and adults. Mary's parents were happy when she was born, and as a young child Mary seemed to thrive on the affection her mother and father gave her. Yet there were indications of negative emotions as well: Mary had crying spells and temper tantrums, and she disliked being blamed for everything. In studying the emotional lives of children, we find that children experience fairly simple, straightforward emotional states early on and then develop more complex feelings that increasingly reflect an understanding of other people's viewpoints. Simple emotions of fear, anger, and happiness in infancy make room for shame, guilt, and pride during early and middle childhood. Children also learn to deal with negative emotions more effectively as they grow older. For instance, Mary's temper tantrums gradually diminished as she learned to channel her anger into other, more productive modes of expression.

Finally, Mary reflected on who she was as an individual. She cast herself in a balanced yet optimistic light. She was concerned that she not appear too conceited, but she perceived herself to have a good personality, to know right from wrong, to be somewhat jealous (though not greedy), and to be receptive to new learning opportunities. In this chapter, we examine how children think about themselves, how they feel about their own worth, and how they evaluate what they can do in life.

The developments we examine in this chapter—attaching to caregivers, effectively expressing and regulating emotions, and constructing a sense of self—are necessary for positive peer interactions, construction of a moral code, healthy family relationships, and the ability to navigate through community and cultural contexts. These assorted social-emotional developments are interrelated, as experiences with peers, family, and the broader cultural community do feed back into how children feel about themselves and how they express their emotions. But we must begin our story somewhere, and it makes sense to start with the very core of children's social-emotional functioning—their first attachments, their emotional expression, and their sense of self.

As you learn about social-emotional development in this and later chapters, we invite you to look for the basic developmental issues we have raised in previous chapters. For instance, attachments, emotions, and understandings of self grow out of the interacting forces of nature and nurture. Their manifestations show some universality and much diversity, and they change in both qualitative and quantitative ways.

Early Attachments

By **attachment** we mean an enduring emotional tie that unites one person to another (Ainsworth, 1973). During infancy and early childhood, attachment to parents and other family members serves an important protective function (Ainsworth, 1963; Bowlby, 1958). Young children use their caregivers as a secure base from which to explore their world. They typically stay close by, and when they do venture out, they routinely return whenever they feel worried or afraid.

In the last few decades, the dominant theoretical perspective on caregiver-infant relationships has been **ethological attachment theory,** a perspective originally suggested by John Bowlby (1951, 1958), fleshed out by Mary Ainsworth (1963, 1973; Ainsworth, Blehar, Waters, & Wall, 1978), and tested and refined by many contemporary psychologists. Ethological attachment theory describes the significance of children's social-emotional bonds with parents in terms of evolutionary function; as such, it is an example of the *evolutionary perspectives* described in Chapter 1. Evolutionary perspectives remind us that human infants, who are unable to feed themselves or protect themselves from harm, must depend on their parents to survive. Parents are biologically predisposed to care for their infants, and infants are biologically programmed to stay close to their parents, especially in times of danger. Infants have many tools at their disposal to maintain this proximity: They can cry, cling, and crawl when distressed, and they can show their affection with snuggles, smiles, and cooing under less stressful conditions.

Initial theorizing about attachment emphasized infants' relationships with their mothers, but contemporary perspectives have been more inclusive of other attachment figures, such as fathers, other family members, and caregivers outside the family. It is becoming increasingly apparent that infants and young children can, and often do, form lasting attachments to a variety of caring individuals.

Evolutionary pressures for adult-child bonding lead us to conclude that attachment is a universal human capacity. Nonetheless, attachment does not happen automatically; rather, it depends squarely on caregivers' capacity to be nurturing and attend to children's welfare (Thompson, 1998). Parents and others who provide sensitive care pick up on infants' signals, drawing inferences about states of discomfort, hunger, fatigue, and so on. They then do what it takes to make things better, perhaps offering bottle or breast, changing a diaper, or giving reassurance. Caregivers also focus on what young children care about and attend to, whether it be the blades of a fan, the rumble of the dryer, the texture of a fabric, or the scent of a flower.

The nature of social-emotional bonds between caregivers and children changes over time. Early on, parents and other caregivers appear to do most of the work. Keep in mind, though, that nature has made infants alluring partners in this social dance; for instance, few parents can resist the chance to cuddle their young babies, and many drop everything to respond to their infants' urgent cries. With time and experience, the relationship changes. Parents increasingly hear the subtle nuances in cries and vocalizations, and infants become more competent participators in social interaction. Face-to-face exchanges evolve from one-sided, parent-directed affairs into two-sided, turn-taking activities. Within their first year, infants show an emerging understanding that they can influence their social world ("If I cry, Daddy comes"; "When I smile, Mommy smiles back"). They also begin to attend to and interpret adults' emotional expressions and associate them with particular contexts ("When I crawl toward the stairs, Mommy looks scared"; "When Grampa drops me off at daycare, he smiles at my teacher").

Attachments are probably most evident when children sense danger, pain, or uncertainty (Bowlby, 1988). An intruding stranger, a stubbed toe, and sheer exhaustion are the kinds of events that send children fleeing to parents or, if they're not yet mobile, crying and thrashing for cuddling and comfort. But attachments reveal themselves under happier circumstances as well. Perhaps you've witnessed the energetic wiggling, cooing, and laughter that a 6-month-old baby shows when a parent walks into the room. It's as if the baby is saying, "Look at me! I'm happy to see you! Come play with me!"

The attachments that infants form with their parents or other primary caregivers provide a foundation for later social-emotional relationships.

attachment
An enduring emotional tie uniting one person to another.

ethological attachment theory
Theoretical perspective that emphasizes the functional importance of caregiver-child bonds in protecting children and giving them a secure base from which to explore their surroundings.

Individual Differences in Attachment

If you look around at young children you know, you may notice variations in how they respond to their parents. Some children are less inclined than others to seek out parents when distressed, and they may have a hard time accepting comfort. Others cling to parents constantly and are reluctant to venture from protective arms. To study such differences in the laboratory, Mary Ainsworth created a mildly stressful situation for 1-year-old infants. First, a mother and her infant were brought to a playroom and left alone. A stranger (a research assistant) soon entered the room and attempted to play with the baby. After 3 minutes, the mother left the room, so that the baby was alone with the stranger. Subsequently, the mother returned and the stranger departed, leaving mother and baby together. Next, mother departed, and baby was alone; the stranger returned at this point. Finally, the mother returned and the stranger departed (Ainsworth et al., 1978). This sequence, commonly known as the *Strange Situation,* has become a classic research tool for assessing attachment in young children.

In the Strange Situation, attention is focused primarily on the child's behavior. Observers rate the child's attempts to seek contact with the mother, the physical proximity of the child to mother, the child's resistance to or avoidance of mother, and the child's apparent level of distress. From such ratings, the child is given one of four classifications:

- Infants who exhibit **secure attachment** seem to use mother as a secure base. When she is present, they actively explore new toys and surroundings. When she returns after leaving the room, they smile at or talk to her, move over to greet her, or in other ways seek proximity with her. About 65% of infants from typical middle-class backgrounds are classified as securely attached (Thompson, 1998).

- Infants who exhibit **insecure-avoidant attachment** fail to greet mother when she comes back and perhaps even look away upon her return. Even before their mother departs, these children appear indifferent to her presence; instead, they go about their business independently, and they are somewhat superficial in their interactions with toys. About 20% of children participating in Strange Situation studies are classified as insecure-avoidant (Thompson, 1998).

- Infants who exhibit **insecure-resistant attachment** seem preoccupied with their mother, but they are not easily comforted during reunions. Even when mother returns, they remain distressed and angry; they may rush to her yet quickly struggle to be released. Insecure-resistant infants comprise about 15% of participants in Strange Situation studies (Thompson, 1998).

- Not part of Ainsworth's original classification, a fourth type—**disorganized and disoriented attachment**—has since been identified (Main & Solomon, 1986, 1990). Infants in this group lack a coherent way of responding to stressful events such as those in the Strange Situation. These infants may be calm and contented one minute yet, without provocation, become angry the next minute. They may interrupt their own actions midstream, for example by crawling toward mother and then suddenly freezing with apprehension. It is difficult to estimate the percentage of children in this category, as it has only recently been identified. It seems safe to say that only a small minority of children would be classified as having a disorganized and disoriented attachment.

Teachers of young children, especially those working in daycare and preschool settings, may occasionally want to make inferences about the quality of children's attachment to parents. Teachers can observe how children and their caregivers typically behave toward one another, recognizing, of course, that "bad days" and unusual events may temporarily disrupt normal patterns of interaction in even the most affectionate of families. In the table that follows, we offer some Observation Guidelines that provide clues about the quality of child-caregiver attachments.

Origins of Attachment Security

What factors lead to different patterns of attachment? Research has shown that the quality of the caregiver-child relationship, the cultural setting, and the child's own behavior each plays a role in the patterns that develop.

secure attachment
Attachment classification in which children use attachment figures as a secure base from which to explore and as a source of comfort in times of distress.

insecure-avoidant attachment
Attachment classification in which children appear somewhat indifferent to attachment figures.

insecure-resistant attachment
Attachment classification in which children are preoccupied with their attachment figures but gain little comfort from them when distressed.

disorganized and disoriented attachment
Attachment classification in which children lack a single coherent way of responding to attachment figures.

Assessing Young Children's Security of Attachment

CHARACTERISTIC	LOOK FOR	EXAMPLE	IMPLICATION
Secure Attachment to Caregivers	• Active, intentional exploration of the environment in the presence of the caregiver • Protest at being separated from a caregiver; ability to be soothed when the caregiver returns • Initial wariness of strangers, with subsequent acceptance if reassured by the caregiver	Luis cries when his father drops him off at daycare in the morning. After a few minutes, he settles down and seeks comfort from a familiar and affectionate daycare provider, who appears to be becoming a target of his attachment as well.	It is natural for young children to resist separation from their parents. Help them establish a routine of saying goodbye in the morning, and give them extra attention during this time. Reassure parents by describing children's daily activities and behaviors, and inform them of how long it takes their children to settle into a relaxed routine after their departure. (Oftentimes parents witness a dramatic protest as they say goodbye, but the distress is usually more short-lived than parents realize.)
Insecure-Avoidant Attachment to Caregivers	• Superficial exploration of the environment • Indifference to a caregiver's departure; failure to seek comfort upon the caregiver's return • Apparent discomfort around strangers, but without an active resistance of their overtures	Jennifer walks around her new preschool with a frown on her face. She parts easily with her mother, and after a short time she seems to settle into her new environment. She glances up and smiles briefly when her mother comes at the end of the day, but she doesn't seem particularly happy about her mother's return.	Independence from parents is often a sign of children's familiarity with daycare or preschool settings. If children seem truly at ease with separation, support their relaxed state by welcoming them in the morning, sending them off warmly in the afternoon, and keeping parents informed of their activities. If children instead appear indifferent to their parents, offer special encouragement to the parents, who may be struggling with issues in their own lives and so find it difficult to invest in their children emotionally. In addition, form your own affectionate relationships with children, with the hopes that such support will lead to secure attachments.
Insecure-Resistant Attachment	• Exceptional clinginess and anxiety when with the caregiver • Agitation and distress at the caregiver's departure; continued crying or fussing after the caregiver returns • Apparent fear of strangers; tendency to stay close to the caregiver in a new situation	Irene tightly clutches her mother's skirt as the two enter the preschool building, and she stays close by as mother signs her in for the morning. She is quite upset when her mother leaves yet finds little comfort in mother's return a few hours later.	If insecure-resistant children appear anxious when they enter a new daycare or preschool setting, give them extra time to part with their parents, and perhaps give them a "comfort" object, such as a teddy bear or blanket from home. Be patient and reassuring as you interact with these children, knowing that such children can eventually form a secure attachment to you.
Disorganized and Disoriented Attachment	• Unpredictable emotional responses (e.g., calmness one moment followed by anger the next, without any obvious provocation) • Tendency to approach a caregiver cautiously and with an appearance of uncertainty, as if wary about the kind of response the caregiver will make	Myles seems lost at school. He arrives hungry, walks aimlessly for some time, and eventually sits to play with blocks. He is aggressive with his peers, and his teacher sees bruises on his arms.	Provide special attention and monitoring to students who seem disorganized and disoriented in their attachment. Be on the lookout for signs of abuse, and be ready to seek advice from authorities. Remember that these children are *not* doomed to serious lifelong problems, and work hard to establish positive, trusting relationships with them.

The quality of the relationship between primary caregivers and their children appears to be the factor that most influences attachment. When caregivers are sensitive and responsive to young children, protect them, and provide for their needs, children are inclined to develop secure attachments (Chisholm, 1996; NICHD Early Child Care Research Network, 1997). With a secure attachment in place, they then feel safe enough to get on with other important matters, such as exploring the physical environment and forming social bonds with other adults and children. Less productive forms of attachment appear to be related to other parenting behaviors (Thompson, 1998). Children with insecure attachments often have parents who either have difficulty caring for them or are unwilling to invest energy in them. Such parents may be struggling with serious emotional issues, may have limited financial resources, or may need to spread their attention among many children. Some children—those who are insecure-avoidant—become independent early on and find creative ways to obtain needed care and comfort from others. Other children—those who are insecure-resistant—cling tenaciously to their caregivers, thereby increasing their chances of gaining access to needed resources. Children with disorganized and disoriented attachments may, in many cases, live with people whose behaviors are unpredictable from one occasion to the next; oftentimes these children are the victims of abuse or maltreatment. These children typically approach their parents slowly and cautiously, unsure if they will get an affectionate response or a punitive one.

Although nonsecure attachment patterns are almost certainly adaptive over the short run, they may be counterproductive over the long run. For instance, children who become demanding and clingy may end up with adequate nourishment and care even under extremely impoverished conditions (DeVries & Sameroff, 1984). Yet they may remain excessively dependent on their parents long after they should be establishing some independence, or they may become overly demanding and competitive with other children (Thompson, 1998).

A second factor affecting the nature of children's attachments is the cultural setting in which they live (Rothbaum, Weisz, Pott, Miyake, & Morelli, 2000). Cultures differ appreciably in their emphasis on a close, exclusive relationship between parents and infants. Here are some examples:

- In some studies with Japanese children, a high proportion of the children have shown behaviors that researchers categorize as reflecting insecure-resistant attachment. Many infants in these studies became quite upset when their mothers left the room, perhaps in part because the Japanese emphasis on physical closeness, intimacy, and strong mother-child bonds leaves children unprepared for separation (Miyake, Chen, & Campos, 1985; Takahashi, 1990). Separation from mother is not a common circumstance in Japan; babysitters are rare, and when mothers leave their children, they often seek the assistance of grandparents (Saarni, Mumme, & Campos, 1998).
- Behaviors consistent with an insecure-resistant attachment classification are also fairly common in Israeli kibbutz–raised infants (Sagi & Lewkowicz, 1987). Infants raised on the kibbutz are accustomed to contact with a small group of children and adults. They rarely see strangers, and adults are suspicious of outsiders. A historical record of unexpected terrorist attacks makes security measures a prudent necessity (Saarni et al., 1998). Infants pick up adults' wary feelings toward strangers, and so, when they encounter a stranger in their midst, they understandably withdraw or communicate distress.
- In northern Germany, many infants display behaviors that, on the surface, would seem to indicate an insecure-avoidant attachment (Grossmann, Grossmann, Huber, & Wartner, 1981). These babies do not fret much when their mothers leave the playroom, nor do they move frantically toward mothers when they return. In northern Germany, infants are regularly left at home alone or outside supermarkets as mothers go about their errands. The time alone is not lengthy, but it happens often enough to be routine. These children seem to understand that their mothers will return shortly and that they can get along just fine in the meantime.

Furthermore, many cultural groups in the United States and elsewhere depend on multiple caregivers, such as aunts, uncles, grandparents, and family friends. Distributing responsibility for child care may have an evolutionary function (Dunbar, 1992; Fisher, Jackson, & Villarruel, 1998). More specifically, the human race has evolved in such a way that children reach out to multiple adults in their community, especially when they have lost their mothers to rampant contagious diseases or other uncontrollable circumstances (Meindl, 1992). In essence, then, cross-cultural data support the value of a tight emotional bond between mother and infant, but having other family and community members stand by as backup has obvious survival value.

A third factor affecting the security of children's attachment is the children themselves (you may recall our discussion of *organismic influences* in Chapter 1). It certainly takes two to form an attachment. Accordingly, children help to strengthen their relationship with parents by reciprocating their affection: snuggling up to them, allowing themselves to be comforted, smiling and rubbing their faces, and so on. Children also contribute to their own attachment security through their unique ways of handling stress and relating to parents. While some children kick up quite a fuss when scared, others are less adamant in their protests. Perhaps those who are prone to be fearful, irritable, anxious, and fussy are more difficult to care for and to interact with, whereas those who are more even-tempered and sociable invite positive interactions. Perhaps, too, mismatches between dispositions of parents and those of children make attachments less smooth. However, available research suggests that differences in infants' behaviors play only a minor role in attachment security (Thompson, 1998). Parents are generally able to be sensitive to a wide range of dispositions and ability levels in children; thus, "fussy" or "difficult" babies are not necessarily destined to become insecure children.

Children's attachments to parents or other caregivers provide the foundation for later social-emotional relationships. With healthy attachments in place, children feel secure and fortified to confront the demons and discomforts of everyday life. Yet some children do not seem able to use the adults in their lives as a source of reassurance. In the next section, we consider the long-term effects of secure and insecure attachment.

Developmental Course of Early Social Ties

As children gain experience with their primary caregivers, they begin to form an internal understanding, or *mental representation,* of what relationships with other people are usually like (Bowlby, 1969/1982, 1973; Ryan, Stiller, & Lynch, 1994). Their understanding of "typical" relationships then influences the kinds of relationships they form with other individuals—particularly with other adults, such as teachers (Ryan et al., 1994). If you've ever visited a preschool, perhaps you know what we're talking about. Some children, curious and affectionate, flock to you with books and puzzles in hand, assuming you will want to join them in their chosen activities (we certainly urge you to do so!). In making these social overtures, children convey their expectations: "Unfamiliar adults are interesting people who will like me and care for me." Such a positive expectation is not universal, however, as you might expect from the attachment literature we've reviewed thus far. A few children may look at you suspiciously, not because they're shy, but because they wonder, "Who are you? What do you want from me? What harm might you cause me?"

Generally speaking, early attachment security is associated with positive long-term outcomes. In Western cultures, children who are securely attached in infancy tend to become relatively independent, empathic, socially competent preschoolers, particularly in comparison with children who are insecurely attached (Kestenbaum, Farber, & Sroufe, 1989; Sroufe, 1983; Vaughn, Egeland, Sroufe, & Waters, 1979). In middle childhood and adolescence, they tend to be self-confident, adjust easily to the school environment, establish productive relationships with teachers and peers, and be motivated to do well at classroom tasks (Elicker, Englund, & Sroufe, 1992; Ryan et al., 1994; Shulman, Elicker, & Sroufe, 1994; Sroufe, Carlson, & Schulman, 1993; Urban, Carlson, Egeland, & Sroufe, 1991). It is important to note, however, that not all of these findings apply to children in non-Western cultures. For instance, in Japan, caregivers encourage dependence on others, reservedness, and avoidance of strangers. Thus, for Japanese children, close and affectionate relationships with caregivers are not as likely to lead to independence and sociability (Rothbaum et al., 2000).

At least two factors may be at the root of the positive outcomes of secure attachment. First, parents who are sensitive to their children's needs during infancy usually continue to be affectionate and responsive as their children grow older; in other words, secure attachments evolve into solid, loving relationships. Second, children with secure attachments form positive expectations about other people, and they take these expectations into new relationships. A self-fulfilling element is at work here: Children expect other people to be trustworthy, and they give second chances to those who initially let them down—actions that feed and sustain healthy emotional ties.

Social-emotional well-being is not necessarily set in stone in infancy, however. Initially, attachment theorists suggested that an infant's early attachment to primary caregivers (especially the mother) sets the tone of all future relationships (e.g., Bowlby, 1973). More recently, however, researchers have discovered that infants often form very different, yet perhaps equally potent, attachments to their mothers and fathers (Bridges, Connell, & Belsky, 1988). Furthermore, as youngsters grow older, their attachments to important peers—perhaps to best friends and, eventually, to romantic partners—may be significantly different from those they have previously formed with their parents (Baldwin, Keelan, Fehr, Enns, & Koh-Rangarajoo, 1996; La Guardia, Ryan, Couchman, & Deci, 2000). To some extent, the strength and quality of their attachments to various other individuals depend on how supportive and responsive those individuals are (La Guardia et al., 2000). Apparently, growing children and adolescents form not one, but several mental representations (perhaps in the form of the mental *schemas* and *scripts* described in Chapter 5) of what interpersonal relationships can sometimes be like (Baldwin et al., 1996).

Stressful life events affect the course of children's attachments. For instance, children who initially form secure attachments to caregivers and then later live through one or more traumatic events (perhaps their parents get divorced, a family member dies or suffers a debilitating illness, or they are physically or sexually abused by a family member) may have difficulty forming attachments as adolescents or adults (Lewis, Feiring, & Rosenthal, 2000; Waters, Merrick, Treboux, Crowell, & Albersheim, 2000; Weinfield, Sroufe, & Egeland, 2000). It is important to note, however, that many children and adolescents maintain their ability to form healthy emotional bonds with others *despite* stressful events in their lives. To illustrate, let's return once again to our opening case study. As an infant, Mary formed a secure attachment to each of her parents. A few years later, her mother's behavior became erratic and occasionally abusive, apparently as the result of an emerging mental illness. Mary's attachment to her mother waned ("we're not really close"), but her attachment to her father remained strong ("I feel very close to him"), and she was sociable and well-adjusted at school.

Educational Implications of Attachment Research

As we have seen, attachments formed during infancy provide the foundation for later social relationships. Nevertheless, this foundation can be rebuilt if it's shaky, and it must occasionally be bolstered if, despite a solid beginning, it later disintegrates in the face of adverse circumstances (Thompson, 1998).

In essence, secure attachment is like a multivitamin: It increases the chances of, but does not guarantee, good health. Conversely, a child with an early insecure attachment may, with help and guidance, become a happy, productive adult. The past *and* the present matter in children's well-being. Based on the existing attachment literature, we formulate these recommendations for teachers:

■ *Cultivate strong relationships with young children in your care.* Although parents and other family members are usually the recipients of children's first attachment bonds, young children often form intensely emotional bonds with daycare providers and preschool teachers as well. Furthermore, high-quality attachments in child-care situations can to some extent compensate for poor parenting (Howes & Ritchie, 1998; NICHD Early Child Care Research Network, 1997). Thus, the recipe for good bonding—sensitive, responsive, and reliable care—is applicable in daycare and school settings as well as at home. By providing consistent warmth and support, teachers can give students needed reassurance to stay on—or get on—the path toward social and emotional well-being.

■ *Acknowledge and encourage multiple attachments.* As children grow older and venture out into the world, they gradually increase the number of social-emotional bonds they form. Children may talk about a variety of people in their lives—brothers and sisters, aunts and uncles, grandparents, neighbors—and invite such individuals to parent-teacher conferences, concerts, and school performances. Teachers and school administrators should acknowledge the importance of these people in children's lives and make them feel welcome at school events.

Unfortunately, some students have few if any supportive, affectionate relationships at home. Such students often have less developed social skills than their more "attached" classmates and so may, in many teachers' eyes, be the most difficult students to love. Yet these students are the ones most in need of affectionate relationships with responsible, dependable adults and peers. In our own experiences working with troubled children, we have found that persistence pays off: Although initial overtures are sometimes rebuffed, a regular, ongoing pattern of kindness, attention, and support eventually fosters relationships of trust and affection with children who may not have believed such relationships were possible. Children benefit, too, from learning more appropriate ways of interacting with their peers; we will offer suggestions for teaching such skills in Chapter 13.

■ *Be alert to signs of maltreatment.* We will discuss child abuse more fully in Chapter 12. For the present, simply note that the attachment literature suggests that abused children may show a disorganized and disoriented attachment pattern, including ambivalent responses to parents and nonproductive social behaviors (e.g., social withdrawal, aggression, or frequent expressions of anger). Teachers who notice such behaviors in children may wish to keep their eyes open for other possible indications of a serious family problem.

■ *When appropriate, seek the assistance of experts.* Children who have serious attachment problems often need the help of a professional therapist (Booth & Koller, 1998; Levy & Orlans, 2000). If students seem unwilling or unable to form emotional bonds with others, teachers should consult with a school psychologist or counselor for guidance about how best to meet the students' needs.

Having bonded with family members and other caregivers, children are ready to take on other social-emotional tasks, such as forming productive relationships with teachers and peers and learning how to treat other people fairly and compassionately. To establish and maintain healthy social relationships, children must be able to "read" other people's emotional cues and express their own emotions appropriately. They must also have a meaningful sense of who they are—where they fit into family and social groups, what is distinctive about them as individuals, and where their strengths and limitations lie. These two areas of development are our focus for the remainder of the chapter.

Emotional Development

Emotions (sometimes referred to as *affect*) are the feelings, both physiological and psychological, that people have in response to events that are personally relevant to their needs and goals. Emotional states energize thinking and acting in ways that are often adaptive to the circumstances (Goleman, 1995; Saarni et al., 1998). For example, if you are being chased by a lion, nature instills you with fear so that you can mobilize energy, focus intently on escape, and run furiously to safety. Stopping to think and reflect on the lion's behavior is *not* an adaptive response; immediately feeling scared and fleeing for your life *is*.

What functions do emotions serve in the classroom? Most of the time, physical survival is not at stake (sadly, we can recall a few tragic exceptions making national headlines in recent years). But even in non-life-threatening situations, emotions are important in guiding behavior. In the following vignettes, we examine some basic emotional states and the kinds of adaptive responses that may grow out of them (Saarni et al., 1998).

- *Happiness.* Paul, age 17, chatters and laughs with his friends during his school's end-of-the-year athletic field day. He is happy about having most of the year's schoolwork behind him and looking forward to his summer job and the paychecks it will bring. Happiness helps people to enjoy life and to seek similar pleasurable experiences.
- *Anger.* Aranya, age 14, sits at her desk frowning, her lips tightly pressed together. She is furious that she wasn't admitted into the elective course, "International Events and Conflicts," which she desperately wanted to take. To make matters worse, her two closest friends did get into the class. Aranya is angry with her teacher, who she thinks dislikes her, and with her mother, who lost the enrollment forms and caused a delay in her request for admission.

emotion
Affective response to an event that is personally relevant to one's needs and goals.

Anger helps people deal with obstacles to their goals, often spurring them to try new tactics and exert pressure. Aranya's anger leads her to think about what she can do to change the situation.

- *Fear.* Tony, age 2½, sits on the mat he has brought from home, eyes wide, body tense. He stares at a poster of a clown on the wall of his preschool classroom. He is afraid of clowns and is particularly anxious at nap time, when the lights are dimmed and the blinds are closed. On this particular day, he becomes downright scared; he runs to his teacher and buries his head in her lap. Fear occurs when people feel threatened and believe that their physical safety and psychological well-being are potentially at stake. Fear motivates people to flee, escape from harm, seek reassurance, and perhaps fight back.

- *Sadness.* Greta, age 15, sits quietly on a bench near her locker. With her head hung low, she rereads the letter from a regional cheerleading organization. She has not been admitted to the prestigious cheerleading summer camp. Since she started high school, cheerleading has given her much joy and satisfaction. People are sad when they realize that they cannot attain a desired goal or when they experience a loss, such as a parent dying or a friend moving to a distant city. Sadness often causes people to reassess their goals: Greta realizes that she can remain on the school's cheerleading squad even though she can't go to cheerleading camp. It also provokes others to be nurturing: When Greta's parents and friends see her tears, they realize how much cheerleading means to her and shower her with affection and reassurance.

- *Disgust.* Norton, age 8, peers at the lunch he has just purchased in the school cafeteria. He wrinkles his nose and averts his gaze from the "tuna melt" on his plate. He doesn't like tuna to begin with, and this particular preparation smells way too "fishy" to him. Disgust occurs when people encounter food, smells, and sights that they sense are contaminating to them. What is "disgusting" is partly in the eye of the beholder, and Norton's tuna melt is probably just fine. Nonetheless, having an aversion response is nature's way of getting people to be wary of substances that are *potentially* troublesome.

- *Anxiety.* Kanesha, age 16, has to give an oral report about the industrial revolution in her history class tomorrow. She has read several books on the topic and thinks she knows quite a bit about it. But she is worried that, when she is standing all by herself in front of the class, she might get so nervous that she will forget everything she wants to say. To make sure that she doesn't look "stupid" in front of her teacher and classmates, she writes the most important ideas on several index cards. She plans to give her report from memory, but she will have the cards as a backup in case she needs them. Anxiety often motivates people to behave in ways that increase their chances of success.

- *Shame.* Luke, age 7, is stunned. He's just had an accident, urinating on the floor. He had felt a bit antsy beforehand but wasn't aware that he needed to go to the bathroom. He doesn't know what to do; his pants are wet, and there is a puddle under his chair. Twenty pairs of eyes are glued on him. How embarrassing! When students feel ashamed, they are aware of other people's standards for behavior and know they have violated these standards. The adaptive function of shame is that it motivates students to try harder. In the short run, they may withdraw and avoid others, but in the long run, they are likely to behave more appropriately. Shame works only when it comes from within; teachers should *never* ridicule students in attempts to shame them. Derisive, hurtful comments don't motivate more responsible behavior; they provoke only anger, withdrawal, and escape.

- *Guilt.* A.J., age 12, regrets bad-mouthing his friend Pete to some other classmates. A.J. had thought his friend was "sucking up" to their teacher, but rather than say something to Pete directly, he instead complained to Tom, Noel, and Isaiah. The other boys promptly teased Pete, taunting "Hey, Petey-Wetey! A.J. says you're the teacher's pet!" A.J. sinks down low in his chair, feeling guilty for what he's said behind Pete's back and for the unanticipated repercussions of his remarks. Guilt occurs when people do something—in this case, betray a friend—that violates their own standards. It leads people to right the wrong, to make things better for the person they've hurt. More generally, it causes people to behave in socially appropriate ways that protect others from harm.

- *Pride.* Jacinda, age 5, is beaming. For the last 20 minutes, she's painstakingly pasted sequins, stars, and feathers onto a mask. Her final product is a fanciful, colorful, delicately adorned creation. She is happy with her work, evident from her ear-to-ear grin. Jacinda looks up at the teacher and her classmates, expecting that others will admire the beauty of her mask. People are proud when they earn others' respect and meet their own goals. Pride fosters continued commitment to behaving appropriately and achieving high standards. It also motivates people to share their accomplishments with others.

In the vignettes just presented, each child's emotional state is a natural, immediate response to a personally meaningful event. Happiness, anger, fear, anxiety, and other emotional responses focus children's attention on important aspects of their lives; they also help children develop new ideas, goals, and plans. Emotions are not just means for venting excess energy; instead, they help students redirect their actions and relationships.

Individual Differences in Emotional Responding

Emotionally, children seem to be different from one another even in early infancy. Some infants are fussy and demanding; others, like Mary in our opening case, are cheerful and easy to care for. Some are fearful and anxious; others actively seek novelty and adventure. Some are quiet and shy; others are more sociable and outgoing. Such differences reflect **temperament**—constitutional ways of responding to emotional events and novel stimulation, as well as ways of regulating impulses (Kagan, 1998; Rothbart & Bates, 1998).

Researchers suspect that cultural differences in temperament result partly from differing approaches to parenting. Many Japanese mothers comfort their infants in a very peaceful and soothing manner—an approach that may partly explain a tendency for Japanese children to be quiet and subdued.

Many aspects of temperament, such as cheerfulness, outgoingness, moodiness, and anxiety, probably have a genetic basis; for example, identical twins reared in different homes often have similar personalities (Henderson, 1982; Rothbart & Bates, 1998; Tellegren, Lykken, Bouchard, & Wilcox, 1988). Yet the genetic basis for temperament is best thought of as only a *predisposition* to behave in a certain way. That predisposition is then molded and modified by experience (Thompson, 1998). For example, temperamentally shy children have more opportunities to interact with other children—and thus are more likely to overcome their shyness—if they attend preschool rather than remain at home until kindergarten or first grade.

Furthermore, parents, teachers, and peers may intentionally cultivate certain ways of responding. In other words, children's emotional responses are the targets of **socialization**—systematic efforts by adults, other children, and institutions (e.g., schools and churches) to prepare youngsters to act in ways their society perceives to be appropriate and responsible. Different cultural groups may socialize children differently, in part by encouraging certain kinds of behaviors (Harwood, Miller, & Irizarry, 1995). For instance, among Navajo Native Americans and in many Middle Eastern societies, it is common for adults to swaddle babies, tightly bundling them in wrapped layers of fabric (Whiting, 1981). Swaddling keeps mothers and their infants near one another, makes it easier for mothers to respond to their infants' cries, and helps infants relax and remain calm in noisy environments (Saarni et al., 1998). In mainstream Western societies, swaddling is not commonly practiced, as many adults believe it engenders passivity. As another example, Japanese parents do much to keep their babies pacified and quiet, in part out of regard for a cultural ideal of harmony and in part out of consideration for neighbors who live on the other side of thin walls. Japanese mothers therefore talk infrequently, speak softly, and gently stroke their babies (Miyake, Campos, Kagan, & Bradshaw, 1986). In contrast, American mothers talk to their infants frequently, often in an expressive and evocative manner, perhaps in an effort to stimulate cognitive development or strengthen the caregiver-infant relationship (e.g., Trainor, Austin, & Desjardins, 2000).

Research on temperamental characteristics suggests some stability over time, such that we can, to some degree, predict children's later personality characteristics and social behaviors from their earlier ones (Caspi, 1998; Kagan, 1998; Rothbart & Bates, 1998). For example, children who are inhibited and fearful as toddlers and preschoolers also tend to become fairly anxious adolescents and adults (Caspi, 1998). Children who freely show negative affect (e.g., irritability, fussiness, frequent anger) in the early years are more likely

temperament
Constitutional ways of responding to emotional events and novel stimulation, and of regulating impulses.

socialization
Systematic efforts by other people and by institutions to prepare youngsters to act in ways deemed by society to be appropriate and responsible.

to show negative affect (e.g., depression, anxiety, aggression) later in life (Caspi, 1998). Such stability is undoubtedly due both to genetic factors and to ongoing, persistent characteristics in children's social environments.

Developmental Changes in Emotional Functioning

As children grow older, they acquire a broader range of emotions; they also become increasingly aware of their own and others' feelings. More specifically, their emotional development is characterized by the following trends:

■ *Children become increasingly sophisticated interpreters of emotions.* From the early days of infancy, children respond to emotional states in others. If you've ever visited an infant daycare center, you may have noticed the **emotional contagion** of babies: When one starts crying, others soon join in with tears of their own (Hatfield, Cacioppo, & Rapson, 1994). In the first year or two of life, children also show the ability to monitor the emotions of others, particularly parents and trusted caregivers. Children who engage in **social referencing** watch their parents' faces, especially in the presence of a novel or puzzling phenomenon (Boccia & Campos, 1989; Sorce, Emde, Campos, & Klinnert, 1985). Creeping to a stand in a slippery bathtub, a toddler may quickly sit when she sees the horrified expression on Mommy's face. Likewise, this same toddler may glance at Daddy's face when a new babysitter enters the house: Is the stranger trustworthy? How does Daddy react to her? Does he seem to recognize her? Is he smiling or frowning?

With age, children become increasingly adept at "reading" people's facial expressions. For instance, when her sons Alex and Connor were 5 and 13, respectively, Teresa asked them to draw pictures of faces showing various emotional expressions. Although she had to give Alex examples of circumstances that might provoke feelings of being "ashamed" and "guilty," both boys found the task to be an easy one. Their drawings, shown in Figure 9–1, indicate clear differentiations among facial expressions that reflect such negative emotions as anger, sadness, fear, disgust, and guilt.

As children grow older, they also become more thoughtful about emotions. As early as age 2 or 3, they talk about emotional states that they and others experience ("Daniel got mad and pushed me"), and they realize that emotions are connected to people's desires ("I'm angry that Kurt ate the last cookie") (Bretherton, Fritz, Zahn-Waxler, & Ridgeway, 1986; Dunn, Bretherton, & Munn, 1987; Wellman, Harris, Banerjee, & Sinclair, 1995). By middle childhood, they realize that their thoughts and interpretations determine how they feel about a particular situation and that other people have different interpretations and, as a result, different feelings ("Arlene feels bad because she thinks I don't like her") (Harris, 1989).

By the upper elementary grades, children begin to realize that emotional expressions do not always reflect people's true feelings (Selman, 1980). For instance, a 9-year-old may observe the smile and cheerful demeanor of his teacher yet know that this teacher just lost her brother to cancer and so is probably very sad. Finally, during the end of middle childhood and the beginning of adolescence, children appreciate that people can have ambivalent feelings toward people and events (Donaldson & Westerman, 1986; Harter & Whitesell, 1989). For instance, a 12-year-old girl may love her father but be angry at him for moving out of the house when her parents divorced; she may like going to see him during custodial visits but not like the feelings of turmoil these visits provoke in her.

■ *Children expand their repertoire of basic emotions to include self-conscious emotions.* Infants seem to be born with a full arsenal of emotional states. Anger, fear, happiness, and disgust are evident from the first days of life; an ability to detect basic emotions in others is present in infancy as well (Caron, Caron, & MacLean, 1988; Emde, Gaensbauer, & Harmon, 1976; Haviland & Lelwica, 1987; Hiatt, Campos, & Emde, 1979; Schwarz, Izard, & Ansul, 1985; Stenberg & Campos, 1990). By preschool age, children also show evidence of **self-conscious emotions,** affective states that reflect awareness of social standards and other people's concerns about adherence to these standards (Lewis, 1993, 1995). Self-conscious emotions include guilt, shame, embarrassment, and pride. Teresa recalls early displays of guilt and shame in both of her sons. As toddlers and preschoolers, the boys would often respond angrily when a misbehavior resulted in their being sent to their rooms or having a privilege taken away. Occa-

emotional contagion
Tendency for infants to cry spontaneously when they hear other infants crying.

social referencing
Observing emotional cues of others and using such cues to interpret the possible implications of an event for oneself.

self-conscious emotion
Affective state that reflects awareness of a community's social standards (e.g., pride, guilt, shame).

FIGURE 9–1 Drawings of basic emotional expressions by Alex (age 5) and Connor (age 13)

sionally they'd swat at her or stomp out of the room in a snit. However, they'd return a few minutes later, scrutinizing her face for signs of sadness and affectionately rubbing her arm as they apologized for their misdeeds.

■ *Children and adolescents gradually learn to regulate their emotions.* **Emotional regulation** (also called *coping*) refers to the strategies children use to manage stressful situations (Brenner & Salovey, 1997). As children grow older, experience a breadth of emotionally significant events, and observe the role models around them, they acquire an increasing number of coping strategies for dealing with difficult situations (Saarni et al., 1998). As an example, they may observe their parents controlling their anger physically yet expressing it verbally: "I'm angry that you said you were going to make dinner and didn't keep your commitment!" They may then use a similar strategy in dealing with peer conflicts: "You said you would meet me at four o'clock but you never showed up. Where *were* you?!" Youngsters who appropriately control and express their emotions are those most likely to be popular with their peers (Fabes et al., 1999).

Children also become better able to appraise the advantages and disadvantages of particular coping strategies. For instance, a 14-year-old may observe a best friend becoming entangled in a fight or an intoxicated neighbor heading for her car with keys in hand; in such circumstances, the teenager quickly identifies a range of possible solutions and considers the potential benefits and risks of each one. As children and adolescents evaluate the various

emotional regulation
Using strategies to manage responses to stressful events (also called *coping*).

Despite gains in emotional regulation, adolescents can be more emotionally volatile than younger children, in part because they feel self-conscious about their changing bodies, develop more complex relationships with peers, and have increasing responsibilities both during and after school.

strategies they might use, they seek the social support of others, perhaps by soliciting direct assistance or perhaps by presenting themselves in ways that will gain others' sympathy. In general, younger children are more inclined to go to adults (especially parents, other family members, and teachers) for help and guidance, whereas older children and adolescents are more likely to seek the support of peers (Rossman, 1992).

Sometimes children's appraisals of emotionally charged events enable them to deal directly with a problem—for instance, by confronting a peer. At other times, when they cannot change the situation, they instead try to deal with their emotions. For example, a child might alleviate his anxiety about an upcoming test by reminding himself that he has done well in the past on such examinations.

A final component of emotional regulation is determining when to express emotions publicly. Children gradually learn to curb their emotional reactions to protect themselves and other people (Cole, 1986). For example, many preschoolers realize that they should not reveal their true feelings when disappointed by a gift from a well-meaning relative. They instead conceal their disappointment with a big "thank you," realizing that the relative had good intentions and might be hurt by a more honest reaction ("Does she *really* think I'd wear that hat?").

In the opening case study, Mary had several strategies for coping with troubling events. She entered new situations cautiously, trying to gather more information before committing herself to a particular course of action. She shied away from open conflicts with others, and she kept her distance from her overly critical and punitive mother. As Mary grew older, she became able to put herself in her mother's shoes—for instance, by realizing that her mother was probably lonely and may have been in the midst of early menopause—and this strategy may have made her relationship with mother more tolerable.

■ *Adolescence brings new anxieties and pressures.* Adolescents tend to be more emotionally volatile than younger children: They more often report feeling lonely, embarrassed, or anxious, and they have more extreme mood swings (Arnett, 1999). The hormonal changes that accompany puberty may account for some of this volatility, but environmental factors probably have a more significant effect (Arnett, 1999).

Adolescence ushers in many new situations and problems that children haven't encountered before. As young teenagers undergo rapid, uncontrollable physical changes, they may feel self-conscious and awkward, perhaps even alienated from their own bodies (Rudlin, 1993). As they grow more independent, they may find their own needs and desires conflicting with those of their parents and other authority figures (Arnett, 1999). As peer relationships become more important, their interpersonal problems become an increasing source of anxiety and inner turmoil. School provides additional pressures: Worries about completing homework, getting along with teachers, achieving good grades, and "fitting in" with classmates are common sources of concern for secondary school students (Phelan, Yu, & Davidson, 1994). All of these factors come into play for even the most "normal" of adolescents, but some have additional challenges—perhaps living in poverty, experiencing ongoing family conflict, or being abused by a family member—that they must deal with (Cicchetti & Toth, 1998; Rutter & Garmezy, 1983).

Not surprisingly, then, many (though by no means all) adolescents perceive their lives as being quite stressful, particularly in highly developed Western countries (Arnett, 1999; Masten, Neemann, & Andenas, 1994). They may turn to their peers for understanding and guidance, or perhaps for distraction from their troubles. They may also express their frustrations through poetry and art. For example, early in his senior year of high school, 17-year-old Jeff felt "locked in" by the combined pressures of a demanding course load, impending due dates for college applications, and his role as confidant for several troubled friends. Late one night, he put his schoolwork aside to create the picture shown in Figure 9–2. Because he had trouble drawing human figures, he combined two favorite things—a soft drink and black-and-white cow hide—to represent himself. As you can see, a cage and gigantic boulder hold him in, and so he cannot join in as his peers (represented by other soft drink cans) frolic freely in the distance.

Some adolescents believe that the problems they face exceed their capabilities to cope effectively (Masten et al., 1994). The sad result is that suicide is more common in adolescence than in the earlier years (Durkin, 1995).

Group Differences in Emotional Responding

All children show developmental progression in the expression and control of their emotions. To some degree, their developmental pathways are influenced by their group membership—by their gender, their culture, and their socioeconomic status.

Gender Differences On average, male and female babies tend to be similar in temperament; any gender differences in infancy are subtle and situation-dependent (Eisenberg, Martin, & Fabes, 1996). After the age of 2, however, consistent gender differences begin to emerge. For instance, boys show more anger than girls beginning in the preschool years, and girls more often report feeling sad, fearful, or guilty beginning in the elementary grades (Eisenberg et al., 1996). Girls also respond more negatively to their failures, to the point where their subsequent performance may suffer (Dweck, 1986). As early as elementary school, boys begin to hide their true feelings, oftentimes even from themselves (Eisenberg et al., 1996; Sadker & Sadker, 1994).

Biology may be the source of some gender differences in emotions; for instance, rising hormonal levels at puberty are associated with increases in moodiness and depression in girls, but with aggressiveness and rebelliousness in boys (Buchanan, Eccles, & Becker, 1992; Susman et al., 1987). Yet many theorists suspect that differences in socialization are a more significant cause of gender differences in emotional responding (Durkin, 1995; Eisenberg et al., 1996; Sadker & Sadker, 1994). For instance, parents are more likely to discourage overt anger in daughters than in sons (Birnbaum & Croll, 1984; Malatesta & Haviland, 1982). Parents are apt to discourage sons from expressing emotions yet may encourage daughters to talk about how they are feeling (Block, 1979; Eisenberg et al., 1996). At school, many teachers seem to prefer the passive, compliant nature that girls are more likely to exhibit (Bennett, Gottesman, Rock, & Cerullo, 1993; Pollack, 1998). Witness Pollack's (1998) observations of a fourth-grade classroom:

> [O]n several occasions I had observed the fourth-grade class of Ms. Callahan. She was particularly skillful, modern, and warm in her approach, universally beloved by her students. I have every reason to believe that Ms. Callahan was a teacher who would want both boys and girls to derive all they could from the classroom experience.
>
> On this visit, some boys and girls who had been organized into "teams" were working together on a writing project about friendship. Adult volunteers were consultants for these teams and were helping them with their computer skills. I was surprised to see that instead of focusing on the writing project, Ms. Callahan's attention was almost entirely taken up by disciplining the boys. Several lively boys were making a commotion in one corner near the computer. Ms. Callahan cautioned them about making too much noise, and told them to return to their desks and wait their turns. With long faces, the boys meandered across the room and slumped into their seats. A moment later one of the boys could not resist calling out about something. Ms. Callahan gave him a stern second warning. "I don't want to have to caution you again," Ms. Callahan said. "If I do, you're heading for the principal's office."
>
> I had observed the class before, and now I noticed that two of the more creative male students—Robert and Shawn—were not in evidence. I asked Ms. Callahan if they were sick that day.
>
> "No," she explained. "Robert is too excitable for the group process. He's working on an entirely different project." She pointed him out—sitting alone on the floor, tucked out of view, banished from the team endeavor.
>
> "And where's Shawn?" I inquired.
>
> "He was telling inappropriate jokes about Albert Einstein earlier in the day and distracting the entire class. So, he's sitting outside working on his spelling," Ms. Callahan sighed. "Some kids just seem unable to fit into this more quiet team-based teaching."

FIGURE 9–2 Drawing himself as a cow-patterned soda can, 17-year-old Jeff dramatically depicts how the pressures in his life prevent him from doing the things he would like to do.

I wish I had asked her what those jokes about Albert Einstein were, but I was too concerned about her attitude toward these boys. She clearly felt that they could not "fit in" and that they were "unable" to participate appropriately, when I knew (as she did) that these were bright boys with a lot to offer. Although I doubt that Ms. Callahan would agree, I think the prevailing method in class that day was structured around the way girl students prefer to work, and that boys were at a disadvantage. (Pollack, 1998, pp. 240–241)

Cultural Differences Earlier we suggested that temperamental differences in infants may be partly a function of how parents in different cultures care for and respond to their babies. Cultural differences in socialization practices continue throughout childhood and adolescence, resulting in noticeable differences in emotional responding. For instance, in China and Japan, many children are raised to be shy and restrained, whereas in Zambia, smiling and sociability are apt to be the norm (Chen, Rubin, & Sun, 1992; Hale-Benson, 1986; Ho, 1986, 1994; Rothbaum et al., 2000). Many Mexican American parents encourage obedience rather than self-assertiveness (Trawick-Smith, 1997). Girls in India are more likely than British girls to be deferential and controlled, and to hide negative feelings such as anger and sadness, especially in the presence of adults (Joshi & MacLean, 1994).

Socioeconomic Differences Children from lower-income families are more prone to emotional difficulties than children from middle-income families (Caspi, Taylor, Moffitt, & Plomin, 2000; McLoyd, 1998). Environmental factors are almost certainly to blame for the major portion of these differences. Children living in impoverished circumstances have more than their share of reasons to feel sad, fearful, and angry; for instance, they may not know where their next meal is coming from, and they are more likely to encounter violence and drug addiction in their neighborhoods. Their parents have limited resources (and perhaps limited energy) to address their needs and may apply inconsistent and unpredictable nurturance and discipline (McLoyd, 1998). Furthermore, many children from low-income backgrounds, particularly those with a history of learning problems, have few if any positive interactions with teachers at school (Clark, 1983).

Teachers, in fact, are in a strategic position to ensure that much goes *right,* rather than wrong, in children's lives. We now consider some strategies that teachers can use to promote their students' emotional development.

Promoting Emotional Development in the Classroom

Emotions are an important part of classroom dynamics, yet many educators are uneasy about how to deal with them, as Sylvester (1995) lamented:

[W]e know emotion is very important to the educative process because it drives attention, which drives learning and memory. We've never really understood emotion, however, and so don't know how to regulate it in school—beyond defining too much or too little of it as misbehavior and relegating most of it to the arts, PE, recess, and the extracurricular program. (Sylvester, 1995, p. 2)

We propose that teachers can perhaps best promote emotional development if they consider emotional reactions, interpretations, and regulation as *competencies*—that is, as valuable skills that can improve over time. Indeed, some theorists have argued that the ability to interpret and use emotions effectively is a kind of "intelligence" (Bodine & Crawford, 1999; Gardner, 1983; Goleman, 1995). In Chapter 6, we defined intelligence as "the ability to benefit from experiences and thereby modify future behaviors in order to accomplish new tasks successfully." This definition has a practical ring to it: It is action-oriented and conveys the importance of learning from everyday experience. Emotions are clearly action-oriented in that, as we've previously noted, they guide behavior toward personally relevant needs and goals.

People certainly differ from one another in how insightful they are about their own and other individuals' emotions. We invite you to think about "smart" people you know who often do not-so-smart things. Perhaps you can think of academically "bright" classmates who seem to be clueless about other people's thoughts and feelings, insult others without knowing it, and in other ways undermine every attempt to establish productive interpersonal relationships. Smart? In some areas of life, definitely, but in other areas they seem to lack essential skills.

How can emotional competencies be cultivated in the classroom? We offer the following suggestions:

- *Create an atmosphere of warmth, acceptance, and trust.* Students learn and perform more successfully when they have positive emotions—for instance, when they feel secure, happy, and excited about the subject matter (Boekaert, 1993; Isen, Daubman, & Gorgoglione, 1987; Oatley & Nundy, 1996). And they are more likely to confide in a teacher about troublesome issues if they know that the teacher will continue to like and respect them no matter what they may reveal about themselves in heart-to-heart conversations.

- *Encourage students to express their feelings.* Children and adolescents can better deal with their feelings when they are aware of what their feelings *are*. Some teachers successfully incorporate discussions about feelings into everyday classroom routines. For example, when Teresa's son Connor was in first grade, his teacher ended each day with "circle time." She asked the children to hold hands and communicate how they felt about their day: one squeeze for happy, two squeezes for sad, three squeezes for bored, and so on. They took turns, and without words, these young students communicated how they felt to their partners, and to the rest of the class, with all eyes glued on the single hand doing the squeezing at the moment. This simple exercise gave the children a chance to reflect on, and then communicate, their basic emotional states.

Some students may, for a variety of reasons, be reluctant to share their feelings so publicly. In such cases, writing about them, perhaps in essays or journals shared only with the teacher, can provide a more confidential alternative. In the essay in Figure 9–3, 10-year-old

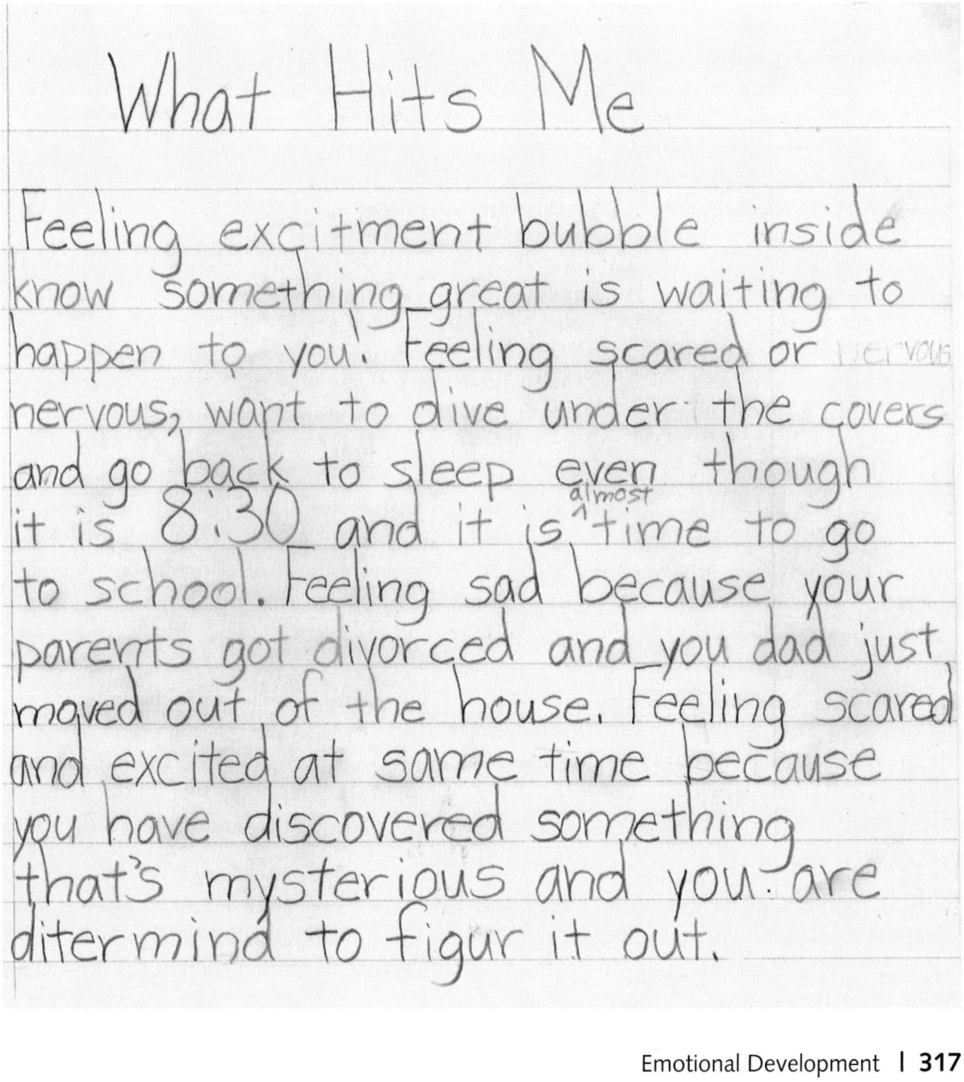

What Hits Me

Feeling excitment bubble inside
know something great is waiting to
happen to you. Feeling scared or nervous
nervous, want to dive under the covers
and go back to sleep even though
it is 8:30 and it is almost time to go
to school. Feeling sad because your
parents got divorced and you dad just
moved out of the house. Feeling scared
and excited at same time because
you have discovered something
that's mysterious and you are
ditermind to figur it out.

FIGURE 9–3 In this "What Hits Me" essay, 10-year-old Shea describes her experiences with various emotions.

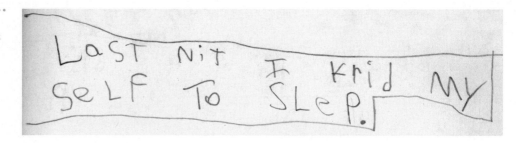

Shea describes her growing awareness of the various emotions she experiences. In the journal entry in Figure 9–4, 8-year-old Noah—ordinarily a happy, energetic student—reveals how upset he is about his parents' divorce.

■ *Help students become astute observers of others' emotional cues.* Children and adolescents are more successful in their interpersonal relationships when they learn to pick up on the subtle cues that reveal other people's emotional states. As an example, the following classroom discussion between the teacher (T) and various children (C) took place in a third-grade art lesson. The class was beginning to consider possible ways of capturing people's facial expressions on paper.

T: Have you ever noticed that people's faces change depending on how they are feeling?
C: When my mom is mad, her eyes get real skinny and her mouth closes up tight.
C: I can tell when my grandmother is really happy, because her face goes all soft looking.
T: What parts of our faces are important for showing how we feel? Which parts change? How do those parts change?
C: When my little brother gets surprised, his mouth just drops wide open.
C: When I'm scared, my eyes get much rounder and look as if they are going to drop right out.
T: You've been describing some very strong feelings in which your face changes a lot. What are some other feelings that can make your face change? How can it change? . . .
C: If I'm confused, my eyes squint, and my mouth feels all wrinkly.
T: So what parts of your face are most important for showing how you are feeling?
C: Eyes. Mouth.
C: But sometimes if I'm puzzled, my eyebrows go crooked instead of straight.
C: And when my sister smells something bad, her nose twitches. . . .
T: Here are some mirrors. Let's try to imagine some of the feelings we talked about and see how our faces change. Try out two or three very different feelings. How do your eyes change? What happens to your mouth? Do other parts of your face change too? (Smith et al., 1998, pp. 71–72)

■ *Discuss emotions of the characters you study in literature and history.* The innumerable stories that students encounter in the classroom—whether the stories are fiction or nonfiction—provide many opportunities for students to draw inferences about emotional states. We have found in our own experience that even children in the elementary grades are quite able to draw inferences about characters' emotional states and to speculate about how various emotions led to particular courses of action. For instance, in *Frog and Toad Are Friends* (Lobel, 1979), a book for 4- to 8-year-olds, Frog waits impatiently to play with his hibernating friend, Toad, and plays a trick on him to get him up early. The story provides a forum for discussions about friendships, feeling tricked and teased, and sharing feelings with friends (Solomon, Watson, Battistich, Schaps, & Delucchi, 1992). Similarly, the study of history yields many tales of inequities, hostilities, and societal transformations—good fodder for discussions about feelings and coping.

■ *Take cultural differences into account.* As we have seen, some cultures encourage open expression of feelings, whereas others actively *discourage* such expressiveness. Teachers working with children from diverse cultures must continually be mindful of such differences when interpreting the emotional displays (or lack thereof) of their students.

■ *Help students keep their anxiety at a manageable level.* **Anxiety** is an emotional state characterized by worry and apprehension, often about future events with unknown outcomes. Almost all of us feel anxious at one time or another, perhaps when we are performing in public or taking an important test. In such situations, we may experience such physiological symptoms as muscle tension and headaches and may have trouble concentrating on and remembering important information.

Small amounts of anxiety are often beneficial. For instance, anxiety can spur students to take action to make sure undesirable events (e.g., looking "stupid" in front of classmates) don't happen. But many children and adolescents sometimes become excessively anxious, especially when they are taking tests, speaking in public, or in other ways subjecting themselves to the potential evaluation of others.

Teachers can do a variety of things to keep anxiety at a manageable level. For instance, when they assign oral reports, they can encourage students to create index cards or other memory "crutches." Before giving an important test (such as the standardized tests that many school districts require), they can administer a practice test that gives students a general idea of what to expect. And teachers should make sure that in their own classrooms, no single assessment is so important that a student's ultimate success or failure depends on it.

Teachers can serve as exemplary models for staying calm in stressful situations, and they can help relieve students' anxiety by talking through problems in a warm and supportive manner.

■ *Model appropriate ways of dealing with negative emotions.* Students often struggle with how to deal with anger, fear, and sadness and can certainly benefit from seeing adults express their emotions appropriately. Teresa vividly remembers how her fifth-grade teacher expressed anger: Rather than raise her voice, she lowered it to a whisper. Her approach worked quite well: Students sensed her anger and disappointment, responded with concern and guilt, and tried to make amends for their misdeeds. Teachers can enhance the benefits of modeling controlled, honest emotional reactions by explaining what they're doing: "I'm really angry now. Let's talk this out when we've both calmed down"; "I can't believe the School Board cut our budget for new science equipment. I'm going to give the Board a piece of my mind . . . *after* I compose myself."

Some children have such strong emotions that simply talking about feelings and modeling appropriate ways of coping will have limited, if any, effect. We now look at serious emotional problems that some children and adolescents have, as well as at strategies that teachers can use in such situations.

Emotional Problems in Children and Adolescents

In the opening case study, Mary's mother suffered from an "emotional disturbance." Moods fluctuate for everyone—adults and children alike—but some people have more than their share of negative emotional experiences, to the point where such experiences disrupt the quality of their lives and their ability to tackle everyday problems and developmental tasks.

Some emotional problems are manifested in **externalizing behaviors,** behaviors that have direct or indirect effects on other people; examples are aggression, destructiveness, lying, stealing, defiance, and lack of self-control. Others are manifested in **internalizing behaviors,** behaviors that typically affect only the individual who has the problem; examples are depression, anxiety, withdrawal from social interaction, eating disorders, and suicidal tendencies. When distressed, boys are more likely to display externalizing behaviors, such as aggression and destructiveness; girls are more likely to develop internalizing disorders, such as depression and anxiety (Rutter & Garmezy, 1983). Although students with externalizing behaviors are more likely to be referred by teachers for evaluation and possible special services (Kerr & Nelson, 1989), students with internalizing behaviors are often at just as much risk for school failure.

Many emotional problems are believed to result from environmental factors, such as child abuse, inconsistent parenting practices, stressful living conditions, exposure to violence, and family drug or alcohol abuse (Johnson & Friesen, 1993; Patterson, DeBaryshe, & Ramsey, 1989; Shaffer, 1988). At the same time, biological causes, such as heredity,

anxiety
Emotional state characterized by worry and apprehension.

externalizing behavior
Undesirable emotion, behavior, or a combination that affects other people (e.g., aggression, stealing, lack of self-control).

internalizing behavior
Undesirable emotion, behavior, or a combination that primarily affects oneself (e.g., depression, social withdrawal, and suicidal tendencies).

chemical imbalances, brain injuries, and illnesses, may also contribute to emotional and behavioral problems (Hallowell, 1996; Johnson & Friesen, 1993). Overall, it appears that no single factor—biological, psychological, or environmental—accounts for the emergence of serious emotional difficulties, except in extreme conditions (Cicchetti & Toth, 1998). Rather, nature and nurture interact to create problematic emotional conditions for a particular child in a particular cultural setting.

Three emotional-behavioral disorders are fairly common in children and adolescents: depression, anxiety disorder, and conduct disorder. We look at each of these conditions and then formulate some general recommendations for working with students who have ongoing emotional problems.

Depression People with **depression** feel exceptionally sad, discouraged, and hopeless: they may also feel restless, sluggish, helpless, worthless, or guilty (American Psychiatric Association, 1994; Seligman, 1991). Seriously depressed individuals may have trouble concentrating, lose interest in their usual activities, have little appetite, and have difficulty sleeping (American Psychiatric Association, 1994; Hertel, 1994). In children and adolescents, irritability may be more evident than sadness. Other common characteristics of depression in young people include complaints about physical pain, withdrawal from social relationships, significant substance abuse, and talk of suicide. In a variation of depression, **bipolar disorder** (also known as *manic-depression*), individuals experience periods of extreme elation (*mania*) as well as periods of deep depression.

The specific symptoms of depression vary somewhat from culture to culture. The American Psychiatric Association provides several examples of how depression might manifest itself in different cultures:

> Complaints of "nerves" and headaches (in Latino and Mediterranean cultures), of weakness, tiredness, or "imbalance" (in Chinese and Asian cultures), of problems of the "heart" (in Middle Eastern cultures), or of being "heartbroken" (among Hopi). (American Psychiatric Association, 1994, p. 324)

Many instances of depression and bipolar disorder probably have biological, and possibly genetic, roots (Cicchetti, Rogosch, & Toth, 1997; Griswold & Pessar, 2000). These conditions tend to run in families, are often foreshadowed by temperamental moodiness and insecure attachment, and may reflect chemical imbalances (Cicchetti et al., 1997; Griswold & Pessar, 2000). Yet environmental factors often play a role as well; for instance, the death of a loved one, mental illness or marital conflict in parents, child maltreatment, poverty, inadequate schools, and negative social relationships may bring about or exacerbate depressive symptoms (Cicchetti et al., 1997). When individuals yield to extreme stress with a depressive episode, the event may alter their neurological chemistry, making it more likely for them to suffer another depressive episode in the future (Akiskal & McKinney, 1973; Antelman & Caggiula, 1977; Siever & Davis, 1985).

Before adolescence, depression and bipolar disorder are relatively rare. Their prevalence increases during adolescence; for instance, 5% to 10% of teenagers have one or more major depressive episodes (Cicchetti et al., 1997). During childhood, depression rates are approximately equal for boys and girls, but by age 16, rates are considerably higher for girls than for boys, perhaps because girls are more likely to think about and dwell on their problems (Cicchetti et al., 1997; Eisenberg et al., 1996; Nolen-Hoeksema, 1987).

How might depression emerge in the life of a child? Let's consider Billy, a 5-year-old boy who's just entered kindergarten. His single mother suffers from depression and seems inconsistent in her gestures of affection. She occasionally gives in to his persistent demands, but at other times she vacillates between indifference and anger. When Billy first comes to school, he clings to his mother and is anxious about separating from her. When she does leave, he seems irritable and tired, and he has trouble focusing on activities and interacting with peers. He is not diagnosed with depression for another 10 years, when he shows more classic symptoms—missing school, sleeping irregularly, abusing alcohol, and forecasting his own death to the few friends he has. Billy exemplifies some of the internal vulnerability factors for depression: a possible genetic predisposition (inherited from his mother), uneven temperament, and insecure attachment.

depression
Emotional condition characterized by significant sadness, discouragement, and hopelessness.

bipolar disorder
Condition characterized by cyclical mood swings, including periods of elation (mania) and periods of deep depression.

Suicide is an ever-present risk for youth with serious depression or bipolar disorder. Depressed individuals who contemplate suicide often believe that they face problems they cannot solve or have extreme emotional pain that they wish to end (Miller, 1994). Approximately 15% of individuals with a major depressive disorder die by their own hand (American Psychiatric Association, 1994).

The overwhelming despair and high frequency of suicide that characterize depression make it a condition that educators must take seriously. Through their daily contact with students, teachers have numerous opportunities to observe fluctuations in mood and performance and so are often in a position to spot cases of possible depression in students. (Friends and family, though they may have closer ties to students, may not comprehend how serious a problem is or may possibly even deny its existence.) Teachers will want to offer emotional reassurance to students who appear troubled, but they should consult with principals and school counselors if they suspect serious depression or related emotional disturbance.

Anxiety Disorders In its milder forms, anxiety is a common and very "normal" emotion. But some people, including some children and adolescents, worry excessively and find it difficult to control their worrisome thoughts and feelings; in other words, they have an **anxiety disorder** (American Psychiatric Association, 1994). Children with a *generalized anxiety disorder* tend to worry excessively about a wide variety of things—perhaps including their academic achievement, their performance in sports, and potential catastrophic events such as wars or hurricanes. Some individuals have more specific anxiety disorders—perhaps worrying excessively about gaining weight, having a serious illness, being away from family and home, or feeling embarrassed in public (American Psychiatric Association, 1994).

Anxiety as a trait does tend to run in families, and individuals with anxiety disorders also tend to have biological relatives with other affective disorders, such as major depression (American Psychiatric Association, 1994; Last, Hersen, Kazdin, Francis, & Grubb, 1987). Furthermore, children with anxiety disorders are themselves more susceptible to other emotional difficulties, such as serious depression (Mattison, 1992). There are hints in the research that family environment may play a role in the onset of anxiety disorders, but more investigation is needed in this area (Famularo, Kinscherff, & Fenton, 1992; Mattison, 1992).

Conduct Disorder When children and adolescents display a chronic pattern of externalizing behaviors, they are sometimes identified as having a **conduct disorder.** Youngsters who display a conduct disorder ignore the rights of others in ways that are unusual for their age. Common symptoms include aggression to people and animals (e.g., initiating physical fights, forcing someone into sexual activity, torturing animals), destruction of property (e.g., setting fires, painting graffiti), theft and deceitfulness (e.g., breaking into cars, lying about shoplifting so as not to be caught), and serious violations of rules (e.g., ignoring reasonable curfews, being truant from school) (American Psychiatric Association, 1994).

One or two antisocial acts do not necessarily indicate a serious emotional problem. Conduct disorders are more than a matter of "kids being kids" or "sowing wild oats." Instead, they represent deep-seated and persistent disregard for the rights and feelings of others, as reflected in a *consistent* pattern of antisocial behavior, often beginning in the early elementary years. Youth with conduct disorder tend to see the world through conflict-colored glasses, for example by always assuming that others have hostile intentions toward them (Crick & Dodge, 1994).

Approximately 2% to 6% of school-age youth could be classified as having conduct disorder, with the rates being three or four times higher for boys than for girls (Kazdin, 1997). Particular manifestations of conduct disorder also vary by gender: Boys are more likely to engage in theft and aggression, whereas girls are apt to engage in sexual misbehavior. When boys and girls exhibit conduct disorders in childhood and adolescence, they are also likely to have problems in adulthood, including antisocial behavior and criminal behavior, frequent changes in employment, high divorce rates, little participation in families and community groups, and early death (Kazdin, 1997).

As is true for the emotional disorders we've previously considered, biology may be partly to blame for conduct disorders; for instance, children and adolescents with conduct disorders may have difficulty inhibiting aggressive impulses, perhaps as a result of brain damage

anxiety disorder
Chronic emotional condition characterized by excessive, debilitating worry.

conduct disorder
Chronic emotional condition characterized by lack of concern for the rights of others.

or other neurological abnormalities (Dempster & Corkill, 1999; Gladwell, 1997; Kazdin, 1997). Family environments may be influential as well: Conduct disorders are more common when children's parents provide little love and affection, are highly critical, and unpredictably administer harsh physical punishment (Blackson et al., 1999; DeKlynen, Speltz, & Greenberg, 1998; Kazdin, 1997; Patterson et al., 1989; Webster-Stratton & Hammond, 1999). School environments may further contribute to the problem. Conduct disorders are more frequently observed in situations where teachers have low expectations for students, provide little encouragement or praise for schoolwork, and put little effort into planning lessons (Kazdin, 1997).

Working with Students Who Have Serious Emotional Problems Effective educational programs for students with emotional disorders are usually individualized and tailored to the unique needs of each student. Without such adaptations, schools are difficult places for students with serious emotional problems. As a telling statistic, less than half of these students graduate from high school (Bassett et al., 1996; Koyanagi & Gaines, 1993). Teachers should work closely with psychologists and special education professionals to design specific support systems. In addition, they can consider the following general strategies:

■ *Show an interest in students' well-being.* Many students with emotional disorders have few positive and productive relationships with individuals outside of school, and so their relationships with caring and supportive teachers may become all the more important (Diamond, 1991). The many "little things" teachers do each day—greeting students warmly in the hallway, expressing concern when they seem worried or upset, and lending a ready ear when they want to share their ideas, opinions, feelings, or frustrations—can make a world of difference (Diamond, 1991).

■ *Teach and encourage interpersonal skills.* Many students with emotional problems have difficulty establishing and maintaining friendships (Asher & Coie, 1990; Cartledge & Milburn, 1995; Schonert-Reichl, 1993). Training and practice in effective social skills seem to improve both the interpersonal relationships *and* the emotional functioning of these students (e.g., Gillham, Reivich, Jaycox, & Seligman, 1995). We will look at specific strategies for teaching social skills in our discussion of peer relationships in Chapter 13.

■ *Provide extra structure and support for students who have high levels of anxiety about classroom tasks and activities.* One effective strategy is to communicate expectations for performance in clear and concrete terms; highly anxious students perform better in well-structured classrooms, those in which expectations for academic achievement and social behavior are explicitly laid out (Hembree, 1988; Stipek, 1993; Tobias, 1977). Teachers can also talk with students about specific sources of anxiety, such as separating from parents or giving oral presentations in public. Students often appreciate a teacher's assistance in overcoming their concerns. For instance, a preschool teacher might make it a familiar routine to stand with children at the window to wave goodbye to parents in the morning. A high school teacher might give students the opportunity to give oral presentations to a small group of friends before giving them to the entire class.

■ *Be alert for signs that a student may be contemplating suicide.* Seriously depressed students often give signs that they may be thinking about taking their own lives. Such warning signs include the following (Kerns & Lieberman, 1993):
- Sudden withdrawal from social relationships
- Disregard for personal appearance
- A dramatic personality change
- A sudden elevation in mood
- A preoccupation with death and morbid themes
- Overt or veiled threats (e.g., "I won't be around much longer")
- Actions that indicate "putting one's affairs in order" (e.g., giving away prized possessions)

Teachers must always be alert for signs that a student is seriously depressed. If they suspect that a student may be contemplating suicide, they should seek trained help immediately.

Teachers must take any of these behaviors seriously. They should show genuine caring and concern for potentially suicidal students, and they should also seek trained help, such as from the school psychologist or counselor, *immediately* (McCoy, 1994).

■ *Set reasonable limits for behavior.* Even though the misbehaviors that accompany conduct disorders may have a biological basis, children need to learn that certain actions—aggression, destructiveness, stealing, and so on—are simply unacceptable. Establishing rules for appropriate behavior and applying appropriate consequences (e.g., loss of privileges) for infractions provide the structure and guidance that some students need to keep undesirable behaviors in check (Turnbull et al., 1999).

■ *Give students a sense that they have some control.* Some students, especially those who consistently defy authority figures, often respond to efforts to control them by behaving even *less* appropriately than they have previously. With such students, it is important that teachers not get into power struggles—situations where only one person "wins" and the other inevitably loses. Instead, teachers might create situations in which students conform to classroom expectations yet also feel that they have some control over what happens to them. For instance, students can learn and apply techniques for observing and monitoring their own actions with the goal of developing more productive classroom behavior (Kern, Dunlap, Childs, & Clark, 1994). They can also be given choices (within reasonable limits) about how to proceed in particular situations (Knowlton, 1995). We will examine such approaches in more depth in Chapter 11.

To some extent, children's emotional well-being is related to how they perceive themselves—for instance, whether they see themselves as capable or incapable of handling life's daily challenges, whether they compare favorably or unfavorably with those around them, and whether they like or dislike the person they see in the mirror. We turn our attention now to children's knowledge, beliefs, and feelings about themselves as human beings.

Development of a Sense of Self

Let's look once again at 18-year-old Mary's description of herself:

> If I say how I am, it sounds like bragging—I have a good personality and people like me. I'm not the greedy type—I'm jealous a lot of times, yes. And I don't like it when people think they can run my own life——I like to be my own judge. I know right and wrong, but I feel I have a lot more to learn and go through. Generally, I hope I can make it—I hope. (Werner & Smith, 1982, p. 140)

Like Mary, children and adolescents often have very definite beliefs and feelings about themselves. The term **self-concept** refers to the beliefs that people have about themselves, their personal attributes, and their strengths and weaknesses. Mary's self-concept included her reflection that she was likeable, independent, and prone to jealousy. **Self-esteem** is based on the judgments and feelings students have of their capabilities and worth. Mary seemed to have positive feelings about herself—so much so that she thought she might come across as "bragging."[1]

Children and adolescents tend to have an overall, general feeling of self-worth: They believe either that they are good, capable individuals or that they are somehow inept and unworthy (Harter, 1990a; Marsh & Craven, 1997). At the same time, they are usually aware that they have both strengths and weaknesses—that they do some things well and other things poorly (Harter, Whitesell, & Junkin, 1998; Marsh & Craven, 1997; Wigfield, 1994). Consider 9-year-old Shea's *Song of Myself,* presented in Figure 9–5. Note the multiplicity of domains that Shea addresses; for instance, she says, "I am kind, responsible, pretty, smart; I think, plan, help, research. . . ."

By the time they reach adolescence, young people have distinctly differing beliefs about themselves in at least eight domains: cognitive competence, behavioral conduct, physical appearance, romantic appeal, positive regard from peers, relationships with close friends, athletic competence, and job performance (Harter et al., 1998). They view some of these domains

---

[1]Theorists often have difficulty distinguishing between *self-concept* and *self-esteem,* as the two constructs clearly overlap (Hart, 1988; Marsh & Craven, 1997; Wigfield & Karpathian, 1991). In general, however, they tend to use *self-concept* to refer to cognition (beliefs, theories) about the self and *self-esteem* to refer to affect (emotions).

self-concept
Beliefs that people have about themselves, their characteristics, and their abilities.

self-esteem
Feelings that people have about their own capabilities and self-worth.

FIGURE 9–5 Shea's *Song of Myself.* Shea and her classmates were given "stems" to guide their writing (e.g., "Above me . . . ," "I feel . . . ," "I am . . . ," "I dream . . .").

Song of Myself

I am Shea
Above me are the bright colored leaves on the trees
Below me are seeds waiting to become flowers next spring
Before me are years to come full of new things to be learned
Behind me are memories I've forgotten
All around me are my friends lending me a helping hand
I see children having fun
I smell the sweet scent of flowers
I hear the birds talking to each other
I feel the fur of a helpless baby bunny
I move like wind as I run through the grass
I am old like the planets who have been here from the beginning
I am young like a seed waiting to sprout
I am the black of a panda's patches
I am the gold of the sun
I am the green of a cat's eye
I am the many colors of the sunset
I am a parrot, kangaroo, tiger, turtle
I am kind, responsible, pretty, smart
I think, plan, help, research
I give ideas to people that need them
I fear lightning
I believe that we all are equal
I remember my dreams
I dream of bad things as well as the good
I do not understand why some people pollute the Earth
I am Shea, a child of honesty
May I walk in peace

as being more important than others, and their proficiency in domains that they think *are* important has a greater influence on their overall sense of self-worth (Bender, 1997; Harter et al., 1998; Marsh & Craven, 1997).

Especially as they get older, individuals may even have differing beliefs about themselves regarding specific tasks and situations *within* a particular domain. For instance, Jeanne doesn't perceive herself to be a very good athlete—she's not very strong, and she has little endurance—but she knows that she's a proficient racquetball player (when she and Teresa lived in the same city, she routinely beat Teresa at racquetball). Teresa doesn't perceive herself to be a good athlete either, but she is a fairly decent runner (she wishes Jeanne would join her in a running race). Children, too, develop these kinds of refined ideas about their skills within any domain, such as athletics or academics: They are good at some things and not so good at others.

When we talk about people's self-beliefs at this level of specificity, we are often talking about their **self-efficacy**—their beliefs about whether they are capable of achieving certain goals or outcomes (e.g., Bandura, 1982, 1994). Students' expectations about their probable success or failure at particular tasks influence their choices of tasks, their effort and persistence, and (in part as a result of their effort and persistence) their *actual* success or failure (Bandura, 1982).

self-efficacy
Belief that one is capable of executing certain behaviors or reaching certain goals in a particular task or domain.

(Judging from what you've learned about self-efficacy, who do you think would be more likely to initiate a racquetball game, Jeanne or Teresa?)

Students' self-perceptions are important factors influencing behavior and achievement in school: Students tend to behave in ways that are consistent with their beliefs about themselves and their expectations for future success or failure (Pintrich & Garcia, 1994; Yu, Elder, & Urdan, 1995). For instance, those who believe that they are capable of high academic achievement are more likely to pay attention in class, use effective learning strategies, seek out challenges, and persist in the face of difficulty (Eccles, Wigfield, & Schiefele, 1998; Meyer, Turner, & Spencer, 1994; Zimmerman & Bandura, 1994). In contrast, those who believe they are "poor students" are likely to misbehave in class, study infrequently or not at all, ignore homework assignments, and avoid taking difficult subjects. Along a similar vein, students who see themselves as friendly and likable are apt to seek the company of their classmates and to run for student council, whereas those who believe they are disliked by classmates may keep to themselves or perhaps even act with hostility and aggression toward their peers. Students with a high sense of physical competence will go out for extracurricular athletics, whereas those who see themselves as total klutzes probably will not. More generally, students who have positive beliefs about themselves in particular domains or tasks are those most likely to succeed in those domains (Assor & Connell, 1992; Ma & Kishor, 1997; Marsh & Yeung, 1998; Pajares, 1996).

Factors Influencing the Development of Self-Perceptions

Several factors affect the development of children's self-concepts and self-esteem. Perhaps most influential is children's *own past behaviors and performance*. We noted earlier that children's beliefs about themselves influence the ways in which they behave. Yet the reverse is true as well: To some extent, children's self-concepts and self-esteem depend on how successfully they have behaved in the past (Damon, 1991; Marsh, 1990a). Children are more likely to believe they have an aptitude for mathematics if they have been successful in previous math classes, to believe that they are capable athletes if they have been victorious in athletic competitions, or to believe that they are likable individuals if they have been able to establish and maintain friendly peer relationships.

In addition, the *behaviors of other people,* both adults and peers, play a crucial role in the development of students' self-concepts (Durkin, 1995; Harter, 1983b, 1988; Hartup, 1989). How other individuals behave toward a child communicates their evaluations of the child and their beliefs about his or her worth as a person. For example, parents who accept their children as they are and treat their children's concerns as important are likely to have children with positive self-concepts and high self-esteem. Parents who punish their children for the things they cannot do, without also praising for things done well, are likely to have children with low self-esteem (Harter, 1983b). Teacher behaviors have an impact as well; for example, the relative proportion of positive and negative feedback that teachers give influences students' expectations for future academic success (e.g., Little, Oettingen, Stetsenko, & Baltes, 1995). And students' classmates communicate information about their social competence through a variety of behaviors—for example, by seeking out their companionship or by ridiculing them in front of others. Some adolescents are especially preoccupied with peers' approval, basing their own sense of self-worth largely on what peers think of them (Harter, Stocker, & Robinson, 1996).

Given the preceding discussion, you might predict that praising children should always lead to a higher self-concept and that criticizing children should inevitably lead to a lower one. As it turns out, the effects of praise and criticism are not so simple (Parsons, Kaczala, & Meece, 1982; Stipek, 1996). For instance, when adults praise children for successes on *easy* tasks, children may conclude that they are not capable of handling anything more difficult. Conversely, when adults criticize children's performance on difficult tasks, they may, in the process, communicate the message that the children *can* succeed on such challenges. The key factor appears to be the *expectations* that adults communicate through their statements and actions. When parents and teachers communicate high expectations and offer support and encouragement for the attainment of challenging goals, children tend to have more positive self-concepts (Eccles, Jacobs, Harold-Goldsmith, Jayaratne, & Yee, 1989; Harris & Rosenthal, 1985).

So far our discussion has focused primarily on the effects of children's experiences—that is, on environment—in the development of their self-perceptions. Yet biology also has its say, albeit indirectly. For one thing, inherited temperamental predispositions and physical and intellectual capabilities contribute to children's successes in social, athletic, and academic pursuits. Furthermore, physical appearance is a highly influential factor in the self-esteem of people of all ages (Harter, 1998); for instance, adults respond differently to children (even to infants!) depending on their perceived physical attractiveness (Langlois, 1981; Maccoby & Martin, 1983). And children with disabilities—conditions that usually have biological roots—report less positive self-concepts, on average, than their nondisabled peers (e.g., Harter et al., 1998).

Developmental Trends in Children's Self-Concepts

Children's and adolescents' physical, cognitive, and social capabilities change with age, and their perceptions of themselves shift accordingly. Yet we see several other age-related changes in children's self-concepts as well:

■ *Self-concepts become increasingly abstract.* Young children tend to define themselves in terms of external and concrete characteristics. As they grow older, they begin to define themselves more in terms of internal and abstract characteristics (Harter, 1983a, 1988; Livesley & Bromley, 1973; Rosenberg, 1986). For example, Jeanne once asked her three children to describe themselves. Their responses were as follows:

Jeff (age 6):
I like animals. I like making things. I do good in school. I'm happy. Blue eyes. Yellow hair. Light skin.

Alex (age 9):
I have brown hair, brown eyes. I like wearing short-sleeved shirts. My hair is curly. I was adopted. I was born in Denver. I like all sorts of critters. The major sport I like is baseball. I do fairly well in school. I have a lizard, and I'm going to get a second one.

Tina (age 12):
I'm cool. I'm awesome. I'm way cool. I'm 12. I'm boy crazy. I go to Brentwood Middle School. I'm popular with my fans. I play viola. My best friend is Lindsay. I have a gerbil named Taj. I'm adopted. I'm beautiful.

Notice how Jeff and Alex mostly talked about how they looked, how they behaved, and what they liked. In contrast, Tina described more abstract qualities—cool, awesome, boy crazy, popular, beautiful—that she had apparently derived from many specific, concrete experiences over time. (Appropriately, her list of self-descriptors did not include "modest.")

■ *Self-concepts become both increasingly differentiated and increasingly integrated.* As children grow older, they make increasingly finer distinctions among various aspects of themselves (Harter, 1983a; Rosenberg, 1986). Eventually, they also pull these distinctions together into an integrated conception of who they are (Harter, 1988). Somewhere around age 15, they identify aspects of their self-definitions that are potentially contradictory and then develop higher-level understandings that resolve such contradictions (Harter, 1988). For instance, they may resolve their perceptions of being both "cheerful" and "depressed" into a realization that they are "moody," or they may explain their inconsistent behaviors in different situations by concluding that they are "flexible" or "open-minded" (Harter, 1988).

■ *Children increasingly base their self-assessments on comparisons with peers.* Young children (e.g., second graders) tend to base their self-evaluations largely on their own improvement over time. Older children (e.g., sixth graders) are more likely to consider how well classmates are performing when they evaluate their own capabilities (Marsh, 1990b; Nicholls, 1984; Pintrich & Schunk, 1996). Thus, at the middle and secondary school levels especially, students who think they are doing better than others are likely to develop a relatively positive self-concept, whereas those who think they perform less well are likely to develop a more negative self-concept.

■ *With age, self-concepts become more stable.* Children with the most positive self-concepts in the early years also tend to have the most positive self-concepts in later years. Conversely, students who think poorly of themselves in elementary school also tend to have lower self-esteem in high school (Marsh & Craven, 1997; O'Malley & Bachman, 1983; Savin-Williams & Demo, 1984). As children get older, their self-perceptions become increasingly stable, probably for several reasons. First, as mentioned earlier, people usually behave in ways that are consistent with what they believe about themselves, so their behaviors are likely to produce reactions from others that confirm their self-concepts. Second, people tend to seek out information that confirms what they already believe about themselves: Those with positive self-concepts are more likely to seek out positive feedback, whereas those with negative self-concepts may actually look for information about their weaknesses and limitations (Epstein & Morling, 1995; Swann, 1997). Third, people seldom put themselves in situations where they believe they won't succeed, thereby eliminating any possibility of discovering that they *can* succeed. For example, if a teenager believes he is a poor athlete and so refuses to go out for the baseball team, he may never learn that, in fact, he has the potential to become a skillful player. And fourth, many outside factors that contribute to one's self-concept—for example, parental behaviors, socioeconomic circumstances, and one's physical attractiveness—usually remain relatively stable throughout childhood (O'Malley & Bachman, 1983).

This is *not* to say that once children acquire low self-concepts, they will always think poorly of themselves. Quite the contrary can be true, particularly when circumstances change significantly—for instance, when, after a history of failures, children begin experiencing regular success (Marsh & Craven, 1997). We will look at specific strategies for enhancing children's and adolescents' self-concepts a bit later in the chapter.

Development of the Self Across Childhood and Adolescence

The developmental trends just listed reflect gradual changes in the nature of self-concepts over time. Yet we also see qualitative differences among preschoolers, elementary students, middle schoolers, and high school students. We now look at unique aspects of self-perceptions at four age levels: early childhood, middle childhood, early adolescence, and late adolescence.

Early Childhood (Ages 2–6) Most young children have positive self-concepts, to the point where they may believe they are more capable than they actually are (Flavell et al., 1993; Paris & Cunningham, 1996). They probably make such overestimations because they base their self-assessments on their improvement in various activities over time, rather than on a comparison to age-mates. A small amount of overconfidence is probably beneficial for children's development, in that it motivates children to try and to persist at new and challenging tasks (Bjorklund & Green, 1992; Pintrich & Schunk, 1996).

Not all young children are so naively optimistic, however. Some quickly become pessimists in the face of failure. For instance, in a series of studies by Carol Dweck and her colleagues, preschoolers, kindergartners, and first graders worked on several picture puzzles that were either unsolvable (the pieces didn't fit together) or too difficult to complete in the time provided. Later, when the children were given a second opportunity to work on these puzzles, some chose to do so, but others preferred to work on puzzles they had already completely successfully. Of these "nonpersisting" youngsters, many showed signs of *learned helplessness*—a belief that their efforts would simply not pay off for them (Burhans & Dweck, 1995). (We will revisit the phenomenon of learned helplessness in Chapter 11.)

Middle Childhood (Ages 6–10) Research indicates that children's self-concepts sometimes drop soon after they begin elementary school (Harter, 1990a; Stipek, 1981), probably as a result of the many new academic and social challenges that school presents. Elementary school gives children many occasions to compare their performance with that of peers, and so their self-assessments gradually become more realistic (Hart, 1988; Paris & Cunningham, 1996; Wigfield, 1994). Yet this comparative approach inevitably creates "winners" and "losers." Children who routinely find themselves at the bottom of the heap must do some fancy footwork to keep their self-esteem intact. Often, they focus on performance areas in which they excel (e.g., sports, social relationships, or hobbies) and discount areas that give them trouble (e.g., "Reading is dumb"). Perhaps because they have so many domains and experiences to consider as they look for strengths in their own performance, most children maintain fairly high and stable self-esteem during the elementary school years (Wigfield & Eccles, 1994).

Early Adolescence (Ages 10–14) Another drop in self-concept occurs at about the time that students move from elementary school to junior high school; this drop is especially pronounced for girls (Eccles & Midgley, 1989; Marsh, 1990b; Sadker & Sadker, 1994; Simmons & Blyth, 1987; Wigfield & Eccles, 1994). The physiological changes that occur with puberty may be a factor: Students' self-concepts depend increasingly on their beliefs about their appearance and their popularity, yet boys and girls alike tend to think of themselves as being somewhat less attractive once they reach adolescence (Cornell et al., 1990; Hart, 1988; Harter, 1990a; Harter et al., 1998). The changing school environment probably also has a negative impact. Traditional junior high schools often differ from elementary schools in several ways (Eccles & Midgley, 1989). For one thing, students don't have the opportunity to form the close-knit, supportive relationships with teachers that many of them had in elementary school. Students may also discover that their school grades are based more on competitive criteria—that is, on how well they perform in comparison with their classmates. Furthermore, at a time when they probably have an increased need for close friendships, students may find themselves in classes with many people they don't know.

With all of these unsettling changes occurring simultaneously, it is not surprising that we see a temporary drop in young adolescents' self-perceptions. Fortunately, with the advent of the *middle school* concept, many school districts now take great pains to ease students' transition into a more socially complex and academically challenging secondary school environment. For instance, large schools may split up the student body into smaller and more intimate "clusters" of perhaps 60–90 students, and many schools provide explicit guidance in the skills and habits necessary for self-regulated learning. Once students have successfully adjusted to their changing school environment, most adolescents enjoy positive self-concepts and general mental health (Durkin, 1995; Nottelmann, 1987; Powers, Hauser, & Kilner, 1989; Wigfield & Eccles, 1994).

Yet in early adolescence, two new phenomena appear. First, many young adolescents believe that, in any social situation, everyone else's attention is focused squarely on them (Elkind, 1981; Lapsley, 1993; Ryan & Kuczkowski, 1994). This self-centered aspect of the adolescent self-concept is sometimes called the **imaginary audience.** Because they believe themselves to be the center of attention, teenagers (girls especially) are often preoccupied with their physical appearance and are quite critical of themselves, assuming that everyone else is going to be equally observant and critical. Extreme sensitivity to embarrassment, when coupled with inadequate social skills, can lead some adolescents to respond with undue violence when their peers insult or verbally attack them (Lowry, Sleet, Duncan, Powell, & Kolbe, 1995).

A second noteworthy phenomenon in early adolescence is the **personal fable:** Young teenagers often believe themselves to be completely unlike anyone else (Elkind, 1981; Lapsley, 1993). For instance, they often think that their own feelings are completely unique—that those around them have never experienced such emotions. Hence, they may insist that no one else, least of all parents and teachers, can possibly know how they feel. Furthermore, they may have a sense of invulnerability and immortality, believing that they are not susceptible to the normal dangers of life. Thus, many adolescents take seemingly foolish risks, such as driving at high speeds, experimenting with drugs and alcohol, or having unprotected sexual intercourse (Arnett, 1995; DeRidder, 1993; Packard, 1983; Thomas, Groër, & Droppleman, 1993).

imaginary audience
Belief that one is the center of attention in any social situation.

personal fable
Belief that one is completely unlike other people, cannot be understood, and is impervious to danger.

A frequently observed phenomenon in early adolescence is the *personal fable:* Young teenagers often believe that they are completely unique, to the point where no one else—least of all their parents and teachers—can possibly understand their thoughts and feelings.

Zits by Jerry Scott and Jim Borgman. Reprinted with special permission of King Features Syndicate.

The development of both the imaginary audience and personal fable may to some extent reflect students' changing cognitive abilities during the adolescent years. Elkind (1981) has proposed that both the imaginary audience and the personal fable are a function of the *formal operational egocentrism* that Piaget described (see Chapter 4). More specifically, young adolescents have difficulty distinguishing between their own perspectives on the world and those of others and so assume that because their *own* thoughts are focused on themselves, everyone else's thoughts must be focused on them as well. Yet researchers have found no correlation between measures of youngsters' formal thinking capabilities and measures of the imaginary audience and personal fable (Lapsley, 1993; Lapsley, Milstead, Quintana, Flannery, & Buss, 1986). An alternative explanation is that the two phenomena serve adaptive purposes as young adolescents strive for increasing independence from their families. The personal fable—in particular, the sense of invulnerability—may encourage young people to venture out into the world and try new things (Bjorklund & Green, 1992; Lapsley, 1993). At the same time, the imaginary audience keeps them "connected" to their larger social context, so that they are continually considering how others might judge their actions (Lapsley, 1993; Ryan & Kuczkowski, 1994). Whatever the origins of these phenomena, they appear to peak in early adolescence and then slowly decline (Lapsley, 1993; Lapsley, Jackson, Rice, & Shadid, 1988).

Late Adolescence (Ages 14–18) As their worlds broaden in the teenage years, young people have a greater variety of social experiences and so are apt to get conflicting messages about their characteristics and capabilities (Hart, 1988). The result is that their self-concepts may include contradictory views of themselves (Harter, 1990b; Wigfield, Eccles, & Pintrich, 1996). As they reach high school age, they begin to wrestle with such contradictions and, with luck, eventually establish a sense of **identity**—a self-constructed definition of who they are, what things they find important, and what goals they want to accomplish in life.

Membership in groups—perhaps informal cliques at school, organized clubs or teams, ethnic neighborhoods, and the community at large—often plays a key role in adolescents' identities (Durkin, 1995; Lave & Wenger, 1991; Trawick-Smith, 1997; Wigfield et al., 1996). Not only do such groups help teenagers define who they are, but they also endorse values and goals that teenagers may adopt for themselves.

Before adolescents achieve a true sense of their adult identity, most need considerable time to explore their various options for careers, political beliefs, religious affiliations, and so on. Marcia (1980) has observed four distinct patterns of behavior that may characterize the status of an adolescent's search for identity:

- *Identity diffusion.* The adolescent has made no commitment to a particular career path or ideological belief system. Possibly there has been some haphazard experimentation with

identity
People's self-constructed definition of who they are, what they find important, and what goals they want to accomplish in life.

Development of a Sense of Self | **329**

Emotional and Personal Development at Different Age Levels

DEVELOPMENTAL TRENDS

AGE	WHAT YOU MIGHT OBSERVE	DIVERSITY	IMPLICATIONS
Early Childhood (2–6) 	• Desire to be close to parents when afraid, hurt, or uncertain • Wide variety of emotions (e.g., happiness, sadness, fear, anger, disgust) • Emergence of self-conscious emotions (e.g., pride, shame, guilt) • Only a rudimentary sense of one's unique characteristics, talents, and weaknesses • Optimism about what academic and physical tasks can be accomplished	• Children vary in the number of close attachments they form, the extent to which they find reassurance in these attachment figures, and their responses to strangers. Some cling tightly to caregivers, others venture confidently to explore new environments and check out strangers. • Children vary in how they express their emotions. Some are very controlled, especially in masking anger and sadness. Others are more expressive.	• Realize that young children may initially be cautious or fearful in a new classroom environment; they will become more confident as they begin to form attachments to their teachers. • Be patient in establishing relationships with young children; some may form attachments quickly, but others make take several weeks or months before they begin to trust adults outside the home. • Teach appropriate ways of handling negative emotions. For example, encourage children to "use their words" rather than physically pushing and hitting when angry or frustrated.
Middle Childhood (6–10) 	• Increasing number of emotional bonds with teachers and peers • Increasing ability to regulate emotions • Increasing tendency to base self-perceptions of ability on how others perform • Generally positive self-concept in most children	• Children are affected by major family disruptions (e.g., divorce of parents, death or illness of a family member). Such risk factors may provide opportunities for social-emotional growth, but they often undermine children's sense of well-being and security, at least temporarily. • Some children have strong role models for emotional regulation (e.g., a parent may work out negative feelings in productive ways, resolve conflicts with others constructively, etc.). • Different children derive their sense of self-worth from different arenas—perhaps from social relationships, academic performance, or physical accomplishments.	• Incorporate discussions of emotional states into the curriculum; for example, address the feelings of characters in literature and history. • Model appropriate ways of expressing feelings. • Praise children for their talents and accomplishments in numerous areas (e.g., in physical activities, social relationships, and specific academic subjects).

particular roles or beliefs, but the individual has not yet embarked on a serious exploration of issues related to self-definition.

- *Foreclosure.* The adolescent has made a firm commitment to an occupation and/or a particular set of beliefs. The choices have been based largely on what others (especially parents) have prescribed, without an earnest exploration of other possibilities.
- *Moratorium.* The adolescent has no strong commitment to a particular career or set of beliefs but is actively exploring and considering a variety of professions and ideologies. In essence, the individual is undergoing an **identity crisis.**
- *Identity achievement.* The adolescent has previously gone through a period of moratorium and emerged with a clear choice regarding occupation and/or commitment to particular political or religious beliefs.

identity crisis
Period during which an individual actively struggles to choose a course in life.

Perhaps the ideal situation is to proceed through moratorium, a period of searching and experimentation that may continue into early adulthood, before finally settling on a clear identity (Berzonsky, 1988; Marcia, 1988). Foreclosure—identity choice *without* prior exploration—rules

DEVELOPMENTAL TRENDS

AGE	WHAT YOU MIGHT OBSERVE	DIVERSITY	IMPLICATIONS
Early Adolescence (10–14)	• Frequent fluctuations in mood, partly as a result of hormonal changes • Careful regulation of emotions (e.g., hiding joy about a good grade in order to appear "cool" to peers) • Possible temporary drop in self-concept after the transition to middle school or junior high • Preoccupation with appearance (often reflected in conformity in dress, behavior, etc.) • Increased risk taking, accompanied by a sense of invulnerability	• Adolescents differ in the extent to which they strive to conform to gender stereotypes. • Drops in self-esteem, when sizable and not followed by a rebound, can signal a serious problem. • Some serious emotional problems, such as depression and bipolar disorder, first appear during adolescence. • Some students tend to internalize their stresses (e.g., experiencing depression or anxiety); other respond with externalizing behaviors (e.g., being violent, breaking the law).	• Be a willing and supportive "ear" when students want to share concerns or anxieties. • Keep in mind that some moodiness is normal in the middle school grades. However, talk with parents and trained professionals (e.g., the school psychologist or counselor) about your concerns for the emotional well-being of students who seem especially troubled. • To help students discover that not everyone views the world as they do, plan activities in which they can express their opinions and perspectives.
Late Adolescence (14–18)	• Seeking of intimacy with same-sex and opposite-sex peers • Decrease in the self-consciousness evident in early adolescence • Wrestling with identity issues: Who am I? What do I believe? How do I fit into society?	• Adolescents differ in the extent to which they focus on dating and intimacy. • Some adolescents willingly accept the professional goals and ideologies that their parents offer. Others engage in more soul-searching and exploration as they strive to develop their identity. • Minority youth are more likely than European American youth to reflect on how their ethnic status plays a role in their identity.	• Provide opportunities for students to work closely together on classroom assignments. • Explore diverse belief systems. • Provide service learning and mentoring opportunities that allow adolescents to try on a variety of occupational "hats."

out potentially more productive alternatives, and identity diffusion leaves youth without a clear sense of direction in life.

Even as high school students move rapidly toward independence and self-reliance, their attachment to family members—especially parents—continues to play a significant role in their personal development. Adolescents who have strong emotional bonds with their parents tend to have higher self-esteem and function at more mature levels (Josselson, 1988; Ryan & Lynch, 1989). Such bonds are not overly restrictive or protective, however; parents best foster their children's personal growth by gradually releasing the apron strings as their offspring gain competence (Lapsley, 1993; Ryan & Lynch, 1989). Adolescents who feel alienated from (i.e., have little sense of attachment to) their parents are susceptible to the opinions of others for a longer period of time (i.e., the imaginary audience persists) and have more difficulty establishing a sense of identity (i.e., they are identity-diffused) (Josselson, 1988; Marcia, 1988; Ryan & Kuczkowski, 1994).

In the Developmental Trends table above, we summarize the general course of development of emotions and sense of self across the four age ranges. Keep in mind, however, that such development is characterized by considerable diversity. We now look at group differences in children's and adolescents' sense of self.

Group Differences in Representations of the Self

We have already seen several examples of diversity in children's self-perceptions. For instance, some preschoolers are more optimistic about their own capabilities than others, and adolescents with close attachments to their parents have higher self-esteem than adolescents without such close emotional bonds. To some extent, children's and adolescents' self-perceptions are a function of their group membership. Here we consider research findings related to gender, ethnicity, and cultural background.

Gender Differences As children grow older, their understandings of gender become increasingly sophisticated, and this trend has implications for their self-concepts and behaviors. During their toddler and preschool years, children show a rudimentary understanding of gender. For instance, they realize that there are two sexes, can label them, and know that they personally are either girl or boy (Etaugh, Grinnell, & Etaugh, 1989; Fagot & Leinbach, 1989). But it takes several years for them to appreciate that this state is permanent—in other words, that boys do not become girls if they grow their hair long and wear ribbons, nor do girls become boys if they cut their hair short and wear boys' clothes (Bem, 1989; DeLisi & Gallagher, 1991; Emmerich, Goldman, Kirsh, & Sharabany, 1977; Slaby & Frey, 1975). With this developing concept of gender, young children watch the world around them for further clues about the distinctions between what is "male" and what is "female," and they are especially attentive to role models of their own gender.

During middle childhood, friendships are largely dictated by gender: Although boys may have friends who are girls, and vice versa, children usually prefer same-sex companions. Furthermore, by defining themselves as "boy" or "girl," children tend to choose activities and exhibit behaviors that their society deems to be "gender-appropriate." For example, girls are more concerned about their appearance, but also less satisfied with it, beginning in middle childhood (Maloney, McGuire, & Daniels, 1988; Stein, 1996). Of course, there are individual differences in how strictly children adhere to sex-role stereotypes. **Androgynous** individuals show both feminine and masculine attributes; for instance, they might be nurturing and sensitive with friends (stereotypically "feminine" characteristics) yet assertive and independent in classroom activities (stereotypically "masculine" characteristics) (Bem, 1977). Children, adolescents, and adults who relax the sex-role boundaries seem to be fairly well adjusted, perhaps because they have more choices in the standards by which they evaluate themselves and because others respond favorably to their wide range of skills and dispositions (Piche & Plante, 1991; Williams & D'Alessandro, 1994).

Girls who value being feminine and boys who value being masculine integrate such ideas about gender into their self-concepts.

With the onset of puberty, being "male" or "female" takes on an entirely new meaning. Many young adolescents show an upsurge in gender-specific interests (Galambos, Almeida, & Petersen, 1990). For example, at age 13, Teresa's son Connor displayed a newfound interest in American football—definitely a rough and "manly" sport—and so joined the middle school football team. Also during adolescence, earlier interests may begin to dwindle, particularly if they are emblematic of the opposite sex. For example, both of us recall having mixed feelings about mathematics in adolescence. Although math was something we were clearly good at, we thought of it as a "masculine" domain that would somehow make us look less feminine. (Fortunately, our interest rekindled in college, where we felt more free to "be ourselves" and not conform to sex-role stereotypes.) Even girls who have grown up in more recent and "open-minded" decades than we did tend to have less interest and self-confidence in subject areas that are traditionally "masculine"—notably mathematics, science, and sports (Binns, Steinberg, Amorosi, & Cuevas, 1997; Chandler & Goldberg, 1990; Middleton, 1999; Rowe, 1999; Wigfield et al., 1996).

As young people continue to define themselves throughout childhood and adolescence, they integrate their ideas about gender into their core concepts of self. For instance, they determine how well they measure up to ideal gender roles. If their characteristics and behaviors approximate these ideals, they feel good about themselves, especially if they strongly value being a "manly" man or "womanly" woman. If they don't measure up, their self-concepts and self-esteem may suffer (Harter, 1998).

Children and adolescents learn about and adhere to gender roles through several mechanisms. Biology clearly has some influence. The brain is permanently marked "male" or "female" during prenatal development; for example, a part of the forebrain known as the *hypothalamus* is shaped somewhat differently in boys and girls (Arnold & Gorski, 1984). Sex differences in the brain become more prominent during adolescence, because circulating hormones activate gender-specific structures that have previously remained rather quiet (Ruble & Martin, 1998). As noted earlier, in boys these rising hormones are associated with increased aggression—a stereotypically "male" characteristic (Susman et al., 1987).

androgyny
Tendency to have some characteristics that are stereotypically "female" (e.g., nurturance) and others that are stereotypically "male" (e.g., assertiveness).

But perhaps more importantly, children and adolescents are socialized to conform to sex roles: Family, peers, and the broader community reinforce them for "staying within bounds" and punish them (e.g., by ridicule or exclusion) when they violate accepted gender roles (Pipher, 1994; Ruble & Martin, 1998). For example, a boy who cries after breaking his arm may be called a "sissy," and a girl who excels in mathematics might be teased for being a "math geek." Agents of socialization affect gender differentiation in concepts ("Nurses are almost always women"), self-perceptions ("Like most girls, I'm no good at auto mechanics"), preferences ("I'm a boy, so I like trucks"), and behaviors ("Can I borrow your lipstick?") (Ruble & Martin, 1998).

Finally, gender roles are intensified by children's own thinking and desire to fit into society's structure (Ruble & Martin, 1998). Children help to socialize themselves initially by constructing an understanding of gender as a stable attribute: It doesn't change from day to day, and it doesn't depend on clothing or hairstyle. In addition, they develop mental representations, or schemas, for "what boys do" and "what girls do" (Bem, 1981; Martin, 1991; Martin & Halverson, 1981). With such understandings in place, children are motivated to interpret the world through the lens of gender. They stay vigilant about gender-related roles in their social world and to some degree are motivated to be boylike or girl-like, as the following recollection from Benita Balegh illustrates:

> I was one of seven girls in a family of eight children. The son was like "Big Son," because he was the answer to my parents' prayers and the rest of us—we didn't quite make it.
>
> In our home we had to defer to this boy and, of course, to my father. When my father and my brother would come home, everybody would stand around to serve them, to do anything we could to gain their favor. . . .
>
> It was OK, even feminine, not to be good in math. It was even cute. And so I locked myself out of a very important part of what it is to be a human being, and that is to know all of oneself. I just locked that part out because I didn't think that was an appropriate thing for me to do. . . . [But] it was not OK for the men to not do well in math. It was *not* OK for them to not take calculus. It was not manly. . . .
>
> Another thing that affected me greatly happened when I went to a foreign country. One day I decided that I was going to build a sandbox for my little boy. I went in to get the wood and they told me, "Oh, no! You cannot buy wood. You have to have your husband's permission before you can purchase wood." That was a very big shock to me. But it was a shock that helped me see the insidiousness of what had happened to me in the beginning. And it helped me to open my eyes. When I came back to my country I was very intolerant of what I had swallowed hook, line, and sinker. (Benita Balegh, in Weissglass, 1998, p. 160)

Benita's reluctance to speak her mind is not a problem for all girls, nor is it a problem *only* for girls. Also, when it does appear, it is not always a general trait; for instance, some youth may be reticent in classrooms yet be quite vocal with friends and family (Harter, Waters, Whitesell, & Kastelic, 1998).

In broaching the topic of male-female differences, we don't mean to imply that the two sexes are entirely different, nor do we wish to communicate that the sexes are blandly uniform. In fact, there is *substantial* variation in both groups on all psychological characteristics. Finally, our discussion of gender and self-representations would be remiss if we did not recognize the unique dilemmas faced by students who are homosexual and bisexual in orientation. These students face the added challenge of forming an integrated self-concept and maintaining high self-esteem when they face rampant rejection in society at large and, sadly, occasional rejection from family and peers. Gay and lesbian youngsters who have close relationships with their parents and families tend to have more positive identities and to disclose their orientation ("come out") sooner than those with poor relationships (Beaty, 1999). We will explore the topic of sexual orientation in greater detail in Chapter 13.

Ethnic and Cultural Differences Many children and adolescents from ethnic and racial minority groups have positive self-concepts and high general self-esteem. In fact, researchers often find that, on average, minority youth have more favorable self-perceptions than European American youth (Cooper & Dorr, 1995; Spencer & Markstrom-Adams, 1990; Stevenson, Chen, & Uttal, 1990; van Laar, 2000). Given that members of minority groups are often the victims of prejudice and discrimination in our society, this finding seems quite puzzling, yet theorists have offered possible explanations for it. First, widespread prejudice and discrimination—though certainly not attitudes and practices that we advocate—may, in a backhanded way, actually enhance the self-concepts of some youngsters, who take credit for their successes (they worked hard for them and/or have exceptional talent) but blame outside factors for their failures (others are biased against them and are preventing them from getting ahead) (van Laar, 2000).

A second possible explanation is that some ethnic groups encourage children to take pride in the accomplishments of their families or communities, rather than in their own, individual achievements (Harrison, Wilson, Pine, Chan, & Buriel, 1990; Olneck, 1995; Pang, 1995; Trawick-Smith, 1997). Such groups often encourage a strong **ethnic identity,** an awareness of one's membership in the group and willingness to adopt certain behaviors characteristic of that group. A strong sense of ethnic or racial identity and pride often helps youth from minority groups deal with the racist behaviors of others (McAdoo, 1985; Spencer & Markstrom-Adams, 1990). Consider this statement by Eva, an African American high school student:

> I'm proud to be black and everything. But, um, I'm aware of, you know, racist acts and racist things that are happening in the world, but I use that as no excuse, you know. I feel as though I can succeed. . . . I just know that I'm not gonna let [racism] stop me. . . . Being black is good. I'm proud to be black but you also gotta face reality. And what's going on, you know, black people are not really getting anywhere in life, but I know I will and I don't know—I just know I will. Well, I'm determined to . . . and with God's help, you can't go wrong. (Way, 1998, p. 257)

Not all minority youth identify strongly with their ethnic and cultural backgrounds, however (Phinney, 1989). The strength of their ethnic identity will inevitably depend, in part, on the extent to which their families nurture it and the extent to which they want to assimilate into mainstream society (Dien, 1998; Thornton, Chatters, Taylor, & Allen, 1990).

Another important factor affecting the self-concepts and self-esteem of children and adolescents from ethnic minority groups is the treatment they receive in classrooms. Consider Rogelio López del Bosque's recollection of his first day at an American school in the 1950s:

> As I walked into the school with my sister, I remember smiling with pride and full of that desire to learn. Now that I recall, my sister gave me a sense of security. She had been directed by my Mom to take me to school the first day. (Mom did not feel she could do it herself since she spoke Spanish.) I was ready, and I know my family was proud. My parents were probably very happy that I was the last of 13 children to finally go to school.
>
> Shortly after arriving in the classroom and meeting the teacher, I recall vividly learning that I was no longer going to be called by my name, Rogelio. I was given a new name. I thought it was part of being in school.
>
> Of course, I found out later that the name Rogelio was too difficult for the teacher to pronounce. There was something wrong with me. So my name had to be changed. This was the beginning of my feeling different.
>
> Was there something wrong with my name? It really did not matter. This was what schools did, and it would help me learn—so I thought. I rationalized: Big deal, my Mom does not even call me Rogelio. She calls me "Rogelito." So on my first day of school, I was given a new name so I would fit in with everyone else and I would be ready to learn.
>
> Little did I know that the excitement of that first day of school would soon change to discomfort. I really could not identify exactly what I was feeling. But something was not right.
>
> During my years of school, I experienced low expectations and hostile attitudes on the part of some teachers, administrators, and other students. I had difficulty assimilating into this unfamiliar environment. Continuously, I was made aware that speaking Spanish had bad consequences. I was also told many times that I should not speak Spanish because I used an incorrect form. Was the language I learned at home inferior? I had learned to express my love, desires, and fears in that language. Of course, my parents must have been a very bad influence by teaching me such language, this Tex-Mex. . . .
>
> Like all children, there were so many qualities that I brought with me to school that were valuable. I was eager to learn, eager to please, and eager to do a good job and feel right just like everyone. Instead, like so many other students with similar backgrounds, I was made to feel wrong, unintelligent, and inferior. My whole person was in jeopardy. (López del Bosque, 2000, pp. 3–4)

Although most teachers today are more aware of the need to acknowledge and respect students' ethnic and cultural backgrounds, we have, in our own experience, occasionally seen teachers whose behaviors are as condescending and demeaning as Rogelio's teacher was. At the other

ethnic identity
Awareness of one's membership in a particular ethnic or cultural group, and willingness to adopt certain behaviors characteristic of that group.

Emotional and Personal Characteristics of Children and Adolescents

BASIC DEVELOPMENTAL ISSUES

ISSUE	ATTACHMENT TO CAREGIVERS	EMOTIONAL STATES AND REGULATION	DEVELOPMENT OF THE SELF
Nature and Nurture	Young human beings are biologically predisposed to form close social-emotional bonds with their parents and other primary caregivers, but they are more likely to form attachments to such individuals when they are treated in a socially sensitive and responsible fashion. Parents, in turn, are by nature predisposed to care for their offspring, but they learn specific ways of caring for their children from other family members and from the community and culture in which they live.	The full range of emotions is made possible by human genetic instructions; the brain is wired to experience anger, joy, fear, and so on. Genetic factors also affect individual differences in temperament (e.g., activity level, irritability, and characteristic ways of responding to new stimuli). Nurture affects the specific ways in which emotions are expressed. Children learn to control their expression of negative emotional responses in part from observing other people within their culture and in part from practicing various ways of dealing with their own emotional experiences. Some children who are maltreated or have parents who are emotionally depressed cope in counterproductive ways, yet others show considerable resilience in the face of negative emotional experiences.	The capacities to reflect on oneself as a social agent and to think about how other people view oneself are species-specific and so seem to have a genetic basis. These capacities are not fully functioning at birth, however; rather, they develop with experience and social input. Temperamental predispositions interact with experience and feedback from others to become the fodder for self-reflection (e.g., "I'm always getting in trouble at school") and influence self-concept and self-esteem.
Universality and Diversity	The predisposition to form close social-emotional bonds is probably universal. Moreover, socially sensitive care is the universal trigger for forming emotional attachments. However, not all children form secure attachments to their caregivers, and different environments place differing demands on children. For example, being clingy and demanding may help infants who live in an environment with scarce resources. Similarly, being able to negotiate multiple relationships may enhance adjustment when children are exposed to numerous caregivers during the early years.	All children experience such basic emotions as happiness, sadness, anger, and fear. The tendency for emotional states to energize particular kinds of responses (e.g., fleeing in response to fear) is also universal. But substantial diversity is present in how children regulate their emotions (e.g., when trying to conceal their true feelings). Some children are more likely than others to respond to situations in a positive, "upbeat" fashion.	Self-concept seems to be universal as a multidimensional construct; that is, all children see themselves as good at some things and not so good at other things. The trend toward increasing self-reflection also appears to be universal. But children differ in the particular domains in which they think they are strong and weak, as well as in the importance that they attach to each domain. Gender differences and cultural differences are seen in self-concepts and self-esteem, but there is also considerable variability *within* each gender and cultural group.

(continued)

extreme are well-meaning teachers who take great pains to give positive feedback to students from minority backgrounds, to the point where the feedback greatly overrates students' actual performance and gives little information about areas in which students need to continue refining their skills (Little et al., 1995; Paris & Cunningham, 1996). In our minds, this state of affairs may not be much of an improvement over how things were in López del Bosque's day. Ideally, educators should help students of all ethnic and cultural backgrounds acquire the knowledge, skills, and abilities they need to achieve genuine successes both in the classroom and in the outside world. Such successes will lead to high yet accurate self-concepts.

At this point, we should step back and reconsider what we've learned related to the three basic themes of nature versus nurture, universality versus diversity, and qualitative versus quantitative change. The Basic Developmental Issues table above summarizes how these

BASIC DEVELOPMENTAL ISSUES

ISSUE	ATTACHMENT TO CAREGIVERS	EMOTIONAL STATES AND REGULATION	DEVELOPMENT OF THE SELF
Qualitative and Quantitative Change	The development of attachments largely reflects quantitative change: Children gradually become more active in guiding interactions with their parents, initiating conversations and other exchanges, taking "turns" to keep interactions going, and so on. Qualitative change occurs when young children, who have previously met strangers with no protest, suddenly display "stranger anxiety." During this phase, they are anxious around people they do not know and show a clear preference for their attachment figures.	Children gradually gain knowledge and skills for assessing other people's emotional states. By watching facial expressions, listening to tone of voice, and drawing inferences from behaviors, children learn how others express and control emotions. They also become increasingly reflective about their own emotional states. However, the emergence of self-conscious emotions (pride, shame, guilt, etc.) represents a qualitative change in development. As children become more aware of family and societal standards, they learn to apply these standards to their own actions, are motivated (usually) to adhere to them, and feel shameful or guilty when they have violated them.	Changes in self-esteem are most often quantitative, increasing as children learn new skills and master more complex tasks but occasionally decreasing as children face major transitions in their lives. In the early years, children use self-improvement as a gauge for evaluating their performance, but beginning in middle childhood they begin to compare their performance to that of their peers—a shift that reflects qualitative change.

For positive self-concepts and high self-esteem, students need numerous opportunities to achieve success, perhaps in academic activities, in interpersonal relationships, or on the athletic field.

themes surface not only in the development of the self but also in the formation of attachments and emotional development. We turn now to strategies for enhancing students' sense of self in the classroom.

Enhancing Students' Sense of Self

The interplay between self-concept and behavior can create a vicious downward spiral: A low self-concept leads to less productive behavior, which leads to fewer successes, which perpetuates the low self-concept. Yet simply telling students that they are "good" or "smart" or "popular" is unlikely to make much of a dent in poor self-perceptions (Damon, 1991; Marsh & Craven, 1997; Pajares, 1996). Furthermore, vague, abstract statements such as "You're special" have little meaning in the concrete realities of young children (McMillan, Singh, & Simonetta, 1994). The following strategies are more likely to be effective:

■ *Promote success on academic, social, and physical tasks.* Success experiences are far and away the most powerful catalysts for the development of positive self-concepts and high self-esteem (Damon, 1991; Marsh & Craven, 1997). Thus, teachers should gear assignments to students' developmental levels and cognitive capabilities—for instance, by making sure that students have already mastered any necessary prerequisite knowledge and skills.

Yet success at very *easy* activities is unlikely to have much of an impact. Mastering the significant challenges in life—the hard-won successes that come only with effort, and perhaps with persistence in the face of obstacles—brings more enduring and resilient self-perceptions (Dweck, 1986; B. Lerner, 1985). Thus, teachers are most likely to bolster students' self-concepts when they assign challenging tasks and provide the structure and support (the scaffolding) that students need to accomplish those tasks successfully. They should also help students keep the little "failures" along the way in perspective: Mistakes

ENHANCING STUDENTS' EMOTIONAL WELL-BEING AND SENSE OF SELF

■ Communicate a genuine interest in students' welfare.

When a student is visibly teary-eyed during class, her teacher invites her to take a walk during lunchtime. The student describes the trouble she is having making friends at her new school, and she and her teacher develop a plan to address the problem.

■ Promote success on classroom tasks.

A high school teacher provides a format (scaffolding) for writing an expository paragraph: a sentence expressing the main idea, three sentences that support that idea, and a concluding sentence.

■ Hold reasonably high expectations for students' performance.

A junior high swimming coach encourages students to come out for the swim team regardless of past experience. She works as closely with newcomers as with experienced swimmers so that all team members can improve.

■ Give positive feedback for students' accomplishments. Accompany negative feedback with the message that students can improve.

The same swimming coach tells a student, "Your crawl stroke has really improved. Your timing on the butterfly is a bit off; let's work on that today."

■ Give students opportunities to examine and try out a variety of adultlike roles.

A first-grade teacher develops a list of classroom chores, such as getting a hot-lunch count, delivering messages to the main office, and feeding the class goldfish and rabbit. He assigns these chores to students on a rotating basis.

■ Learn about the domains of performance most important to individual students.

A fifth-grade teacher asks his students to write an essay about the school activities that they like most and least. He makes sure his students have frequent opportunities to engage in their favorite activities and compliments them when they do especially well in their areas of interest.

---

are an inevitable yet very temporary part of learning anything new (Clifford, 1990; Eccles & Wigfield, 1985).

■ *Focus students' attention on their own improvement rather than on how others are performing.* Students are likely to be optimistic about their chances of success if they see that, yes, they are making progress and gaining increasing expertise. They are *un*likely to have much optimism if they see that their own performance doesn't measure up to that of their peers (Deci & Ryan, 1992; Krampen, 1987; Stipek, 1996). To help students develop positive self-concepts, then, teachers should minimize competition and other situations in which students might compare themselves unfavorably with classmates.

■ *Give constructive and encouraging feedback.* In part because of the frequent feedback children and adolescents get from others, their self-perceptions are usually similar to how others perceive them (Harter, 1990a; Shaffer, 1988). For example, students' beliefs about their academic ability are similar to their classroom teachers' beliefs about their intelligence and aptitude. Their beliefs about their physical ability are correlated with the perceptions of their physical education teachers. And their sense of their own competence in social situations is likely to be a reflection of their actual popularity with peers.

Obviously, teachers are going to promote more positive self-concepts if they acknowledge and praise students' accomplishments. At the same time, teachers' feedback should reflect fairly accurate assessments of what students currently can and cannot do; thus, it must inevitably include criticism as well as praise (Marsh, 1990b; Parsons et al., 1982; Stipek, 1996). If teachers provide only praise—and particularly if they provide highly inflated evaluations of students' performance—then students will be unaware of areas that need improvement (Little et al., 1995; Paris & Cunningham, 1996). In fact, occasional criticism can actually bolster students' self-concepts and self-esteem *if* it communicates an expectation that students can do better and *if* it provides guidance about how to improve (Pintrich & Schunk, 1996).

■ *Consider the unique needs of girls and boys.* Many children and adolescents may place little value on characteristics and abilities that they think are more "appropriate" for members of the opposite sex. In addition, they may place *too much* value on qualities they think they need to be "feminine" or "manly." Thus, some teenage girls may strive for impossible standards of physical beauty; some teenage boys may worry that they are maturing too slowly and lack the height and build of some of their classmates.

With these points in mind, teachers should probably use somewhat different tactics in nurturing the self-concepts of girls and boys. For example, they might want to help girls identify realistic standards by which to judge themselves and (given girls' propensity to react more negatively to failures) encourage them to pat themselves on the back for their many successes, even those (and perhaps *especially* those) in traditionally "male" domains such as science and mathematics. But boys, too, have special needs (it's our opinion, in fact, that there is entirely too little literature on the needs of boys). Boys are often brought up to believe that they should be manly, aggressive, and "tough," and that they should hide any self-doubts and feelings of inadequacy. Accordingly, teachers may want to take special pains to acknowledge boys' "softer" sides—perhaps their compassion, gentleness, or skill in interacting with small children—and to communicate that childhood and adolescence are times for trying new activities, developing new skills, and inevitably making a few mistakes along the way.

As you can see, teachers can do many things to promote positive, healthy self-concepts. What seems to be particularly critical is that students succeed in areas that are important to *them*. We should note, however, that the popular educational literature often overrates positive self-concepts and high self-esteem as targets for educational enhancement (Harter, 1998). Certainly we want students to feel good about themselves, but we also want them to study hard, learn a lot, and get along with peers. Promoting healthy representations of self can be valuable, but it needs to take place in a meaningful educational context and not interfere with other instructional objectives for students. We encourage our readers to consider the recommendations in the Development and Practice feature in this section, as well as to formulate implications for the specific age level of students they plan to teach.

As we've explored the topics of attachment, emotional development, and development of the self, we've found that different age groups have different priorities. For instance, forming attachments is a major focus in infancy, whereas establishing a personal identity is a particular concern during adolescence. Erik Erikson has synthesized some of these age-specific issues into a life-span perspective of personal and emotional development. His theory is the final topic of the chapter.

A Life-Span Approach to Personal and Emotional Development: Erikson's Theory

Erikson (1963, 1972) outlined eight developmental periods, or **psychosocial stages,** to characterize the course of personal and emotional development. He proposed that human beings tackle a different developmental task or dilemma at each stage and that their achievements at that stage have lifelong implications. Here we describe his eight stages and relate them to concepts we have previously considered.

Trust Versus Mistrust (Infancy)   According to Erikson, infants' primary developmental task is to learn whether or not they can trust other people to satisfy their basic needs. A child's parents and other primary caregivers play a key role here. When caregivers can be depended on to feed a hungry stomach, change an uncomfortable diaper, and provide physical affection at regular intervals, an infant learns *trust*—that others are consistently dependable and reliable. When caregivers ignore the infant's needs, are inconsistent in attending to them, or are even abusive, the infant may instead learn *mistrust*—that the world is an undependable, unpredictable, and possibly dangerous place.

Erikson's notion of trust aligns closely with the secure attachment we spoke of earlier. His notion of mistrust is more reflective of insecure attachment and, even more so, disorganized and disoriented attachment. But, as you may recall from our discussion of attachment, young children form attachments with other people besides their primary caregivers. Furthermore, throughout their development they continue to have many opportunities to form trusting relationships with others.

psychosocial stages
In Erikson's theory, eight periods of life that involve age-related tasks or dilemmas.

Autonomy Versus Shame and Doubt (Toddler Years) As toddlers gain increased muscular coordination and the mobility that accompanies crawling and walking, they become capable of satisfying some of their own needs. They are learning to feed themselves, wash and dress themselves, and use the bathroom. When parents and other caregivers encourage self-sufficient behavior, toddlers develop *autonomy,* a sense of being able to handle many problems on their own. But when caregivers demand too much too soon, refuse to let children perform tasks of which they are capable, or ridicule early attempts at self-sufficiency, children may instead develop *shame and doubt* about their ability to handle the problems they encounter.

Erikson's concept of autonomy is reminiscent of an idea we considered earlier—that securely attached children are more willing to venture out on their own and explore their environment. His concepts of shame and doubt suggest the beginnings of self-conscious emotions and a poor self-concept.

Initiative Versus Guilt (Preschool Years) If all goes well, children spend their infancy and toddler years learning to trust others and to construct a sense of autonomy: The world is a good place, people love them, and they can make things happen. With these important lessons under their belts, children are ready to face Erikson's third psychosocial stage. With their growing independence, preschoolers begin to get their own ideas about the activities they want to pursue; for example, they may undertake simple art projects, make houses and roadways in the sandbox, or play "house" with other children. When parents and preschool teachers encourage and support such efforts, children develop *initiative*—independence in planning and undertaking activities. When adults discourage such activities, children may instead develop *guilt* about their needs and desires.

Drawing on a concept we considered earlier, we could say that children with high self-efficacy—those who are confident that they can achieve desired goals—are more likely to initiate challenging tasks that will benefit their long-term development. And adults, through the messages they communicate about children's capabilities, play a key role in fostering high self-efficacy.

Industry Versus Inferiority (Elementary School Years) When they reach elementary school, children are expected to master many new skills, and they soon learn that they can gain the recognition of adults through their academic assignments, art projects, athletic accomplishments, and so on. When children are allowed and encouraged to make and do things and when they are praised for their accomplishments, they begin to demonstrate *industry*—a pattern of working hard, persisting at lengthy tasks, and putting work before pleasure. But when children are ridiculed or punished for their efforts or when they find that they cannot meet their teachers' and parents' expectations for performance, they may develop feelings of *inferiority* about their own abilities.

Earlier we discovered that children in the lower elementary grades define themselves largely in terms of concrete, observable characteristics such as physical appearance, behaviors, and the like. In Chapter 4, we learned that elementary school children often have difficulty with abstract ideas. It makes sense, then, that children in this age range should derive satisfaction from concrete, observable accomplishments.

Identity Versus Role Confusion (Adolescence) As they make the transition from childhood to adulthood, adolescents begin to wrestle with the questions of who they are and how they will eventually fit into the adult world. Initially, they are likely to experience some *role confusion*—mixed ideas and feelings about the specific ways in which they will fit into society—and may experiment with a variety of behaviors and activities (e.g., tinkering with cars, baby-sitting for neighbors, engaging in extracurricular activities at school, affiliating with particular political or religious groups). According to Erikson, most adolescents eventually achieve a sense of *identity* regarding who they are and where their lives are headed.

As you may have noticed, Erikson's concept of identity is very similar to Marcia's concept of identity achievement, and his concept of role confusion should remind you of Marcia's concepts of identity diffusion and moratorium. Such parallels are hardly a coincidence. In fact, Marcia used Erikson's theory of psychosocial development as a springboard for his own work on adolescent identity.

Intimacy Versus Isolation (Young Adulthood) Once people have established their identities, they are ready to make commitments to one or more other individuals. They become capable of engaging in *intimacy*—that is, they form close, reciprocal relationships with others (e.g., through marriage, partnerships, or close friendships) and willingly make the sacrifices and compromises that such relationships require. When people cannot form these intimate relationships (perhaps because of their reluctance or inability to forego the satisfaction of their own needs), then a sense of *isolation* may result.

Generativity Versus Stagnation (Middle Age) During middle age, the primary developmental task is one of contributing to society and helping to guide future generations. When an individual makes a contribution during this period, perhaps by raising a family or by working toward the betterment of society, a sense of *generativity*—a sense of productivity and accomplishment—results. In contrast, an individual who is self-centered and unable or unwilling to help society move forward develops a feeling of *stagnation,* a dissatisfaction with the relative lack of production.

Integrity Versus Despair (Retirement Years) According to Erikson, the final developmental task is a retrospective one. Individuals look back on their lives and accomplishments. They develop feelings of contentment and *integrity* if they believe that they have led a happy, productive life. They may instead develop a sense of *despair* if they look back on a life of disappointments and unachieved goals.

Critiquing Erikson's Theory

Erikson's stages nicely summarize some of the ideas we've presented in this chapter. Yet the stages are probably not completely accurate descriptions of what happens at each age period, in part because they ignore the very important role that culture plays in personal and emotional development. For example, many cultures intentionally discourage autonomy, initiative, and self-assertiveness in young children, sometimes as a way of protecting them from the very real dangers of their environments (Chen et al., 1992; Harwood et al., 1995; Powell, 1983). Furthermore, Erikson believed that most people achieve a sense of identity by the end of adolescence. But more recent evidence indicates that, even by the high school years, only a small minority of students have begun to think seriously about the eventual role they will play in society and the lifelong goals they wish to pursue (Archer, 1982; Durkin, 1995; Marcia, 1988). Also problematic is the fact that Erikson based his stages on studies of *men.* For many women, a focus on intimacy occurs simultaneously with, and in some cases may even precede, a focus on identity (Josselson, 1988).

Perhaps a useful perspective to take on Erikson's theory is one similar to the stance we advocated for Piaget's theory in Chapter 4: The eight psychosocial stages provide a general idea of the ages at which various issues in personal and emotional development are likely to emerge. Nevertheless, considerable flexibility and diversity are present in these timelines.

The importance of children's emotions and self-perceptions will continue to be evident as we explore the development of social understanding and morality in Chapter 10 and motivation in Chapter 11. For now, however, we use our closing case study to consider how emotions and self-perceptions influence classroom behavior.

CASE STUDY: THE GIRLY SHIRT

Eight-year-old Tim caused quite a disruption in class this morning. His teacher, Amy Fox, isn't quite sure what caused the disruption, and so she is meeting with Tim while the other students are at lunch so she can better understand what happened.

Ms. Fox:	Things got out of control in class this morning, didn't they, Tim?
Tim:	I guess they did.
Ms. Fox:	Tell me what happened.
Tim:	John and Steven were teasing me about my shirt. They really made me mad.
Ms. Fox:	They were teasing you about your *shirt?* What did they say?
Tim:	That it's too pink. That it's a "girly" color.
Ms. Fox:	Really? I don't think it's too "girly" at all. In fact, I rather like that color on you. But anyway, you say the boys teased you about it. What did you do then?
Tim:	I yelled at them. Then when you gave me that dirty look, they kept on laughing, and so I kept on yelling.

Ms. Fox:	I see. John and Steven were certainly wrong to tease you about your clothes. I'll speak to them later. But right now I'm concerned about how you reacted to the situation. You were so loud that the class couldn't possibly continue with the lesson.
Tim:	I know. I'm sorry.
Ms. Fox:	I appreciate your apology, Tim. And I'd like to make sure that the next time someone hurts your feelings—maybe intentionally, maybe not—you don't blow up the way you did today. Let's come up with a plan for how you might keep your temper under better control.

- In what way does John's and Steven's behavior reflect the process of *socialization?* What effect might their behavior have on Tim's self-concept?
- Considering what you have learned about trends in emotional development, is Tim's reaction typical for his age?
- What kind of plan might be effective in helping Tim control his anger?

SUMMARY

Early Attachments

Early attachments are close and enduring social-emotional bonds that form between infants and their caregivers. Sensitive and responsive nurturance provides the necessary catalyst for the formation of attachments, but children also contribute by returning their caregivers' affection. Secure attachments in the early years are predictive of positive social-emotional outcomes later on. Yet attachments manifest themselves somewhat differently in different cultures, and the nature of people's attachments can and often does change over time.

Emotional Development

Emotions are universally seen in all cultures, and they seem to have an adaptive function. Individual differences in emotional functioning appear to be the result of both biology (e.g., temperament, gender-specific hormones) and environment (e.g., socialization by parents, peers, and culture). Emotions develop in several ways; for instance, children and adolescents become increasingly able to regulate their emotions in ways that are both socially acceptable and personally effective. Dealing with students' emotions is an important part of teaching, and in fact teachers can do many things to promote students' emotional development. Teachers need to be especially alert to the needs of students with serious and chronic emotional needs (depression, anxiety disorders, conduct disorders).

Development of the Self

Children develop a perception of who they are (self-concept) and have feelings about their worthiness (self-esteem). As they encounter various successes and failures, and as other people continue to give them feedback about their performance and worth, they develop increasingly complex understandings of themselves, and such self-perceptions influence their behavior and achievement at school. Most children and adolescents enjoy positive self-concepts and high self-esteem, but temporary declines are often seen at major transition points (e.g., when children begin elementary school and then again when they move on to secondary school). In childhood, the focus is largely on learning what one can and cannot do; in adolescence, the focus shifts to the formation of an identity—a sense of who one is and what course one's life will take. Teachers can most effectively foster positive self-concepts not by telling students that they are "good" or "smart," but rather by helping them succeed at challenging academic, social, and physical tasks.

Erikson's Theory

Erikson proposed that eight stages (the first beginning in infancy and the last occurring in old age) describe the evolution of people's personal and emotional functioning. There are similarities between how Erikson described the stages and what other theorists have learned about

Now go to our Companion Website to assess your understanding of chapter content with Multiple-Choice Questions, apply comprehension in Essay Questions, and broaden your knowledge with links to related Developmental Psychology World Wide Web sites.

attachment, self-concept, and identity. However, some psychologists argue that Erikson's theory does not accurately describe emotional development in some cultures, nor does it adequately account for the interplay of identity and intimacy.

KEY CONCEPTS

attachment (p. 303)
ethological attachment theory (p. 303)
secure attachment (p. 304)
insecure-avoidant attachment (p. 304)
insecure-resistant attachment (p. 304)
disorganized and disoriented attachment (p. 304)
emotion (p. 309)
temperament (p. 311)

socialization (p. 311)
emotional contagion (p. 312)
social referencing (p. 312)
self-conscious emotion (p. 312)
emotional regulation (p. 313)
anxiety (p. 319)
externalizing behavior (p. 319)
internalizing behavior (p. 319)
depression (p. 320)
bipolar disorder (p. 320)
anxiety disorder (p. 321)

conduct disorder (p. 321)
self-concept (p. 322)
self-esteem (p. 322)
self-efficacy (p. 323)
imaginary audience (p. 328)
personal fable (p. 328)
identity (p. 329)
identity crisis (p. 330)
androgyny (p. 332)
ethnic identity (p. 334)
psychosocial stages (p. 338)

Glossary

accommodation   Dealing with a new event by either modifying an existing scheme or forming a new one.

actual developmental level   Extent to which one can successfully perform a task independently.

adaptation   Developmental process of responding to the environment in an increasingly effective manner.

androgyny   Tendency to have some characteristics that are stereotypically "female" (e.g., nurturance) and others that are stereotypically "male" (e.g., assertiveness).

anxiety   Emotional state characterized by worry and apprehension.

anxiety disorder   Chronic emotional condition characterized by excessive, debilitating worry.

apprenticeship   Situation in which a person works intensively with an expert to learn how to accomplish complex tasks.

assimilation   Dealing with a new event in a way that is consistent with an existing scheme.

attachment   An enduring emotional tie uniting one person to another.

attention-deficit hyperactivity disorder (ADHD)   Disability (probably biological in origin) characterized by inattention and/or hyperactivity and impulsive behavior.

authentic activity   Classroom activity similar to one that a student might encounter in the outside world.

autism   Disability (probably biological in origin) characterized by infrequent social interaction, communication impairments, repetitive behaviors, narrowly focused interests, and a strong need for a predictable environment.

automatization   Process of becoming able to respond quickly and efficiently while mentally processing or physically performing certain tasks.

bipolar disorder   Condition characterized by cyclical mood swings, including periods of elation (mania) and periods of deep depression.

central conceptual structure   Integrated network of concepts and cognitive processes that forms the basis for much of one's thinking, reasoning, and learning in specific content domains.

central executive   Component of the human information processing system that oversees the flow of information throughout the system.

class inclusion   Recognition that something simultaneously belongs to a particular category and to one of its subcategories.

clinical method   Procedure whereby a researcher probes a child's reasoning about a task or problem, tailoring questions to what the child has previously said or done.

cognition   The various mental activities in which a person engages.

cognitive apprenticeship   Mentorship in which a teacher and a student work together on a challenging task and the teacher suggests ways to think about the task.

cognitive strategy   Specific mental process that people use to acquire or manipulate information.

comprehension monitoring   Process of checking oneself to make sure one understands what one is learning.

conceptual change   Revising one's knowledge and understanding of a topic in response to new information about the topic.

conduct disorder   Chronic emotional condition characterized by lack of concern for the rights of others.

conservation   Realization that if nothing is added or taken away, amount stays the same regardless of any alterations in shape or arrangement.

constructivism   Theoretical perspective proposing that learners construct a body of knowledge from their experiences, rather than absorbing knowledge at face value.

co-regulated learning   Process through which a teacher and learner share responsibility for directing various aspects of the learning process.

deductive reasoning   Drawing a logical inference about something that must be true given other information that has already been presented as true.

depression   Emotional condition characterized by significant sadness, discouragement, and hopelessness.

disequilibrium   State of being *unable* to explain new events in terms of existing schemes.

disorganized and disoriented attachment   Attachment classification in which children lack a single coherent way of responding to attachment figures.

dynamic assessment   Examining how a student's knowledge or reasoning may change as a result of learning or performing a specific task.

egocentric speech   Speaking without taking the perspective and knowledge of the listener into account.

elaboration   Using prior knowledge to expand on new information and thereby learn it more effectively.

elaborative interrogation   Study strategy in which students develop and answer questions designed to promote elaboration of new material.

emotion   Affective response to an event that is personally relevant to one's needs and goals.

emotional contagion   Tendency for infants to cry spontaneously when they hear other infants crying.

emotional regulation   Using strategies to manage responses to stressful events (also called *coping*).

epistemological beliefs   Beliefs regarding the nature of knowledge and knowledge acquisition.

equilibration   Movement from equilibrium to disequilibrium and back to equilibrium; a process that promotes the development of increasingly complex forms of thought and knowledge.

equilibrium   State of being able to explain new events in terms of existing schemes.

ethnic identity   Awareness of one's membership in a particular ethnic or cultural group, and willingness to adopt certain behaviors characteristic of that group.

ethological attachment theory   Theoretical perspective that emphasizes the functional importance of caregiver-child bonds in protecting children and giving them a secure base from which to explore their surroundings.

externalizing behavior   Undesirable emotion, behavior, or a combination that affects other people (e.g., aggression, stealing, lack of self-control).

formal operational egocentrism   Inability of an individual in Piaget's formal operations stage to separate one's own abstract logic from the perspectives of others and from practical considerations.

goal-directed behavior   Planful behavior intended to bring about an anticipated outcome.

identity   People's self-constructed definition of who they are, what they find important, and what goals they want to accomplish in life.

identity crisis   Period during which an individual actively struggles to choose a course in life.

imaginary audience   Belief that one is the center of attention in any social situation.

individual constructivism   Theoretical perspective that focuses on how people construct meaning from events without the assistance of others.

information processing theory   Theoretical perspective that focuses on the specific ways in which people mentally think about ("process") the information they receive.

inner speech   "Talking" to oneself mentally rather than aloud.

insecure-avoidant attachment   Attachment classification in which children appear somewhat indifferent to attachment figures.

insecure-resistant attachment   Attachment classification in which children are preoccupied with their attachment figures but gain little comfort from them when distressed.

internalization   In Vygotsky's theory, the gradual evolution of external, social activities into internal, mental activities.

internalizing behavior   Undesirable emotion, behavior, or a combination that primarily affects oneself (e.g., depression, social withdrawal, and suicidal tendencies).

knowledge base   One's knowledge about specific topics and the world in general.

learning disability   Significant deficit in one or more cognitive processes, to the point where special educational services are required.

learning strategy   Specific mental process used in acquiring new information.

legitimate peripheral participation   A child's early and somewhat limited involvement in adult activities.

level of potential development Extent to which one can successfully execute a task with the assistance of a more competent individual.

long-term memory Component of memory that holds knowledge and skills for a relatively long time.

mediated learning experience Discussion between an adult and a child in which the adult helps the child make sense of an event they have mutually experienced.

metacognition Knowledge and beliefs about one's own cognitive processes, as well as efforts to regulate those cognitive processes to maximize learning and memory.

metacognitive awareness Extent to which one is able to reflect on the nature of one's own thinking processes.

metacognitive scaffolding Supportive technique that guides students in their use of metacognitive strategies.

mnemonics Special memory aid or trick designed to help students learn and remember a particular piece of information.

multiple classification Recognition that objects may belong to several categories simultaneously.

nativism Theoretical perspective that some knowledge is biologically built in and present at birth.

neo-Piagetian theory Theoretical perspective that combines elements of both Piaget's theory and information processing theory and portrays cognitive development as involving a series of distinct stages.

object permanence Realization that objects continue to exist even after they are removed from view.

operation In Piaget's theory, an organized and integrated system of thought processes.

organization Finding interrelationships among pieces of information as a way of learning them more effectively.

perception Cognitive interpretation of stimuli that the body has sensed.

personal fable Belief that one is completely unlike other people, cannot be understood, and is impervious to danger.

portfolio Systematic collection of a student's work over a lengthy period of time.

preoperational egocentrism Inability of a child in Piaget's preoperational stage to view situations from another person's perspective.

psychosocial stages In Erikson's theory, eight periods of life that involve age-related tasks or dilemmas.

rehearsal Attempt to learn and remember information by repeating it over and over.

scaffolding Support mechanism, provided by a more competent individual, that helps a child successfully perform a task within his or her zone of proximal development.

schema Organized and internalized body of knowledge about a specific topic.

scheme In Piaget's theory, an organized group of similar actions or thoughts.

script Schema that involves a predictable sequence of events related to a common activity.

secure attachment Attachment classification in which children use attachment figures as a secure base from which to explore and as a source of comfort in times of distress.

self-concept Beliefs that people have about themselves, their characteristics, and their abilities. **self-conscious emotion** Affective state that reflects awareness of a community's social standards (e.g., pride, guilt, shame).

self-efficacy Belief that one is capable of executing certain behaviors or reaching certain goals in a particular task or domain.

self-esteem Feelings that people have about their own capabilities and self-worth.

self-regulated learning Directing and regulating one's own cognitive processes in order to learn successfully.

self-talk Talking to oneself as a way of guiding oneself through a task.

sensation Physiological detection of stimuli in the environment.

sensory register Component of memory that holds incoming information in an unanalyzed form for a very brief time (2–3 seconds or less).

situative perspective Theoretical perspective that cognitive abilities are tied to the specific contexts in which they have been acquired.

social constructivism Theoretical perspective that focuses on people's collective efforts to impose meaning on the world.

socialization Systematic efforts by other people and by institutions to prepare youngsters to act in ways deemed by society to be appropriate and responsible.

social referencing Observing emotional cues of others and using such cues to interpret the possible implications of an event for oneself.

sociocognitive conflict Encountering and having to wrestle with ideas and viewpoints different from one's own.

sociocultural perspective Theoretical perspective emphasizing the importance of society and culture for promoting cognitive development.

sociodramatic play Play in which children take on assumed roles and act out a scenario of events.

sounding Friendly, playful exchange of insults.

structure In neo-Piagetian theory, a specific system of concepts and thinking skills that influence thinking and reasoning in a particular content domain.

symbol Mental entity that represents an external object or event, often without reflecting its perceptual and behavioral qualities.

symbolic thought Ability to represent and think about external objects and events in one's mind.

temperament Constitutional ways of responding to emotional events and novel stimulation, and of regulating impulses.

theory of mind Child's integrated beliefs about the existence and nature of thought.

theory theory Theoretical perspective proposing that children construct increasingly integrated and complex understandings of physical and mental phenomena.

working memory Component of memory that enables people to actively think about and process a small amount of information.

zone of proximal development (ZPD) Range of tasks that one cannot yet perform independently but *can* perform with the help and guidance of others.

REFERENCES

Adams, R. J. (1987). An evaluation of color preference in early infancy. *Infant Behavior and Development, 10,* 143–150.

Ainsworth, M. D. S. (1963). The development of infant-mother interaction among the Ganda. In B. M. Foss (Ed.), *Determinants of infant behavior* (Vol. 2, pp. 67–104). New York: Wiley.

Ainsworth, M. D. S. (1973). The development of infant-mother attachment. In B. Caldwell & H. Ricciuti (Eds.), *Review of child development research* (Vol. 3, pp. 1–94). Chicago: University of Chicago Press.

Ainsworth, M. D. S., Blehar, M. C., Waters, E., & Wall, S. (1978). *Patterns of attachment.* Hillsdale, NJ: Erlbaum.

Akiskal, H. S., & McKinney, W. T. (1973). Depressive disorders: Toward a unified hypothesis. *Science, 162,* 20–29.

Alexander, P. A., Graham, S., & Harris, K. R. (1998). A perspective on strategy research: Progress and prospects. *Educational Psychology Review, 10,* 129–154.

Alley, G., & Deshler, D. (1979). *Teaching the learning disabled adolescent: Strategies and methods.* Denver, CO: Love.

American Psychiatric Association (1994). *Diagnostic and statistical manual of mental disorders* (4th ed.). Washington, DC: Author.

Anderson, J. C. (1983). *The architecture of cognition.* Cambridge, MA: Harvard University Press.

Anderson, J. R., Reder, L. M., & Simon, H. A. (1997). Situative versus cognitive perspectives: Form versus substance. *Educational Researcher, 26*(1), 18–21.

Antelman, S., & Caggiula, A. (1977). Norepinephrine-dopamine interactions and behavior. *Science, 195,* 646–651.

Archer, S. L. (1982). The lower age boundaries of identity development. *Child Development, 53,* 1551–1556.

Arnett, J. (1995). The young and the reckless: Adolescent reckless behavior. *Current Directions in Psychological Science, 4,* 67–71.

Arnett, J. J. (1999). Adolescent storm and stress, reconsidered. *American Psychologist, 54,* 317–326.

Arnold, A. P., & Gorski, R. A. (1984). Gonadal steroid induction of structural sex differences in the central nervous system. *Annual Review of Neuroscience, 7,* 413–442.

Artman, L., & Cahan, S. (1993). Schooling and the development of transitive inference. *Developmental Psychology, 29,* 753–759.

Asher, S. R., & Coie, J. D. (Eds.). (1990). *Peer rejection in childhood.* Cambridge, England: Cambridge University Press.

Aslin, R. N. (1993). Perception of visual direction in human infants. In C. E. Granrud (Ed.), *Visual perception and cognition in infancy.* Hillsdale, NJ: Erlbaum.

Assor, A., & Connell, J. P. (1992). The validity of students' self-reports as measures of performance affecting self-appraisals. In D. H. Schunk & J. L. Meece (Eds.), *Student perceptions in the classroom.* Hillsdale, NJ: Erlbaum.

Astington, J. W., & Pelletier, J. (1996). The language of mind: Its role in teaching and learning. In D. R. Olson & N. Torrance (Eds.), *The handbook of education and human development: New models of learning, teaching, and schooling.* Cambridge, MA: Blackwell.

Baillargeon, R. (1994). How do infants learn about the physical world? *Current Directions in Psychological Science, 3,* 133–140.

Baker-Ward, L., Ornstein, P. A., & Holden, D. J. (1984). The expression of memorization in early childhood. *Journal of Experimental Child Psychology, 37,* 555–575.

Baldwin, M. W., Keelan, J. P. R., Fehr, B., Enns, V., & Koh-Rangarajoo, E. (1996). Social-cognitive conceptualization of attachment working models: Availability and accessibility effects. *Journal of Personality and Social Psychology, 71,* 94–109.

Bandura, A. (1982). Self-efficacy mechanism in human agency. *American Psychologist, 37,* 122–147.

Bandura, A. (1994). *Self-efficacy: The exercise of control.* New York: Freeman.

Barga, N. K. (1996). Students with learning disabilities in education: Managing a disability. *Journal of Learning Disabilities, 29,* 413–421.

Barkley, R. A. (1998). *Attention-deficit hyperactivity disorder: A handbook for diagnosis and treatment* (2nd ed.). New York: Guilford Press.

Barton, K. C., & Levstik, L. S. (1996). "Back when God was around and everything": Elementary children's understanding of historical time. *American Educational Research Journal, 33,* 419–454.

Bassett, D. S., Jackson, L., Ferrell, K. A., Luckner, J., Hagerty, P. J., Bunsen, T. D., & MacIsaac, D. (1996). Multiple perspectives on inclusive education: Reflections of a university faculty. *Teacher Education and Special Education, 19,* 355–386.

Bauer, P. J., & Dow, G. A. (1994). Episodic memory in 16- and 20-month-old children: Specifics not generalized, but not forgotten. *Developmental Psychology, 30,* 403–417.

Beaty, L. A. (1999). Identity development of homosexual youth and parental and familial influences on the coming out process. *Adolescence, 34,* 597–601.

Begg, I., Anas, A., & Farinacci, S. (1992). Dissociation of processes in belief: Source recollection, statement familiarity, and the illusion of truth. *Journal of Experimental Psychology: General, 121,* 446–458.

Bell, N., Grossen, M., & Perret-Clermont, A. (1985). Sociocognitive conflict and intellectual growth. In M. W. Berkowitz (Ed.), *Peer conflict and psychological growth.* San Francisco: Jossey-Bass.

Bem, S. L. (1977). On the utility of alternative procedures for assessing psychological androgyny. *Journal of Consulting and Clinical Psychology, 45,* 196–205.

Bem, S. L. (1981). Gender schema theory: A cognitive account of sex typing. *Psychological Review, 88,* 354–364.

Bem, S. L. (1989). Genital knowledge and gender constancy in preschool children. *Child Development, 60,* 649–662.

Bender, T. A. (1997). Assessment of subjective well-being during childhood and adolescence. In G. D. Phye (Ed.), *Handbook of classroom assessment: Learning, achievement, and adjustment.* San Diego, CA: Academic Press.

Bennett, R. E., Gottesman, R. L., Rock, D. A., & Cerullo, F. (1993). Influence of behavior perceptions and gender on teachers' judgments of students' academic skill. *Journal of Educational Psychology, 85,* 347–356.

Bergin, D. A. (1996, April). *Adolescents' out-of-school learning strategies.* Paper presented at the annual meeting of the American Educational Research Association, New York.

Berk, L. E. (1994). Why children talk to themselves. *Scientific American, 271,* 78–83.

Berk, L. E. (1997). *Child development* (4th ed.). Boston: Allyn & Bacon.

Berk, L. E., & Spuhl, S. T. (1995). Maternal interaction, private speech, and task performance in preschool children. *Early Childhood Research Quarterly, 10,* 145–169.

Bertenthal, B. I., & Campos, J. J. (1987). New directions in the study of early experience. *Child Development, 58,* 560–567.

Berzonsky, M. D. (1988). Self-theorists, identity status, and social cognition. In D. K. Lapsley & F. C. Power (Eds.), *Self, ego, and identity: Integrative approaches* (pp. 243–261). New York: Springer-Verlag.

Best, D. L., & Ornstein, P. A. (1986). Children's generation and communication of mnemonic organizational strategies. *Developmental Psychology, 22,* 845–853.

Bijeljac-Babic, R., Bertoncini, J., & Mehler, J. (1993). How do 4-day-old infants categorize multisyllable utterances? *Developmental Psychology, 29,* 711–721.

Binns, K., Steinberg, A., Amorosi, S., & Cuevas, A. M. (1997). *The Metropolitan Life survey of the American teacher 1997: Examining gender issues in public schools.* New York: Louis Harris and Associates.

Birnbaum, D. W., & Croll, W. L. (1984). The etiology of children's stereotypes about sex differences in emotionality. *Sex Roles, 10,* 677–691.

Bivens, J. A., & Berk, L. E. (1990). A longitudinal study of the development of elementary school children's private speech. *Merrill-Palmer Quarterly, 36,* 443–463.

Bjorklund, D. F. (1987). How age changes in knowledge base contribute to the development of children's memory: An interpretive review. *Developmental Review, 7,* 93–130.

Bjorklund, D. F., & Coyle, T. R. (1995). Utilization deficiencies in the development of memory strategies. In F. E. Weinert & W. Schneider (Eds.), *Research on memory development: State of the art and future directions.* Hillsdale, NJ: Erlbaum.

Bjorklund, D. F., & Green, B. L. (1992). The adaptive nature of cognitive immaturity. *American Psychologist, 47,* 46–54.

Bjorklund, D. F., & Jacobs, J. W. (1985). Associative and categorical processes in children's memory: The role of automaticity in the development of organization in free recall. *Journal of Experimental Child Psychology, 39,* 599–617.

Bjorklund, D. F., Schneider, W., Cassel, W. S., & Ashley, E. (1994). Training and extension of a memory strategy: Evidence for utilization deficiencies in high- and low-IQ children. *Child Development, 65,* 951–965.

Blackson, T. C., Butler, T., Belsky, J., Ammerman, R. T., Shaw, D. S., & Tarter, R. E. (1999). Individual traits and family contexts predict sons' externalizing behavior and preliminary relative risk ratios for conduct disorder and substance use disorder outcomes. *Drug & Alcohol Dependence, 56*(2), 115–131.

Block, J. H. (1979). Another look at sex differentiation in the socialization behaviors of mothers and fathers. In J. Sherman & F. L. Denmark (Eds.), *Psychology of women: Future of research.* New York: Psychological Dimensions.

Boccia, M., & Campos, J. J. (1989). Maternal emotional signals, social referencing, and infants' reactions to strangers. In N. Eisenberg (Ed.), *New directions for child development* (Vol. 44, pp. 25–49). San Francisco: Jossey-Bass.

Bodine, R. J., & Crawford, D. K. (1999). *Developing emotional intelligence: A guide to behavior management and conflict resolution in schools.* Champaign, IL: Research Press.

Boekaert, M. (1993). Being concerned with well-being and with learning. *Educational Psychologist, 28,* 149–167.

Booth, P. B., & Koller, T. J. (1998). Training parents of failure-to-attach children. In J. M. Briesmeister & C. E. Schaefer (Eds.), *Handbook of parent training: Parents as co-therapists for children's behavior problems* (2nd ed., pp. 308–342). New York: Wiley.

Bornstein, M. H., Haynes, O. M., Pascual, L., Painter, K. M., & Galperin, C. (1999). Play in two societies: Pervasiveness of process, specificity of structure. *Child Development, 70,* 317–331.

Bowlby, J. (1951). *Maternal care and mental health.* Geneva, Switzerland: World Health Organization.

Bowlby, J. (1958). The nature of the child's tie to his mother. *International Journal of Psycho-Analysis, 39,* 350–373.

Bowlby, J. (1969/1982). *Attachment and loss: Vol. 1. Attachment* (2nd ed.). New York: Basic Books.

Bowlby, J. (1973). *Attachment and loss: Vol. 2. Separation: Anxiety and anger.* New York: Basic Books.

Bowlby, J. (1988). *A secure base: Parent-child attachment and healthy human development.* New York: Basic Books.

Brenner, E. M., & Salovey, P. (1997). Emotion regulation during childhood: Developmental, interpersonal, and individual considerations. In P. Salovey & D. J. Sluyter (Eds.), *Emotional development and emotional intelligence: Educational implications* (pp. 168–195). New York: Basic Books.

Bretherton, I., & Beeghly, M. (1982). Talking about internal states: The acquisition of an explicit theory of mind. *Developmental Psychology, 18,* 906–921.

Bretherton, I., Fritz, J., Zahn-Waxler, C., & Ridgeway, D. (1986). Learning to talk about emotions: A functionalist perspective. *Child Development, 57,* 529–548.

Bridges, L. U., Connell, J. P., & Belsky, J. (1988). Similarities and differences in infant-mother and infant-father interaction in the Strange Situation: A component process analysis. *Developmental Psychology, 24,* 92–100.

Brigham, F. J., & Scruggs, T. E. (1995). Elaborative maps for enhanced learning of historical information: Uniting spatial, verbal, and imaginal information. *Journal of Special Education, 28,* 440.

Bristol, M. M., Cohen, D. J., Costello, E. J., Denckla, M., Eckberg, T. J., Kallen, R., Kraemer, H. C., Lord, C., Maurer, R., McIlvane, W. J., Minsher, N., Sigman, M., & Spence, M. A. (1996). State of the science in autism: Report to the National Institutes of Health. *Journal of Autism and Developmental Disorders, 26,* 121–154.

Britt, M. A., Rouet, J-F., Georgi, M. C., & Perfetti, C. A. (1994). Learning from history texts: From causal analysis to argument models. In G. Leinhardt, I. L. Beck, & C. Stainton (Eds.), *Teaching and learning in history.* Hillsdale, NJ: Erlbaum.

Bronson, M. B. (2000). *Self-regulation in early childhood: Nature and nurture.* New York: Guilford Press.

Brown, A. L., & Palincsar, A. S. (1989). Guided, cooperative learning and individual knowledge acquisition. In L. B. Resnick (Ed.), *Knowing, learning, and instruction: Essays in honor of Robert Glaser.* Hillsdale, NJ: Erlbaum.

Brown, J. S., Collins, A., & Duguid, P. (1989). Situated cognition and the culture of learning. *Educational Researcher, 18*(1), 32–42.

Brownell, M. T., Mellard, D. F., & Deshler, D. D. (1993). Differences in the learning and transfer performance between students with learning disabilities and other low-achieving students on problem-solving tasks. *Learning Disabilities Quarterly, 16,* 138–156.

Bruer, J. T. (1999). *The myth of the first three years: A new understanding of early brain development and lifelong learning.* New York: Free Press.

Bryson, S. E. (1997). Epidemiology of autism: Overview and issues outstanding. In D. J. Cohen & F. R. Volkmar (Eds.), *Handbook of autism and pervasive developmental disorders* (2nd ed.). New York: Wiley.

Buchanan, C. M., Eccles, J. S., & Becker, J. B. (1992). Are adolescents the victims of raging hormones: Evidence for activational effects of hormones on moods and behaviors at adolescence. *Psychological Bulletin, 111*(1), 62–107.

Buchoff, T. (1990). Attention deficit disorder: Help for the classroom teacher. *Childhood Education, 67*(2), 86–90.

Burhans, K. K., & Dweck, C. S. (1995). Helplessness in early childhood: The role of contingent worth. *Child Development, 66,* 1719–1738.

Butler, D. L., & Winne, P. H. (1995). Feedback and self-regulated learning: A theoretical synthesis. *Review of Educational Research, 65,* 245–281.

Byrnes, J. P. (1996). *Cognitive development and learning in instructional contexts.* Boston: Allyn & Bacon.

Calfee, R. C., & Masuda, W. V. (1997). Classroom assessment as inquiry. In G. D. Phye (Ed.), *Handbook of classroom assessment: Learning, achievement, and adjustment.* San Diego, CA: Academic Press.

Carey, S. (1985a). Are children fundamentally different kinds of thinkers and learners than adults? In S. F. Chipman, J. W. Segal, & R. Glaser (Eds.), *Learning and thinking skills: Vol. 2. Research and open questions.* Hillsdale, NJ: Erlbaum.

Carey, S. (1985b). *Conceptual change in childhood.* Cambridge, MA: MIT Press.

Carlson, C. L., Pelham, W. E., Milich, R., & Dixon, J. (1992). Single and combined effects of methylphenidate and behavior therapy on the classroom performance of children with attention deficit hyperactivity disorder. *Journal of Abnormal Child Psychology, 20,* 213–232.

Caron, A. J., Caron, R. F., & MacLean, D. J. (1988). Infant discrimination of naturalistic emotional expressions: The role of face and voice. *Child Development, 59,* 604–616.

Carr, E. G., Levin, L., McConnachie, G., Carlson, J. I., Kemp, D. C., & Smith, C. E. (1994). *Communication-based intervention for problem behavior: A user's guide for producing positive change.* Baltimore: Brookes.

Carr, M., & Schneider, W. (1991). Long-term maintenance of organizational strategies in kindergarten children. *Contemporary Educational Psychology, 16,* 61–72.

Carraher, T. N., Carraher, D. W., & Schliemann, A. D. (1985). Mathematics in the streets and in the schools. *British Journal of Developmental Psychology, 3,* 21–29.

Cartledge, G., & Milburn, J. F. (1995). *Teaching social skills to children and youth: Innovative approaches* (3rd ed.). Needham Heights, MA: Allyn & Bacon.

Case, R. (1985). *Intellectual development: Birth to adulthood.* Orlando, FL: Academic Press.

Case, R., & Edelstein, W. (1993). *The new structuralism in cognitive development: Theory and research on individual pathways.* Basel, Switzerland: Karger.

Case, R., & Okamoto, Y., in collaboration with Griffin, S., McKeough, A., Bleiker, C., Henderson, B., & Stephenson, K. M. (1996). The role of central conceptual structures in the development of children's thought. *Monographs of the Society for Research in Child Development, 61*(1, Serial No. 246).

Case, R., Okamoto, Y., Henderson, B., & McKeough, A. (1993). Individual variability and consistency in cognitive development: New evidence for the existence of central conceptual structures. In R. Case & W. Edelstein (Eds.), *The new structuralism in cognitive development: Theory and research on individual pathways.* Basel, Switzerland: Karger.

Caspi, A. (1998). Personality development across the life course. In W. Damon (Editor-in-Chief) & N. Eisenberg (Vol. Ed.), *Handbook of child psychology: Vol. 3. Social, emotional, and personality development* (5th ed., pp. 311–388). New York: Wiley.

Caspi, A., Taylor, A., Moffitt, T. E., & Plomin, R. (2000). Neighborhood deprivation affects children's mental health: Environmental risks identified in a genetic design. *Psychological Science, 11,* 338–342.

Ceci, S. J., & Roazzi, A. (1994). The effects of context on cognition: Postcards from Brazil. In R. J. Sternberg & R. K. Wagner (Eds.), *Mind in context: Interactionist perspectives on human intelligence.* Cambridge, England: Cambridge University Press.

Cerella, J., & Hale, S. (1994). The rise and fall in information-processing rates over the life span. *Acta Psychologia, 86,* 109–197.

Chafel, J. A. (1991). The play of children: Developmental processes and policy implications. *Child & Youth Care Forum, 20,* 115–132.

Chalfant, J. C. (1989). Learning disabilities: Policy issues and promising approaches. *American Psychologist, 44,* 392–398.

Chambliss, M. J. (1994). Why do readers fail to change their beliefs after reading persuasive text? In R. Garner & P. A. Alexander (Eds.), *Beliefs about text and instruction with text.* Hillsdale, NJ: Erlbaum.

Champagne, A. B., & Bunce, D. M. (1991). Learning-theory-based science teaching. In S. M. Glynn, R. H. Yeany, & B. K. Britton (Eds.), *The psychology of learning science.* Hillsdale, NJ: Erlbaum.

Chan, C., Burtis, J., & Bereiter, C. (1997). Knowledge building as a mediator of conflict in conceptual change. *Cognition and Instruction, 15,* 1–40.

Chandler, M., & Boyes, M. (1982). Social-cognitive development. In B. Wolman (Ed.), *Handbook of developmental psychology.* Upper Saddle River, NJ: Prentice Hall.

Chandler, T. J. L., & Goldberg, A. D. (1990). The academic All-American as vaunted adolescent role-identity. *Sociology of Sport Journal, 7,* 287–293.

Cheatham, S. K., Smith, J. D., Rucker, H. N., Polloway, E. A., & Lewis, G. W. (1995, September). Savant syndrome: Case studies, hypotheses, and implications for special education. *Education and Training in Mental Retardation,* 243–253.

Chen, X., Rubin, K. H., & Sun, Y. (1992). Social reputation and peer relationships in Chinese and Canadian children: A cross-cultural study. *Child Development, 63,* 1336–1343.

Chi, M. T. H. (1978). Knowledge structures and memory development. In R. S. Siegler (Ed.), *Children's thinking: What develops?* Hillsdale, NJ: Erlbaum.

Chinn, C. A., & Brewer, W. F. (1993). The role of anomalous data in knowledge acquisition: A theoretical framework and implications for science instruction. *Review of Educational Research, 63,* 1–49.

Chisholm, J. S. (1996). The evolutionary ecology of attachment organization. *Human Nature, 1,* 1–37.

Christie, J. F., & Johnsen, E. P. (1983). The role of play in social-intellectual development. *Review of Educational Research, 53,* 93–115.

Cicchetti, D., Rogosch, F. A., & Toth, S. L. (1997). Ontogenesis, depressotypic organization, and the depressive spectrum. In S. S. Luthar, J. A. Burack, D. Cicchetti, & J. R. Weisz (Eds.), *Developmental psychopathology: Perspectives on adjustment, risk, and disorder* (pp. 273–313). Cambridge, England: Cambridge University Press.

Cicchetti, D., & Toth, S. L. (1998). Perspectives on research and practice in developmental psychopathology. In W. Damon (Editor-in-Chief), I. E. Sigel, & K. A. Renninger (Vol. Eds.), *Handbook of child psychology: Vol. 4. Child psychology in practice* (5th ed., pp. 479–583). New York: Wiley.

Clark, R. M. (1983). *Family life and school achievement: Why poor black children succeed or fail.* Chicago: University of Chicago Press.

Claude, D., & Firestone, P. (1995). The development of ADHD boys: A 12-year follow-up. *Canadian Journal of Behavioural Science, 27,* 226–249.

Clifford, M. M. (1990). Students need challenge, not easy success. *Educational Leadership, 48*(1), 22–26.

Cole, M., & Schribner, S. (1977). Cross-cultural studies of memory and cognition. In R. V. Kail & J. W. Hagen (Eds.), *Perspectives on the development of memory and cognition.* Hillsdale, NJ: Erlbaum.

Cole, N. S. (1990). Conceptions of educational achievement. *Educational Researcher, 19*(3), 2–7.

Cole, P. (1986). Children's spontaneous control of facial expression. *Child Development, 57,* 1309–1321.

Collins, A., Brown, J. S., & Newman, S. E. (1989). Cognitive apprenticeship: Teaching the crafts of reading, writing, and mathematics. In L. B. Resnick (Ed.), *Knowing, learning, and instruction: Essays in honor of Robert Glaser.* Hillsdale, NJ: Erlbaum.

Conte, R. (1991). Attention disorders. In B. Y. L. Wong (Ed.), *Learning about learning disabilities.* San Diego, CA: Academic Press.

Cooper, H., & Dorr, N. (1995). Race comparisons on need for achievement: A meta-analytic alternative to Graham's narrative review. *Review of Educational Research, 65,* 483–508.

Copeland, R. W. (1979). *How children learn mathematics: Teaching implications of Piaget's research* (3rd ed.). New York: Macmillan.

Cornell, D. G., Pelton, G. M., Bassin, L. E., Landrum, M., Ramsay, S. G., Cooley, M. R., Lynch, K. A., & Hamrick, E. (1990). Self-concept and peer status among gifted program youth. *Journal of Educational Psychology, 82,* 456–463.

Crick, N. R., & Dodge, K. A. (1994). A review and reformulation of social information-processing mechanisms in children's social adjustment. *Psychological Bulletin, 115,* 74–101.

Dalrymple, N. J. (1995). Environmental supports to develop flexibility and independence. In K. A. Quill (Ed.), *Teaching children with autism: Strategies to enhance communication and socialization.* New York: Delmar.

Damon, W. (1984). Peer education: The untapped potential. *Journal of Applied Developmental Psychology, 5,* 331–343.

Damon, W. (1991). Putting substance into self-esteem: A focus on academic and moral values. *Educational Horizons, 70*(1), 12–18.

Danner, F. W., & Day, M. C. (1977). Eliciting formal operations. *Child Development, 48,* 1600–1606.

Deci, E. L., & Ryan, R. M. (1992). The initiation and regulation of intrinsically motivated learning and achievement. In A. K. Boggiano & T. S. Pittman (Eds.), *Achievement and motivation: A social-developmental perspective.* Cambridge, England: Cambridge University Press.

De Corte, E., Greer, B., & Verschaffel, L. (1996). Mathematics teaching and learning. In D. C. Berliner & R. C. Calfee (Eds.), *Handbook of educational psychology.* New York: Macmillan.

DeKlynen, M., Speltz, M. L., & Greenberg, M. T. (1998). Fathering and early onset of conduct problems: Positive and negative parenting, father-son attachment, and the marital context. *Clinical Child & Family Psychology Review, 1*(1), 3–28.

DeLisi, R., & Gallagher, A. M. (1991). Understanding of gender stability and constancy in Argentinian children. *Merrill-Palmer Quarterly, 37,* 483–502.

DeLoache, J. S., Cassidy, D. J., & Brown, A. L. (1985). Precursors of mnemonic strategies in very young children's memory. *Child Development, 56,* 125–137.

DeLoache, J. S., Miller, K. F., & Rosengren, K. S. (1997). The credible shrinking room: Very young children's performance with symbolic and non-symbolic relations. *Psychological Science, 8,* 308–313.

DeLoache, J. S., & Todd, C. M. (1988). Young children's use of spatial categorization as a mnemonic strategy. *Journal of Experimental Child Psychology, 46,* 1–20.

Dempster, F. N., & Corkill, A. J. (1999). Interference and inhibition in cognition and behavior: Unifying themes for educational psychology. *Educational Psychology Review, 11,* 1–88.

Denkla, M. B. (1986). New diagnostic criteria for autism and related behavioral disorders: Guidelines for research protocols. *Journal of the American Academy of Child Psychiatry, 25,* 221–224.

DeRidder, L. M. (1993). Teenage pregnancy: Etiology and educational interventions. *Educational Psychology Review, 5,* 87–107.

Derry, S. J. (1996). Cognitive schema theory in the constructivist debate. *Educational Psychologist, 31,* 163–174.

DeVries, M. W., & Sameroff, A. J. (1984). Culture and temperament: Influences on infant temperament in three East-African societies. *American Journal of Orthopsychiatry, 54,* 83–96.

Diamond, S. C. (1991). What to do when you can't do anything: Working with disturbed adolescents. *Clearing House, 64,* 232–234.

Dien, T. (1998). Language and literacy in Vietnamese American communities. In B. Pérez (Ed.), *Sociocultural contexts of language and literacy.* Mahwah, NJ: Erlbaum.

diSessa, A. A. (1996). What do "just plain folk" know about physics? In D. R. Olson & N. Torrance (Eds.), *The handbook of education and human development: New models of learning, teaching, and schooling.* Cambridge, MA: Blackwell.

Dole, J. A., Duffy, G. G., Roehler, L. R., & Pearson, P. D. (1991). Moving from the old to the new: Research on reading comprehension instruction. *Review of Educational Research, 61,* 239–264.

Donaldson, M. (1978). *Children's minds.* New York: Norton.

Donaldson, S. K., & Westerman, M. A. (1986). Development of children's understanding of ambivalence and causal theories of emotion. *Developmental Psychology, 22,* 655–662.

Dube, E. F. (1982). Literacy, cultural familiarity, and "intelligence" as determinants of story recall. In U. Neisser (Ed.), *Memory observed: Remembering in natural contexts.* San Francisco: Freeman.

Duit, R. (1991). Students' conceptual frameworks: Consequences for learning science. In S. M. Glynn, R. H. Yeany, & B. K. Britton (Eds.), *The psychology of learning science.* Hillsdale, NJ: Erlbaum.

Dunbar, R. (1992). Mating and parental care. In S. Jones, R. Martin, D. Pilbeam, & S. Bunney (Eds.), *Cambridge encyclopedia of human evolution* (pp. 150–154). Cambridge, England: Cambridge University Press.

Dunn, J., Bretherton, I., & Munn, P. (1987). Conversations about feeling states between mothers and their young children. *Developmental Psychology, 23,* 132–139.

Durkin, K. (1995). *Developmental social psychology: From infancy to old age.* Cambridge, MA: Blackwell.

Dweck, C. S. (1986). Motivational processes affecting learning. *American Psychologist, 41,* 1040–1048.

Eacott, M. J. (1999). Memory for the events of early childhood. *Current Directions in Psychological Science, 8,* 46–49.

Eccles, J. S., Jacobs, J., Harold-Goldsmith, R., Jayaratne, T., & Yee, D. (1989, April). *The relations between parents' category-based and target-based beliefs: Gender roles and biological influences.* Paper presented at the Society for Research in Child Development, Kansas City, MO.

Eccles, J. S., & Midgley, C. (1989). Stage-environment fit: Developmentally appropriate classrooms for young adolescents. In C. Ames & R. Ames (Eds.), *Research on motivation in education: Vol. 3. Goals and cognition.* San Diego, CA: Academic Press.

Eccles, J. S., & Wigfield, A. (1985). Teacher expectations and student motivation. In J. B. Dusek (Ed.), *Teacher expectancies.* Hillsdale, NJ: Erlbaum.

Eccles, J. S., Wigfield, A., & Schiefele, U. (1998). Motivation to succeed. In W. Damon (Editor-in-Chief) & N. Eisenberg (Vol. Ed.), *Handbook of child psychology: Vol. 3. Social, emotional, and personality development* (5th ed.). New York: Wiley.

Eden, G. F., Stein, J. F., & Wood, F. B. (1995). Verbal and visual problems in reading disability. *Journal of Learning Disabilities, 28,* 272–290.

Eisenberg, N., Martin, C. L., & Fabes, R. A. (1996). Gender development and gender effects. In D. C. Berliner & R. C. Calfee (Eds.), *Handbook of educational psychology.* New York: Macmillan.

Elicker, J., Englund, M., & Sroufe, L. A. (1992). Predicting peer competence and peer relationships in childhood from early parent-child relationships. In R. D. Parke & G. W. Ladd (Eds.), *Family-peer relationships: Modes of linkage* (pp. 77–106). Hillsdale, NJ: Erlbaum.

Elkind, D. (1981). *Children and adolescents: Interpretive essays on Jean Piaget* (3rd ed.). New York: Oxford.

Elkind, D. (1984). *All grown up and no place to go.* Reading, MA: Addison-Wesley.

Elliott, D. J. (1995). *Music matters: A new philosophy of music education.* New York: Oxford University Press.

Ellis, E. S., & Friend, P. (1991). Adolescents with learning disabilities. In B. Y. L. Wong (Ed.), *Learning about learning disabilities.* San Diego, CA: Academic Press.

Emde, R., Gaensbauer, T., & Harmon, R. (1976). *Emotional expression in infancy: A biobehavioral study* (Psychological Issues, Vol. 10, No. 37). New York: International Universities Press.

Emmerich, W., Goldman, K. S., Kirsch, B., & Sharabany, R. (1977). Evidence of a transitional phase in the development of gender constancy. *Child Development, 48,* 930–936.

Epstein, S., & Morling, B. (1995). Is the self motivated to do more than enhance and/or verify itself? In M. H. Kernis (Ed.), *Efficacy, agency, and self-esteem.* New York: Plenum Press.

Erikson, E. H. (1963). *Childhood and society* (2nd ed.). New York: Norton.

Erikson, E. H. (1972). Eight ages of man. In C. S. Lavatelli & F. Stendler (Eds.), *Readings in child behavior and child development.* San Diego, CA: Harcourt Brace Jovanovich.

Etaugh, C., Grinnell, K., & Etaugh, A. (1989). Development of gender labeling: Effect of age of pictured children. *Sex Roles, 21,* 769–773.

Eysenck, M. W. (1992). *Anxiety: The cognitive perspective.* Hove, England: Erlbaum.

Fabes, R. A., Eisenberg, N., Jones, S., Smith, M., Guthrie, I., Poulin, R., Shepard, S., & Friedman, J. (1999). Regulation, emotionality, and preschoolers' socially competent peer interactions. *Child Development, 70,* 432–442.

Fagot, B. I., & Leinbach, M. D. (1989). Gender-role development in young children: From discrimination to labeling. *Developmental Review, 13,* 205–224.

Fahrmeier, E. D. (1978). The development of concrete operations among the Hausa. *Journal of Cross-Cultural Psychology, 9,* 23–44.

Famularo, R., Kinscherff, R., & Fenton, T. (1992). Psychiatric diagnoses of maltreated children: Preliminary findings. *Journal of the American Academy of Child and Adolescent Psychiatry, 31,* 863–867.

Faraone, S. V., Biederman, J., Chen, W. J., Milberger, S., Warburton, R., & Tsuang, M. T. (1995). Genetic heterogeneity in attention-deficit hyperactivity disorder (ADHD): Gender, psychiatric comorbidity, and maternal ADHD. *Journal of Abnormal Psychology, 104,* 334–345.

Farrar, M. J., & Goodman, G. S. (1992). Developmental changes in event memory. *Child Development, 63,* 173–187.

Fein, G. G. (1979). Play and the acquisition of symbols. In L. Katz (Ed.), *Current topics in early childhood education.* Norwood, NJ: Ablex.

Feuerstein, R. (1979). *The dynamic assessment of retarded performers: The Learning Potential Assessment Device, theory, instruments, and techniques.* Baltimore: University Park Press.

Feuerstein, R. (1980). *Instrumental enrichment: An intervention program for cognitive modifiability.* Baltimore: University Park Press.

Feuerstein, R. (1990). The theory of structural cognitive modifiability. In B. Z. Presseisen (Ed.), *Learning and thinking styles: Classroom interaction.* Washington, DC: National Education Association.

Feuerstein, R., Klein, P. R., & Tannenbaum, A. (Eds.). (1991). *Mediated learning experience: Theoretical, psychosocial, and learning implications.* London: Freund.

Field, D. (1987). A review of preschool conservation training: An analysis of analyses. *Developmental Review, 7,* 210–251.

Fischer, K. W., & Bidell, T. (1991). Constraining nativist inferences about cognitive capacities. In S. Carey & R. Gelman (Eds.), *The epigenesis of mind: Essays on biology and cognition.* Hillsdale, NJ: Erlbaum.

Fischer, K. W., Knight, C. C., & Van Parys, M. (1993). Analyzing diversity in developmental pathways: Methods and concepts. In R. Case & W. Edelstein (Eds.), *The new structuralism in cognitive development: Theory and research on individual pathways.* Basel, Switzerland: Karger.

Fisher, C. B., Jackson, J. F., & Villarruel, F. A. (1998). The study of African American and Latin American children and youth. In W. Damon (Editor-in-Chief) & R. M. Lerner (Vol. Ed.), *Handbook of child psychology: Vol. 1. Theoretical models of human development* (5th ed., pp. 1145–1207). New York: Wiley.

Fivush, R., Haden, C., & Adam, S. (1995). Structure and coherence of preschoolers' personal narratives over time: Implications for childhood amnesia. *Journal of Experimental Child Psychology, 60,* 32–56.

Flavell, J. H. (1963). *The developmental psychology of Jean Piaget.* New York: Van Nostrand Reinhold.

Flavell, J. H. (1994). Cognitive development: Past, present, and future. In R. D. Parke, P. A. Ornstein, J. J. Rieser, & C. Zahn-Waxler (Eds.), *A century of developmental psychology.* Washington, DC: American Psychological Association.

Flavell, J. H. (1996). Piaget's legacy. *Psychological Science, 7,* 200–203.

Flavell, J. H., Friedrichs, A. G., & Hoyt, J. D. (1970). Developmental changes in memorization processes. *Cognitive Psychology, 1,* 324–340.

Flavell, J. H., Green, F. L., & Flavell, E. R. (1995). Young children's knowledge about thinking. *Monographs of the Society for Research in Child Development, 60*(1, Serial No. 243).

Flavell, J. H., Green, F. L., Flavell, E. R., & Lin, N. T. (1999). Development of children's knowledge about unconsciousness. *Child Development, 70,* 396–412.

Flavell, J. H., Miller, P. H., & Miller, S. A. (1993). *Cognitive development* (3rd ed.). Upper Saddle River, NJ: Prentice Hall.

Flieller, A. (1999). Comparison of the development of formal thought in adolescent cohorts aged 10 to 15 years (1967–1996 and 1972–1993). *Developmental Psychology, 35,* 1048–1058.

Folds, T. H., Footo, M., Guttentag, R. E., & Ornstein, P. A. (1990). When children mean to remember: Issues of context specificity, strategy effectiveness, and intentionality in the development of memory. In D. F. Bjorklund (Ed.), *Children's strategies: Contemporary views of cognitive development.* Hillsdale, NJ: Erlbaum.

Forbes, M. L., Ormrod, J. E., Bernardi, J. D., Taylor, S. L., & Jackson, D. L. (1999, April). Children's conceptions of space, as reflected in maps of their hometown. Paper presented at the annual meeting of the American Educational Research Association, Montreal.

Friend, M., & Davis, T. L. (1993). Appearance-reality distinction: Children's understanding of the physical and affective domains. *Developmental Psychology, 29,* 907–914.

Frost, J. L., Shin, D., & Jacobs, P. J. (1998). Physical environments and children's play. In O. N. Saracho & B. Spodek (Eds.), *Multiple perspectives on play in early childhood education.* Albany: State University of New York Press.

Fry, A. F., & Hale, S. (1996). Processing speed, working memory, and fluid intelligence. *Psychological Science, 7,* 237–241.

Galambos, N. L., Almeida, D. M., & Petersen, A. C. (1990). Masculinity, femininity, and sex role attitudes in early adolescence: Exploring gender intensification. *Child Development, 61,* 1905–1914.

Gallimore, R., & Tharp, R. (1990). Teaching mind in society: Teaching, schooling, and literate discourse. In L. C. Moll (Ed.), *Vygotsky and education: Instructional implications and applications of sociohistorical psychology.* Cambridge, England: Cambridge University Press.

Gardner, H. (1983). *Frames of mind: The theory of multiple intelligences.* New York: Basic Books.

Gathercole, S. E., & Hitch, G. J. (1993). Developmental changes in short-term memory: A revised working memory perspective. In A. F. Collins, S. E. Gathercole, M. A. Conway, & P. E. Morris (Eds.), *Theories of memory.* Hove, England: Erlbaum.

Gelman, R. (1972). Logical capacity of very young children: Number invariance rules. *Child Development, 43,* 75–90.

Gelman, R., & Baillargeon, R. (1983). A review of some Piagetian concepts. In J. H. Flavell & E. M. Markman (Eds.), *Handbook of child psychology: Vol. 3. Cognitive development.* New York: Wiley.

Gillberg, I. C., & Coleman, M. (1996). Autism and medical disorders: A review of the literature. *Developmental Medicine and Child Neurology, 38,* 191–202.

Gillham, J. E., Reivich, K. J., Jaycox, L. H., & Seligman, M. E. P. (1995). Prevention of depressive symptoms in schoolchildren: Two-year follow-up. *Psychological Science, 6,* 343–351.

Gillis, J. J., Gilger, J. W., Pennington, B. F., & DeFries, J. C. (1992). Attention deficit disorder in reading-disabled twins: Evidence for a genetic etiology. *Journal of Abnormal Child Psychology, 20,* 303–315.

Gladwell, M. (1997, Feb. 24 and Mar. 3). Crime and science: Damaged. *The New Yorker.*

Glick, J. (1975). Cognitive development in cross-cultural perspective. In F. Horowitz (Ed.), *Review of child development research* (Vol. 4). Chicago: University of Chicago Press.

Glynn, S. M., Yeany, R. H., & Britton, B. K. (1991). A constructive view of learning science. In S. M. Glynn, R. H. Yeany, & B. K. Britton (Eds.), *The psychology of learning science.* Hillsdale, NJ: Erlbaum.

Goldin-Meadow, S. (1997). When gestures and words speak differently. *Current Directions in Psychological Science, 6,* 138–143.

Goleman, D. (1995). *Emotional intelligence.* New York: Bantam Books.

Göncü, A. (1993). Development of intersubjectivity in the dyadic play of preschoolers. *Early Childhood Research Quarterly, 8,* 99–116.

Good, T. L., McCaslin, M. M., & Reys, B. J. (1992). Investigating work groups to promote problem solving in mathematics. In J. Brophy (Ed.), *Advances in research on teaching: Vol. 3. Planning and managing learning tasks and activities.* Greenwich, CT: JAI Press.

Grandin, T. (1995). *Thinking in pictures and other reports of my life with autism.* New York: Random House.

Greenhoot, A. F., Ornstein, P. A., Gordon, B. N., & Baker-Ward, L. (1999). Acting out the details of a pediatric check-up: The impact of interview condition and behavioral style on children's memory reports. *Child Development, 70,* 363–380.

Greeno, J. G. (1997). On claims that answer the wrong questions. *Educational Researcher, 26*(1), 5–17.

Gregg, M., & Leinhardt, G. (1994, April). Constructing geography. Paper presented at the annual meeting of the American Educational Research Association, New Orleans, LA.

Gresham, F. M., & MacMillan, D. L. (1997). Social competence and affective characteristics of students with mild disabilities. *Review of Educational Research, 67,* 377–415.

Griffin, S., Case, R., & Capodilupo, A. (1995). Teaching for understanding: The importance of the central conceptual structures in the elementary mathematics curriculum. In A. McKeough, J. Lupart, & A. Marini (Eds.), *Teaching for transfer: Fostering generalization in learning.* Mahwah, NJ: Erlbaum.

Griffin, S. A., Case, R., & Siegler, R. S. (1994). Rightstart: Providing the central conceptual prerequisites for first formal learning of arithmetic to students at risk for school failure. In K. McGilly (Ed.), *Classroom lessons: Integrating cognitive theory and classroom practice.* Cambridge, MA: MIT Press.

Griffore, R. J. (1981). *Child development: An educational perspective.* Springfield, IL: Charles C Thomas.

Griswold, K. S., & Pessar, L. F. (2000). Management of bipolar disorder. *American Family Physician, 62,* 1343–1356.

Grodzinsky, G. M., & Diamond, R. (1992). Frontal lobe functioning in boys with attention-deficit hyperactivity disorder. *Developmental Neuropsychology, 8,* 427–445.

Grossmann, K. E., Grossmann, K., Huber, F., & Wartner, U. (1981). German children's behavior toward their mothers at 12 months and their father at 18 months in Ainsworth's Strange Situation. *International Journal of Behavioral Development, 4,* 157–181.

Haenan, J. (1996). Piotr Gal'perin's criticism and extension of Lev Vygotsky's work. *Journal of Russian and East European Psychology, 34*(2), 54–60.

Hagen, J. W., & Stanovich, K. G. (1977). Memory: Strategies of acquisition. In R. V. Kail, Jr. & J. W. Hagen (Eds.), *Perspectives on the development of memory and cognition.* Hillsdale, NJ: Erlbaum.

Haight, W. L., & Miller, P. J. (1993). *Pretending at home: Early development in a sociocultural context.* Albany, NY: SUNY Press.

Hale-Benson, J. E. (1986). *Black children: Their roots, culture, and learning styles.* Baltimore: Johns Hopkins University Press.

Halford, G. S. (1989). Cognitive processing capacity and learning ability: An integration of two areas. *Learning and Individual Differences, 1,* 125–153.

Hallowell, E. (1996). *When you worry about the child you love.* New York: Simon and Schuster.

Hammer, D. (1994). Epistemological beliefs in introductory physics. *Cognition and Instruction, 12,* 151–183.

Harris, M. J., & Rosenthal, R. (1985). Mediation of interpersonal expectancy effects: 31 meta-analyses. *Psychological Bulletin, 97,* 363–386.

Harris, P. L. (1989). *Children and emotion: The development of psychological understanding.* Oxford, England: Basil Blackwell.

Harrison, A. O., Wilson, M. N., Pine, C. J., Chan, S. Q., & Buriel, R. (1990). Family ecologies of ethnic minority children. *Child Development, 61,* 347–362.

Hart, D. (1988). The adolescent self-concept in social context. In D. K. Lapsley & F. C. Power (Eds.), *Self, ego, and identity: Integrative approaches* (pp. 71–90). New York: Springer-Verlag.

Harter, S. (1983a). Children's understanding of multiple emotions: A cognitive-developmental approach. In W. F. Overton (Ed.), *The relationship between social and cognitive development.* Hillsdale, NJ: Erlbaum.

Harter, S. (1983b). Developmental perspectives on the self-system. In P. M. Mussen (Series Ed.) & E. M. Hetherington (Vol. Ed.), *Handbook of child psychology: Vol. 4. Socialization, personality, and social development* (4th ed.). New York: Wiley.

Harter, S. (1988). The construction and conservation of the self: James and Cooley revisited. In D. K. Lapsley & F. C. Power (Eds.), *Self, ego, and identity: Integrative approaches* (pp. 43–69). New York: Springer-Verlag.

Harter, S. (1990a). Causes, correlates, and the functional role of global self-worth: A life-span perspective. In R. J. Sternberg & J. Kolligian, Jr. (Eds.), *Competence considered.* New Haven, CT: Yale University Press.

Harter, S. (1990b). Processes underlying adolescent self-concept formation. In R. Montemayer, G. R. Adams, & T. P. Gullotta (Eds.), *From childhood to adolescence: A transitional period?* Newbury Park, CA: Sage.

Harter, S. (1998). The development of self-representations. In W. Damon (Editor-in-Chief) & N. Eisenberg (Vol. Ed.), *Handbook of child psychology: Vol. 3. Social, emotional, and personality development* (5th ed., pp. 553–617). New York: Wiley.

Harter, S., Stocker, C., & Robinson, N. S. (1996). The perceived directionality of the link between approval and self-worth: The liabilities of a looking glad self-orientation among young adolescents. *Journal of Research on Adolescence, 6,* 285–308.

Harter, S., Waters, P. L., Whitesell, N. R., & Kastelic, D. (1998). Level of voice among female and male high school students: Relational context, support, and gender orientation. *Developmental Psychology, 34,* 892–901.

Harter, S., & Whitesell, N. R. (1989). Developmental changes in children's understanding of single, multiple, and blended emotion concepts. In C. Saarni & P. Harris (Eds.), *Children's understanding of emotion* (pp. 81–116). Cambridge, England: Cambridge University Press.

Harter, S., Whitesell, N. R., & Junkin, L. J. (1998). Similarities and differences in domain-specific and global self-evaluations of learning-disabled, behaviorally disordered, and normally achieving adolescents. *American Educational Research Journal, 35,* 653–680.

Hartup, W. W. (1989). Social relationships and their developmental significance. *American Psychologist, 44,* 120–126.

Harwood, R. L., Miller, J. G., & Irizarry, N. L. (1995). *Culture and attachment: Perceptions of the child in context.* New York: Guilford Press.

Hatano, G., & Inagaki, K. (1991). Sharing cognition through collective comprehension activity. In L. B. Resnick, J. M. Levine, & S. D. Teasley (Eds.), *Perspectives on socially shared cognition.* Washington, DC: American Psychological Association.

Hatano, G., & Inagaki, K. (1993). Desituating cognition through the construction of conceptual knowledge. In P. Light and G. Butterworth (Eds.), *Context and cognition: Ways of learning and knowing.* Hillsdale, NJ: Erlbaum.

Hatano, G., & Inagaki, K. (1996). Cognitive and cultural factors in the acquisition of intuitive biology. In D. R. Olson & N. Torrance (Eds.), *The handbook of education and human development: New models of learning, teaching, and schooling.* Cambridge, MA: Blackwell.

Hatfield, E., Cacioppo, J. T., & Rapson, R. L. (1994). *Emotional contagion.* Cambridge, England: Cambridge University Press.

Hattie, J., Biggs, J., & Purdie, N. (1996). Effects of learning skills interventions on student learning: A meta-analysis. *Review of Educational Research, 66,* 99–136.

Haviland, J. M., & Lelwica, M. (1987). The induced affect response: 10-week-old infants' responses to three emotional expressions. *Developmental Psychology, 23,* 97–104.

Hawkins, F. P. L. (1997). *Journal with children: The autobiography of a teacher.* Niwot: University Press of Colorado.

Hembree, R. (1988). Correlates, causes, effects, and treatment of test anxiety. *Review of Educational Research, 58,* 47–77.

Hemphill, L., & Snow, C. (1996). Language and literacy development: Discontinuities and differences. In D. R. Olson & N. Torrance (Eds.), *The handbook of education and human development: New models of learning, teaching, and schooling.* Cambridge, MA: Blackwell Publishers.

Henderson, N. D. (1982). Human behavior genetics. *Annual Review of Psychology, 33,* 403–440.

Hertel, P. T. (1994). Depression and memory: Are impairments remediable through attentional control? *Current Directions in Psychological Science, 3,* 190–193.

Heward, W. L. (1996). *Exceptional children: An introduction to special education* (5th ed.). Upper Saddle River, NJ: Merrill/Prentice Hall.

Hiatt, S., Campos, J., & Emde, R. (1979). Facial patterning and infant emotional expression: Happiness, surprise, and fear. *Child Development, 50,* 1020–1035.

Hickey, D. T. (1997). Motivation and contemporary socio-constructivist instructional perspectives. *Educational Psychologist, 32,* 175–193.

Hickey, T. L., & Peduzzi, J. D. (1987). Structure and development of the visual system. In P. Salapatek & L. Cohen (Eds.), *Handbook of infant perception: Vol. 1. From sensation to perception.* New York: Academic Press.

Hiebert, E. H., & Fisher, C. W. (1992). The tasks of school literacy: Trends and issues. In J. Brophy (Ed.), *Advances in research on teaching: Vol. 3. Planning and managing learning tasks and activities.* Greenwich, CT: JAI Press.

Higgins, A. T., & Turnure, J. E. (1984). Distractibility and concentration of attention in children's development. *Child Development, 55,* 1799–1810.

Hillier, L., Hewitt, K. L., & Morrongiello, B. A. (1992). Infants' perception of illusions in sound localization: Reaching to sounds in the dark. *Journal of Experimental Child Psychology, 53,* 159–179.

Hirsh-Pasek, K., Hyson, M., & Rescorla, L. (1990). Academic environments in preschool: Do they pressure or challenge young children? *Early Education and Development, 1*(6), 401–423.

Ho, D. Y. F. (1986). Chinese pattern of socialization: A critical review. In M. H. Bond (Ed.), *The psychology of Chinese people.* Oxford, England: Oxford University Press.

Ho, D. Y. F. (1994). Cognitive socialization in Confucian heritage cultures. In P. M. Greenfield & R. R. Cocking (Eds.), *Cross-cultural roots of minority child development.* Hillsdale, NJ: Erlbaum.

Hofer, B. K., & Pintrich, P. R. (1997). The development of epistemological theories: Beliefs about knowledge and knowing and their relation to learning. *Review of Educational Research, 67,* 88–140.

Hogan, K. (1997, March). *Relating students' personal frameworks for science learning to their cognition in collaborative contexts.* Paper presented at the annual meeting of the American Educational Research Association, Chicago.

Horgan, D. (1990, April). *Students' predictions of test grades: Calibration and metacognition.* Paper presented at the annual meeting of the American Educational Research Association, Boston.

Howes, C., & Ritchie, S. (1998). Changes in child-teacher relationships in a therapeutic preschool program. *Early Education and Development, 9,* 411–422.

Hunt, E. (1997). Nature vs. nurture: The feeling of *vujà dé.* In R. J. Sternberg & E. L. Grigorenko (Eds.), *Intelligence, heredity, and environment* (pp. 531–551). Cambridge, England: Cambridge University Press.

Inhelder, B., & Piaget, J. (1958). *The growth of logical thinking from childhood to adolescence* (A. Parsons & S. Milgram, Trans.). New York: Basic Books.

Isen, A., Daubman, K. A., & Gorgoglione, J. M. (1987). The influence of positive affect on cognitive organization: Implications for education. In R. E. Snow & M. J. Farr (Eds.), *Aptitude, learning and instruction: Vol. 3. Cognitive and affective process analysis.* Hillsdale, NJ: Erlbaum.

Johnson, H. C., & Friesen, B. (1993). Etiologies of mental and emotional disorders in children. In H. Johnson (Ed.), *Child mental health in the 1990s: Curricula for graduate and undergraduate.* Washington, DC: U.S. Department of Health and Human Services.

John-Steiner, V., & Mahn, H. (1996). Sociocultural approaches to learning and development: A Vygotskian framework. *Educational Psychologist, 31,* 191–206.

Joshi, M. S. & MacLean, M. (1994). Indian and English children's understanding of the distinction between real and apparent emotion. *Child Development, 65,* 1372–1384.

Josselson, R. (1988). The embedded self: I and Thou revisited. In D. K. Lapsley & F. C. Power (Eds.), *Self, ego, and identity: Integrative approaches* (pp. 91–106). New York: Springer-Verlag.

Kagan, J. (1998). Biology and the child. In W. Damon (Editor-in-Chief) & N. Eisenberg (Vol. Ed.), *Handbook of child psychology: Vol. 3. Social, emotional, and personality development* (5th ed., pp. 177–235). New York: Wiley.

Kahl, B., & Woloshyn, V. E. (1994). Using elaborative interrogation to facilitate acquisition of factual information in cooperative learning settings: One good strategy deserves another. *Applied Cognitive Psychology, 8,* 465–478.

Kail, R. (1990). *The development of memory in children* (3rd ed.). New York: Freeman.

Kail, R. (1993). The role of a global mechanism in developmental change in speed of processing. In M. L. Howe & R. Pasnak (Eds.), *Emerging themes in cognitive development: Vol. 1. Foundations.* New York: Springer-Verlag.

Kail, R., & Park, Y. (1994). Processing time, articulation time, and memory span. *Journal of Experimental Child Psychology, 57,* 281–291.

Kardash, C. A. M., & Howell, K. L. (1996, April). *Effects of epistemological beliefs on strategies employed to comprehend dual-positional text.* Paper presented at the annual meeting of the American Educational Research Association, New York.

Karpov, Y. V., & Haywood, H. C. (1998). Two ways to elaborate Vygotsky's concept of mediation: Implications for instruction. *American Psychologist, 53,* 27–36.

Kazdin, A. E. (1997). Conduct disorder across the life-span. In S. S. Luthar, J. A. Burack, D. Cicchetti, & J. R. Weisz (Eds.), *Developmental psychopathology: Perspectives on adjustment, risk, and disorder* (pp. 248–272). Cambridge, England: Cambridge University Press.

Kearins, J. M. (1981). Visual spatial memory in Australian aboriginal children of desert regions. *Cognitive Psychology, 13,* 434–460.

Keating, D. P. (1996). A grand theory of development. In R. Case & Y. Okamoto, in collaboration with S. Griffin, A. McKeough, C. Bleiker, B. Henderson, & K. M. Stephenson. The role of central conceptual structures in the development of children's thought. *Monographs of the Society for Research in Child Development, 61*(1, Serial No. 246).

Keeney, T. J., Canizzo, S. R., & Flavell, J. H. (1967). Spontaneous and induced verbal rehearsal in a recall task. *Child Development, 38,* 953–966.

Keil, F. C. (1987). Conceptual development and category structure. In U. Neisser (Ed.), *Concepts and conceptual development: Ecological and intellectual factors in categorization.* Cambridge, England: Cambridge University Press.

Keil, F. C. (1989). *Concepts, kinds, and cognitive development.* Cambridge, MA: MIT Press.

Keil, F. C. (1991). Theories, concepts, and the acquisition of word meaning. In S. A. Gelman & J. P. Byrnes (Eds.), *Perspectives on language and thought: Interrelations in development.* Cambridge, England: Cambridge University Press.

Keil, F. C., & Silberstein, C. S. (1996). Schooling and the acquisition of theoretical knowledge. In D. R. Olson & N. Torrance (Eds.), *The handbook of education and human development: New models of learning, teaching, and schooling.* Cambridge, MA: Blackwell.

Kern, L., Dunlap, G., Childs, K. E., & Clark, S. (1994). Use of a classwide self-management program to improve the behavior of students with emotional and behavioral disorders. *Education and Treatment of Children, 17,* 445–458.

Kerns, L. L., & Lieberman, A. B. (1993). *Helping your depressed child.* Rocklin, CA: Prima.

Kerr, M. M., & Nelson, C. M. (1989). *Strategies for managing behavior problems in the classroom* (2nd ed.). Upper Saddle River, NJ: Merrill/Prentice Hall.

Kestenbaum, R., Farber, E. A., & Sroufe, L. A. (1989). Individual differences in empathy among preschoolers: Relation to attachment history. In N. Eisenberg (Ed.), *Empathy and related emotional responses* (New Directions for Child Development, No. 44; pp. 51–64). San Francisco: Jossey-Bass.

King, A. (1994). Guiding knowledge construction in the classroom: Effects of teaching children how to question and how to explain. *American Educational Research Journal, 31,* 338–368.

King, A., Staffieri, A., & Adelgais, A. (1998). Mutual peer tutoring: Effects of structuring tutorial interaction to scaffold peer learning. *Journal of Educational Psychology, 90,* 134–152.

Knowlton, D. (1995). Managing children with oppositional behavior. *Beyond Behavior, 6*(3), 5–10.

Koyanagi, C., & Gaines, S. (1993). *All systems failure: An examination of the results of neglecting the needs of children with serious emotional disturbance.* Alexandria, VA: National Mental Health Association.

Kozulin, A., & Falik, L. (1995). Dynamic cognitive assessment of the child. *Current Directions in Psychological Science, 4,* 192–196.

Krampen, G. (1987). Differential effects of teacher comments. *Journal of Educational Psychology, 79,* 137–146.

Kreutzer, M. A., Leonard, C., & Flavell, J. H. (1975). An interview study of children's knowledge about memory. *Monographs of the Society for Research in Child Development, 40*(1, Serial No. 159).

Kuhn, D. (1997). Constraints or guideposts? Developmental psychology and science education. *Review of Educational Research, 67,* 141–150.

Kuhn, D., Amsel, E., & O'Loughlin, M. (1988). *The development of scientific thinking skills.* San Diego, CA: Academic Press.

Kuhn, D., & Phelps, E. (1982). The development of problem-solving strategies. In H. Reese (Ed.), *Advances in child development and behavior* (Vol. 17). New York: Academic Press.

Kuhn, D., Shaw, V., & Felton, M. (1997). Effects of dyadic interaction on argumentative reasoning. *Cognition and Instruction, 15,* 287–315.

Kunzinger, E. L., III (1985). A short-term longitudinal study of memorial development during early grade school. *Developmental Psychology, 21,* 642–646.

La Guardia, J. G., Ryan, R. M., Couchman, C. E., & Deci, E. L. (2000). Within-person variation in security of attachment: A self-determination theory perspective on attachment, need fulfillment, and well-being. *Journal of Personality and Social Psychology, 79,* 367–384.

Lampert, M. (1990). When the problem is not the question and the solution is not the answer: Mathematical knowing and teaching. *American Educational Research Journal, 27,* 29–64.

Landau, S., & McAninch, C. (1993). Young children with attention deficits. *Young Children, 48*(4), 49–58.

Lane, D. M., & Pearson, D. A. (1982). The development of selective attention. *Merrill-Palmer Quarterly, 28,* 317–337.

Lange, G., & Pierce, S. H. (1992). Memory-strategy learning and maintenance in preschool children. *Developmental Psychology, 28,* 453–462.

Langlois, J. H. (1981). Beauty and the beast: The role of physical attractiveness in the development of peer relations and social behavior. In S. S. Brehm, S. M. Kassin, & F. X. Gibbons (Eds.), *Developmental social psychology: Theory and research* (pp. 47–63). New York: Oxford University Press.

Lapsley, D. K. (1993). Toward an integrated theory of adolescent ego development: The "new look" at adolescent egocentrism. *American Journal of Orthopsychiatry, 63,* 562–571.

Lapsley, D. K., Jackson, S., Rice, K., & Shadid, G. (1988). Self-monitoring and the "new look" at the imaginary audience and personal fable: An ego-developmental analysis. *Journal of Adolescent Research, 3,* 17–31.

Lapsley, D. K., Milstead, M., Quintana, S., Flannery, D., & Buss, R. (1986). Adolescent egocentrism and formal operations: Tests of a theoretical assumption. *Developmental Psychology, 22,* 800–807.

Last, C. G., Hersen, M., Kazdin, A. E., Francis, G., & Grubb, H. J. (1987). Psychiatric illness in the mothers of anxious children. *American Journal of Psychiatry, 144,* 1580–1583.

Lautrey, J. (1993). Structure and variability: A plea for a pluralistic approach to cognitive development. In R. Case & W. Edelstein (Eds.), *The new structuralism in cognitive development: Theory and research on individual pathways.* Basel, Switzerland: Karger.

Lave, J. (1991). Situating learning in communities of practice. In L. B. Resnick, J. M. Levine, & S. D. Teasley (Eds.), *Perspectives on socially shared cognition.* Washington, DC: American Psychological Association.

Lave, J. (1993). Word problems: A microcosm of theories of learning. In P. Light and G. Butterworth (Eds.), *Context and cognition: Ways of learning and knowing.* Hillsdale, NJ: Erlbaum.

Lave, J., & Wenger, E. (1991). *Situated learning: Legitimate peripheral participation.* Cambridge, England: Cambridge University Press.

Lazarus, R. S. (1991). *Emotion and adaptation.* New York: Oxford University Press.

Lee, S. (1985). Children's acquisition of conditional logic structure: Teachable? *Contemporary Educational Psychology, 10,* 14–27.

Lehman, D. R., & Nisbett, R. E. (1990). A longitudinal study of the effects of undergraduate training on reasoning. *Developmental Psychology, 26,* 952–960.

Leinhardt, G. (1994). History: A time to be mindful. In G. Leinhardt, I. L. Beck, & C. Stainton (Eds.), *Teaching and learning in history.* Hillsdale, NJ: Erlbaum.

Lennon, R., Eisenberg, N., & Carroll, J. L. (1983). The assessment of empathy in early childhood. *Journal of Applied Developmental Psychology, 4,* 295–302.

Leont'ev, A. N. (1981). *Problems of the development of mind.* Moscow: Progress.

Lerner, B. (1985). Self-esteem and excellence: The choice and the paradox. *American Educator, 9*(4), 10–16.

Lerner, J. W. (1985). *Learning disabilities: Theories, diagnosis, and teaching strategies* (4th ed.). Boston: Houghton Mifflin.

Levy, T. M., & Orlans, M. (2000). Attachment disorder and the adoptive family. In T. M. Levy et al. (Eds.), *Handbook of attachment interventions* (pp. 243–259). San Diego, CA: Academic Press.

Lewis, M. (1993). Self-conscious emotions: Embarrassment, pride, shame, and guilt. In M. Lewis & J. Haviland (Eds.), *The handbook of emotions* (pp. 563–573). New York: Guilford Press.

Lewis, M. (1995). Embarrassment: The emotion of self-exposure and evaluation. In J. Tangney & K. Fischer (Eds.), *Self-conscious emotions: The psychology of shame, guilt, embarrassment and pride* (pp. 198–218). New York: Guilford Press.

Lewis, M., Feiring, C., & Rosenthal, S. (2000). Attachment over time. *Child Development, 71,* 707–720.

Liben, L. S., & Downs, R. M. (1989). Understanding maps as symbols: The development of map concepts in children. In H. W. Reese (Ed.), *Advances in child development and behavior* (Vol. 22). San Diego, CA: Harcourt Brace Jovanovich.

Lidz, C. S. (1997). Dynamic assessment approaches. In D. P. Flanagan, J. L. Genshaft, & P. L. Harrison (Eds.), *Contemporary intellectual assessment: Theories, tests, and issues* (pp. 281–296). New York: Guilford Press.

Light, J. G., & Defries, J. C. (1995). Comorbidity of reading and mathematics disabilities: Genetic and environmental etiologies. *Journal of Learning Disabilities, 28,* 96–106.

Light, P., & Butterworth, G. (Eds.). (1993). *Context and cognition: Ways of learning and knowing.* Hillsdale, NJ: Erlbaum.

Lillard, A. (1999). Developing a cultural theory of mind: The CIAO approach. *Current Directions in Psychological Science, 8,* 57–61.

Lillard, A. S. (1993). Pretend play skills and the child's theory of mind. *Child Development, 64,* 348–371.

Lillard, A. S. (1998). Playing with a theory of mind. In O. N. Saracho & B. Spodek (Eds.), *Multiple perspectives on play in early childhood education.* Albany: State University of New York Press.

Linn, M. C., Clement, C., Pulos, S., & Sullivan, P. (1989). Scientific reasoning during adolescence: The influence of instruction in science knowledge and reasoning strategies. *Journal of Research in Science Teaching, 26,* 171–187.

Linn, M. C., Songer, N. B., & Eylon, B. (1996). Shifts and convergences in science learning and instruction. In D. C. Berliner & R. C. Calfee (Eds.), *Handbook of educational psychology.* New York: Macmillan.

Lipson, M. Y. (1983). The influence of religious affiliation on children's memory for text information. *Reading Research Quarterly, 18,* 448–457.

Little, T. D., Oettingen, G., Stetsenko, A., & Baltes, P. B. (1995). Children's action-control beliefs about school performance: How do American children compare with German and Russian children? *Journal of Personality and Social Psychology, 69,* 686–700.

Livesley, W. J., & Bromley, D. B. (1973). *Person perception in childhood and adolescence.* New York: Wiley.

Lobel, A. (1979). *Frog and Toad are friends.* New York: HarperCollins.

López del Bosque, R. (2000). Sticks and stones: What words are to self-esteem. *Intercultural Development Research Association Newsletter, 27*(5), 4–7, 16.

Lorch, E. P., Diener, M. B., Sanchez, R. P., Milich, R., Welsh, R., & van den Broek, P. (1999). The effects of story structure on the recall of stories in children with attention deficit hyperactivity disorder. *Journal of Educational Psychology, 91,* 251–260.

Lou, Y., Abrami, P. C., Spence, J. C., Poulsen, C., Chambers, B., & d'Apollonia, S. (1996). Within-class grouping: A meta-analysis. *Review of Educational Research, 66,* 423–458.

Lovell, K. (1979). Intellectual growth and the school curriculum. In F. B. Murray (Ed.), *The impact of Piagetian theory: On education, philosophy, psychiatry, and psychology.* Baltimore: University Park Press.

Lovett, S. B., & Flavell, J. H. (1990). Understanding and remembering: Children's knowledge about the differential effects of strategy and task variables on comprehension and memorization. *Child Development, 61,* 1842–1858.

Lowry, R., Sleet, D., Duncan, C., Powell, K., & Kolbe, L. (1995). Adolescents at risk for violence. *Educational Psychology Review, 7,* 7–39.

Lyon, T. D., & Flavell, J. H. (1994). Young children's understanding of "remember" and "forget." *Child Development, 65,* 1357–1371.

Lyytinen, P. (1991). Developmental trends in children's pretend play. *Child: Care, Health, and Development, 17,* 9–25.

Ma, X., & Kishor, N. (1997). Attitude toward self, social factors, and achievement in mathematics: A meta-analytic review. *Educational Psychology Review, 9,* 89–120.

Maccoby, E., & Martin, J. (1983). Socialization in the context of the family: Parent-child interaction. In P. H. Mussen (Series Ed.) & E. M. Hetherington (Vol. Ed.), *Handbook of child psychology: Vol. 4. Socialization, personality and social development* (4th ed., pp. 1–102). New York: Wiley.

Maccoby, E. E., & Hagen, J. W. (1965). Effects of distraction upon central versus incidental recall: Developmental trends. *Journal of Experimental Child Psychology, 2,* 280–289.

Magnusson, S. J., Boyle, R. A., & Templin, M. (1994, April). *Conceptual development: Re-examining knowledge construction in science.* Paper presented at the annual meeting of the American Educational Research Association, New Orleans, LA.

Main, M., & Solomon, J. (1986). Discovery of an insecure-disorganized/disoriented attachment pattern. In T. B. Brazelton & M. W. Yogman (Eds.), *Affective development in infancy* (pp. 95–124). Norwood, NJ: Ablex.

Main, M., & Solomon, J. (1990). Procedures for identifying infants as disorganized/disoriented during the Ainsworth Strange Situation. In M. T. Greenberg, D. Cicchetti, & E. M. Cummings (Eds.), *Attachment in the preschool years* (pp. 121–160). Chicago: University of Chicago Press.

Malatesta, C. Z., & Haviland, J. M. (1982). Learning display rules: The socialization of emotion expression in infancy. *Child Development, 53,* 991–1003.

Maloney, M. J., McGuire, J. B., & Daniels, S. R. (1988). Reliability testing of a children's version of the Eating Attitude Test. *Journal of the American Academy of Child and Adolescent Psychiatry, 27,* 541–543.

Manis, F. R. (1996). Current trends in dyslexia research. In B. J. Cratty & R. L. Goldman (Eds.), *Learning disabilities: Contemporary viewpoints.* Amsterdam: Harwood Academic.

Marcia, J. E. (1980). Identity in adolescence. In J. Adelson (Ed.), *Handbook of adolescent psychology.* New York: Wiley.

Marcia, J. E. (1988). Common processes underlying ego identity, cognitive/moral development, and individuation. In D. K. Lapsley & F. C. Power (Eds.), *Self, ego, and identity: Integrative approaches* (pp. 211–225). New York: Springer-Verlag.

Markman, E. M. (1977). Realizing that you don't understand: A preliminary investigation. *Child Development, 48,* 986–992.

Marsh, H. W. (1990a). Causal ordering of academic self-concept and academic achievement: A multiwave, longitudinal panel analysis. *Journal of Educational Psychology, 82,* 646–656.

Marsh, H. W. (1990b). A multidimensional, hierarchical model of self-concept: Theoretical and empirical justification. *Educational Psychology Review, 2,* 77–172.

Marsh, H. W., & Craven, R. (1997). Academic self-concept: Beyond the dustbowl. In G. D. Phye (Ed.), *Handbook of classroom assessment: Learning, achievement, and adjustment.* San Diego, CA: Academic Press.

Marsh, H. W., & Yeung, A. S. (1997). Coursework selection: Relations to academic self-concept and achievement. *American Educational Research Journal, 34,* 691–720.

Marsh, H. W., & Yeung, A. S. (1998). Longitudinal structural equation models of academic self-concept and achievement: Gender differences in the development of math and English constructs.

American Educational Research Journal, 35, 705–738.

Martin, C. L. (1991). The role of cognition in understanding gender effects. *Advances in Child Development and Behavior, 23,* 113–149.

Martin, C. L., & Halverson, C. F. (1981). A schematic processing model of sex typing and stereotyping in children. *Child Development, 52,* 1119–1134.

Masten, A. S., Neemann, J., & Andenas, S. (1994). Life events and adjustment in adolescents: The significance of event independence, desirability, and chronicity. *Journal of Research on Adolescence, 4,* 71–97.

Mastropieri, M. A., & Scruggs, T. E. (1992). Science for students with disabilities. *Review of Educational Research, 62,* 377–411.

Masur, E. F., McIntyre, C. W., & Flavell, J. H. (1973). Developmental changes in apportionment of study time among items in a multitrial free recall task. *Journal of Experimental Child Psychology, 15,* 237–246.

Mattison, R. E. (1992). Anxiety disorders. In S. R. Hooper, G. W. Hynd, & R. E. Mattison (Eds.), *Child psychopathology: Diagnostic criteria and clinical assessment* (pp. 179–202). Hillsdale, NJ: Erlbaum.

Mayer, R. E. (1992). *Thinking, problem solving, cognition* (2nd ed.). New York: Freeman.

Mayer, R. E. (1996). Learning strategies for making sense out of expository text: The SOI model for guiding three cognitive processes in knowledge construction. *Educational Psychology Review, 8,* 357–371.

McAdoo, H. P. (1985). Racial attitude and self-concept of young Black children over time. In H. P. McAdoo & J. L. McAdoo (Eds.), *Black children: Social, educational, and parental environments.* Newbury Park, CA: Sage.

McCaslin, M., & Good, T. L. (1996). The informal curriculum. In D. C. Berliner & R. C. Calfee (Eds.), *Handbook of educational psychology.* New York: Macmillan.

McCoy, K. (1994). *Understanding your teenager's depression.* New York: Perigee.

McDevitt, T. M., Spivey, N., Sheehan, E. P., Lennon, R., & Story, R. (1990). Children's beliefs about listening: Is it enough to be still and quiet? *Child Development, 61,* 713–721.

McKeown, M. G., & Beck, I. L. (1994). Making sense of accounts of history: Why young students don't and how they might. In G. Leinhardt, I. L. Beck, & C. Stainton (Eds.), *Teaching and learning in history.* Hillsdale, NJ: Erlbaum.

McLoyd, V. C. (1998). Socioeconomic disadvantage and child development. *American Psychologist, 53,* 185–204.

McMillan, J. H., Singh, J., & Simonetta, L. G. (1994). The tyranny of self-oriented self-esteem. *Educational Horizons, 72,* 141–145.

Meichenbaum, D. (1977). *Cognitive-behavior modification: An integrative approach.* New York: Plenum Press.

Meichenbaum, D. (1985). Teaching thinking: A cognitive-behavioral perspective. In S. F. Chipman, J. W. Segal, & R. Glaser (Eds.), *Thinking and learning skills: Vol. 2. Research and open questions.* Hillsdale, NJ: Erlbaum.

Meichenbaum, D., & Goodman, J. (1971). Training impulsive children to talk to themselves: A means of developing self-control. *Journal of Abnormal Psychology, 77,* 115–126.

Meindl, R. S. (1992). Human populations before agriculture. In S. Jones, R. Martin, D. Pilbeam, & S. Bunney (Eds.), *Cambridge encyclopedia of human evolution* (pp. 406–410). Cambridge, England: Cambridge University Press.

Meltzoff, A. N. (1988). Infant imitation after a 1-week delay: Long-term memory for novel acts and multiple stimuli. *Developmental Psychology, 24,* 470–476.

Mercer, C. D. (1997). *Students with learning disabilities* (5th ed.). Upper Saddle River, NJ: Merrill/Prentice Hall.

Mercer, C. D., Jordan, L., Allsopp, D. H., & Mercer, A. R. (1996). Learning disabilities definitions and criteria used by state education departments. *Learning Disabilities Quarterly, 19,* 217–231.

Metz, K. E. (1995). Reassessment of developmental constraints on children's science instruction. *Review of Educational Research, 65,* 93–127.

Metz, K. E. (1997). On the complex relation between cognitive developmental research and children's science curricula. *Review of Educational Research, 67,* 151–163.

Meyer, D. K., Turner, J. C., & Spencer, C. A. (1994, April). *Academic risk taking and motivation in an elementary mathematics classroom.* Paper presented at the annual meeting of the American Educational Research Association, New Orleans, LA.

Middleton, M. J. (1999, April). *Classroom effects on the gender gap in middle school students' math self-efficacy.* Paper presented at the annual meeting of the American Educational Research Association, Montreal, Canada.

Miller, D. (1994). Suicidal behavior of adolescents with behavior disorders and their peers without disabilities. *Behavioral Disorders, 20*(1), 61–68.

Miller, J. G. (1997). A cultural-psychology perspective on intelligence. In R. J. Sternberg & E. L. Grigorenko (Eds.), *Intelligence, heredity, and environment* (pp. 269–302). Cambridge, England: Cambridge University Press.

Mintzes, J. J., Trowbridge, J. E., Arnaudin, M. W., & Wandersee, J. H. (1991). Children's biology: Studies on conceptual development in the life sciences. In S. M. Glynn, R. H. Yeany, & B. K. Britton (Eds.), *The psychology of learning science.* Hillsdale, NJ: Erlbaum.

Miyake, K., Campos, J., Kagan, J., & Bradshaw, D. (1986). Issues in socioemotional development in Japan. In H. Azuma, K. Hakuta, & H. Stevenson (Eds.), *Kodomo: Child development and education in Japan* (pp. 238–261). San Francisco: Freeman.

Miyake, K., Chen, S.-J., & Campos, J. J. (1985). Infant temperament, mother's mode of interaction, and attachment in Japan: An interim report. In I. Bretherton & E. Waters (Eds.), Growing points of attachment theory and research. *Monographs of the Society for Research in Child Development, 50*(1–2, Serial No. 209), 276–297.

Morgan, M. (1985). Self-monitoring of attained subgoals in private study. *Journal of Educational Psychology, 77,* 623–630.

Murray, F. B. (1978). Teaching strategies and conservation training. In A. M. Lesgold, J. W. Pellegrino, S. D. Fokkema, & R. Glaser (Eds.), *Cognitive psychology and instruction.* New York: Plenum Press.

National Joint Committee on Learning Disabilities (1994). Learning disabilities: Issues on definition, a position paper of the National Joint Committee on Learning Disabilities. In *Collective perspectives on issues affecting learning disabilities: Position papers and statements.* Austin, TX: Pro-Ed.

Newcombe, N., & Huttenlocher, J. (1992). Children's early ability to solve perspective-taking problems. *Developmental Psychology, 28,* 635–643.

Newson, J., & Newson, E. (1975). Intersubjectivity and the transmission of culture: On the origins of symbolic functioning. *Bulletin of the British Psychological Society, 28,* 437–446.

NICHD Early Child Care Research Network (1997). The effects of infant child care on infant-mother attachment security: Results of the NICHD study of early child care. *Child Development, 68,* 860–879.

Nicholls, J. G. (1984). Conceptions of ability and achievement motivation. In R. Ames & C. Ames (Eds.), *Research on motivation in education: Vol. 1. Student motivation.* San Diego, CA: Academic Press.

Nolen-Hoeksema, S. (1987). Sex differences in unipolar depression: Evidence and theory. *Journal of Personality and Social Psychology, 101,* 259–282.

Nottelmann, E. D. (1987). Competence and self-esteem during transition from childhood to adolescence. *Developmental Psychology, 23,* 441–450.

Oatley, K., & Nundy, S. (1996). Rethinking the role of emotions in education. In D. R. Olson & N. Torrance (Eds.), *The handbook of education and human development: New models of learning, teaching, and schooling.* Cambridge, MA: Blackwell.

Oliver, J. M., Cole, N. H., & Hollingsworth, H. (1991). Learning disabilities as functions of familial learning problems and developmental problems. *Exceptional Children, 57,* 427–440.

Olneck, M. R. (1995). Immigrants and education. In J. A. Banks & C. A. M. Banks (Eds.), *Handbook of research on multicultural education.* New York: Macmillan.

O'Malley, P. M., & Bachman, J. G. (1983). Self-esteem: Change and stability between ages 13 and 23. *Developmental Psychology, 19,* 257–268.

O'Reilly, A. W. (1995). Using representations: Comprehension and production of actions with imagined objects. *Child Development, 66,* 999–1010.

Ormrod, J. E., & Jenkins, L. (1989). Study strategies in spelling: Correlations with achievement and developmental changes. *Perceptual and Motor Skills, 68,* 643–650.

Ormrod, J. E., & Wagner, E. D. (1987, October). *Spelling conscience in undergraduate students: Ratings of spelling accuracy and dictionary use.* Paper presented at the annual meeting of the Northern Rocky Mountain Educational Research Association, Park City, UT.

Owens, R. E., Jr. (1996). *Language development* (4th ed.). Boston: Allyn & Bacon.

Packard, V. (1983). *Our endangered children: Growing up in a changing world.* Boston: Little, Brown.

Pajares, F. (1996). Self-efficacy beliefs in academic settings. *Review of Educational Research, 66,* 543–578.

Pang, V. O. (1995). Asian Pacific American students: A diverse and complex population. In J. A. Banks & C. A. M. Banks (Eds.), *Handbook of research on multicultural education.* New York: Macmillan.

Panksepp, J. (1998). Attention deficit hyperactivity disorders, psychostimulants, and intolerance of childhood playfulness: A tragedy in the making? *Current Directions in Psychological Science, 7,* 91–98.

Paris, S. G., & Ayres, L. R. (1994). *Becoming reflective students and teachers with portfolios and authentic assessment.* Washington, DC: American Psychological Association.

Paris, S. G., & Cunningham, A. E. (1996). Children becoming students. In D. C. Berliner & R. C. Calfee (Eds.), *Handbook of educational psychology.* New York: Macmillan.

Parsons, J. E., Kaczala, C. M., & Meece, J. L. (1982). Socialization of achievement attitudes and beliefs: Classroom influences. *Child Development, 53,* 322–339.

Pascarella, E. T., & Terenzini, P. T. (1991). *How college affects students: Findings and insights from twenty years of research.* San Francisco: Jossey-Bass.

Patterson, G. R., DeBaryshe, B. D., & Ramsey, E. (1989). A developmental perspective on antisocial behavior. *American Psychologist, 44,* 329–335.

Pederson, D. R., Rook-Green, A., & Elder, J. L. (1981). The role of action in the development of pretend play in young children. *Developmental Psychology, 17,* 756–759.

Pellegrini, A. D., & Bjorklund, D. F. (1997). The role of recess in children's cognitive performance. *Educational Psychologist, 32,* 35–40.

Pellegrini, A. D., & Horvat, M. (1995). A developmental contextualist critique of attention deficit hyperactivity disorder. *Educational Researcher, 24*(1), 13–19.

Perkins, D. (1992). *Smart schools: From training memories to educating minds.* New York: Free Press/Macmillan.

Perner, J. (1991). *Understanding the representational mind.* Cambridge, MA: MIT Press.

Perry, N. E. (1998). Young children's self-regulated learning and contexts that support it. *Journal of Educational Psychology, 90,* 715–729.

Perry, W. G., Jr. (1968). *Forms of intellectual and ethical development in the college years.* Cambridge, MA: President and Fellows of Harvard College.

Peterson, P. L. (1992). Revising their thinking: Keisha Coleman and her third-grade mathematics class. In H. H. Marshall (Ed.), *Redefining student learning: Roots of educational change.* Norwood, NJ: Ablex.

Pettito, A. L. (1985). Division of labor: Procedural learning in teacher-led small groups. *Cognition and Instruction, 2,* 233–270.

Phelan, P., Yu, H. C., & Davidson, A. L. (1994). Navigating the psychosocial pressures of adolescence: The voices and experiences of high school youth. *American Educational Research Journal, 31,* 415–447.

Phinney, J. (1989). Stages of ethnic identity development in minority group adolescents. *Journal of Early Adolescence, 9,* 34–39.

Piaget, J. (1928). *Judgment and reasoning in the child* (M. Warden, Trans.). New York: Harcourt, Brace.

Piaget, J. (1929). *The child's conception of the world.* New York: Harcourt, Brace.

Piaget, J. (1952a). *The child's conception of number* (C. Gattegno & F. M. Hodgson, Trans.). London: Routledge & Kegan Paul.

Piaget, J. (1952b). *The origins of intelligence in children.* New York: International Universities Press.

Piaget, J. (1959). *The language and thought of the child* (3rd ed.; M. Gabain, Trans.). London: Routledge & Kegan Paul.

Piaget, J. (1970). Piaget's theory. In P. H. Mussen (Ed.), *Carmichael's manual of psychology.* New York: Wiley.

Piaget, J., & Inhelder, B. (1969). *The psychology of the child* (H. Weaver, Trans.). New York: Basic Books.

Piche, C., & Plante, C. (1991). Perceived masculinity, femininity, and androgyny among primary school boys: Relationships with the adaptation level of these students and the attitudes of the teachers towards them. *European Journal of Psychology of Education, 6,* 423–435.

Pick, A. D., & Frankel, G. W. (1974). A developmental study of strategies of visual selectivity. *Child Development, 45,* 1162–1165.

Pintrich, P. R., & Garcia, T. (1994). Regulating motivation and cognition in the classroom: The role of self-schemas and self-regulatory strategies. In D. Schunk & B. Zimmerman (Eds.), *Self-regulation of learning and performance: Issues and educational applications.* Hillsdale, NJ: Erlbaum.

Pintrich, P. R., & Schunk, D. H. (1996). *Motivation in education: Theory, research, and applications.* Upper Saddle River, NJ: Merrill/Prentice Hall.

Pipher, M. (1994). *Reviving Ophelia: Saving the selves of adolescent girls.* New York: Putnam.

Plumert, J. M. (1994). Flexibility in children's use of spatial and categorical organizational strategies in recall. *Developmental Psychology, 30,* 738–747.

Pogrow, S., & Londer, G. (1994). The effects of an intensive general thinking program on the motivation and cognitive development of at-risk students: Findings from the HOTS program. In H. F. O'Neil, Jr., & M. Drillings (Eds.), *Motivation: Theory and research.* Hillsdale, NJ: Erlbaum.

Pollack, W. (1998). *Real boys: Rescuing our sons from the myths of boyhood.* New York: Henry Holt.

Posner, G. J., Strike, K. A., Hewson, P. W., & Gertzog, W. A. (1982). Accommodation of a scientific conception: Toward a theory of conceptual change. *Science Education, 66,* 211–227.

Powell, G. J. (1983). *The psychosocial development of minority children.* New York: Brunner/Mazel.

Powers, S. I., Hauser, S. T., & Kilner, L. A. (1989). Adolescent mental health. *American Psychologist, 44,* 200–208.

Prawat, R. S. (1989). Promoting access to knowledge, strategy, and disposition in students: A research synthesis. *Review of Educational Research, 59,* 1–41.

Pressley, M. (1982). Elaboration and memory development. *Child Development, 53,* 296–309.

Pressley, M., El-Dinary, P. B., Marks, M. B., Brown, R., & Stein, S. (1992). Good strategy instruction is motivating and interesting. In K. A. Renninger, S. Hidi, & A. Krapp (Eds.), *The role of interest in learning and development.* Hillsdale, NJ: Erlbaum.

Pressley, M., Levin, J. R., & Ghatala, E. S. (1984). Memory strategy monitoring in adults and children. *Journal of Verbal Learning and Verbal Behavior, 23,* 270–288.

Pressley, M., Ross, K. A., Levin, J. R., & Ghatala, E. S. (1984). The role of strategy utility knowledge in children's strategy decision making. *Journal of Experimental Child Psychology, 38,* 491–504.

Price-Williams, D. R., Gordon, W., & Ramirez, M. (1969). Skill and conservation. *Developmental Psychology, 1,* 769.

Pritchard, R. (1990). The effects of cultural schemata on reading processing strategies. *Reading Research Quarterly, 25,* 273–295.

Pulos, S., & Linn, M. C. (1981). Generality of the controlling variables scheme in early adolescence. *Journal of Early Adolescence, 1,* 26–37.

Purdie, N., & Hattie, J. (1996). Cultural differences in the use of strategies for self-regulated learning. *American Educational Research Journal, 33,* 845–871.

Purdie, N., Hattie, J., & Douglas, G. (1996). Student conceptions of learning and their use of self-regulated learning strategies: A cross-cultural comparison. *Journal of Educational Psychology, 88,* 87–100.

Rabinowitz, M., & Glaser, R. (1985). Cognitive structure and process in highly competent performance. In F. D. Horowitz & M. O'Brien (Eds.), *The gifted and the talented: Developmental perspectives.* Washington, DC: American Psychological Association.

Radziszewska, B., & Rogoff, B. (1991). Children's guided participation in planning imaginary errands with skilled adult or peer partners. *Developmental Psychology, 27,* 381–389.

Renninger, K. A., Hidi, S., & Krapp, A. (Eds.). (1992). *The role of interest in learning and development.* Hillsdale, NJ: Erlbaum.

Resnick, L. B. (1989). Developing mathematical knowledge. *American Psychologist, 44,* 162–169.

Reyna, V. F. (1996, May 2). Fuzzy-trace theory, reasoning, and decision-making. Presentation at the University of Northern Colorado, Greeley.

Reynolds, R. E., Taylor, M. A., Steffensen, M. S., Shirey, L. L., & Anderson, R. C. (1982). Cultural schemata and reading comprehension. *Reading Research Quarterly, 17,* 353–366.

Roberge, J. J. (1970). A study of children's abilities to reason with basic principles of deductive reasoning. *American Educational Research Journal, 7,* 583–596.

Rogoff, B. (1990). *Apprenticeship in thinking: Cognitive development in social context.* New York: Oxford University Press.

Rogoff, B. (1991). Social interaction as apprenticeship in thinking: Guidance and participation in spatial planning. In L. B. Resnick, J. M. Levine, & S. D. Teasley (Eds.), *Perspectives on socially shared cognition.* Washington, DC: American Psychological Association.

Rogoff, B., Mistry, J., Göncü, A., & Mosier, C. (1993). Guided participation in cultural activity by toddlers and caregivers. *Monographs of the Society for Research in Child Development, 58* (8, Serial No. 236).

Rosenberg, M. (1986). Self-concept from middle childhood through adolescence. In S. Suls & A. Greenwald (Eds.), *Psychological perspectives on the self* (Vol. 3, pp. 107–135). Hillsdale, NJ: Erlbaum.

Rosenshine, B., & Meister, C. (1992). The use of scaffolds for teaching higher-level cognitive strategies. *Educational Leadership, 49*(7), 26–33.

Rosenshine, B., Meister, C., & Chapman, S. (1996). Teaching students to generate questions: A review of the intervention studies. *Review of Educational Research, 66,* 181–221.

Rosenstein, D., & Oster, H. (1988). Differential facial responses to four basic tastes in newborns. *Child Development, 59,* 1555–1568.

Ross, J. A. (1988). Controlling variables: A meta-analysis of training studies. *Review of Educational Research, 58,* 405–437.

Rosser, R. (1994). *Cognitive development: Psychological and biological perspectives.* Boston: Allyn & Bacon.

Rossman, B. B. R. (1992). School-age children's perceptions of coping with distress: Strategies for emotion regulation and the moderation of adjustment. *Journal of Child Psychology and Psychiatry, 33,* 1373–1397.

Roth, K. J. (1990). Developing meaningful conceptual understanding in science. In B. F. Jones & L. Idol (Eds.), *Dimensions of thinking and cognitive instruction.* Hillsdale, NJ: Erlbaum.

Roth, K. J., & Anderson, C. (1988). Promoting conceptual change learning from science textbooks. In P. Ramsden (Ed.), *Improving learning: New perspectives.* London: Kogan Page.

Roth, W., & Bowen, G. M. (1995). Knowing and interacting: A study of culture, practices, and resources in a grade 8 open-inquiry science classroom guided by a cognitive apprenticeship metaphor. *Cognition and Instruction, 13,* 73–128.

Rothbart, M. K., & Ahadi, S. A. (1994). Temperament and the development of personality. *Journal of Abnormal Psychology, 103,* 55–66.

Rothbart, M. K., & Bates, J. E. (1998). Temperament. In W. Damon (Editor-in-Chief) &

N. Eisenberg (Vol. Ed.), *Handbook of child psychology: Vol. 3. Social, emotional, and personality development* (5th ed., pp. 105–176). New York: Wiley.

Rothbaum, F., Weisz, J., Pott, M., Miyake, K., & Morelli, G. (2000). Attachment and culture: Security in the United States and Japan. *American Psychologist, 55,* 1093–1104.

Rowe, E. (1999, April). *Gender differences in math self-concept development: The role of classroom interaction.* Paper presented at the annual meeting of the American Educational Research Association, Montreal, Canada.

Rubin, K., Fein, G., & Vandenberg, B. (1983). Play. In E. M. Hetherington (Ed.), *Handbook of child psychology: Vol. 4. Socialization, personality, and social development* (pp. 693–774). New York: Wiley.

Ruble, D. N., & Martin, C. L. (1998). Gender development. In W. Damon (Editor-in-Chief) & N. Eisenberg (Vol. Ed.), *Handbook of child psychology: Vol. 3. Social, emotional, and personality development* (5th ed., pp. 933–1016). New York: Wiley.

Rudlin, C. R. (1993). Growth and sexual development: What is normal, and what is not? *Journal of the American Academy of Physician Assistants, 6,* 25–35.

Ruff, H. A., & Lawson, K. R. (1990). Development of sustained, focused attention in young children during free play. *Developmental Psychology, 26,* 85–93.

Ruffman, T., Perner, J., Olson, D. R., & Doherty, M. (1993). Reflecting on scientific thinking: Children's understanding of the hypothesis-evidence relation. *Child Development, 64,* 1617–1636.

Rutter, M., & Garmezy, N. (1983). Developmental psychopathology. In P. H. Mussen (Series Ed.) & E. M. Hetherington (Vol. Ed.), *Handbook of child psychology: Vol. 4. Socialization, personality, and social development* (4th ed., pp. 775–911). New York: Wiley.

Ryan, E. B., Ledger, G. W., & Weed, K. A. (1987). Acquisition and transfer of an integrative imagery strategy by young children. *Child Development, 58,* 443–452.

Ryan, R. M., & Kuczkowski, R. (1994). The imaginary audience, self-consciousness, and public individuation in adolescence. *Journal of Personality, 62,* 219–237.

Ryan, R. M., & Lynch, J. H. (1989). Emotional autonomy versus detachment: Revisiting the vicissitudes of adolescence and young adulthood. *Child Development, 60,* 340–356.

Ryan, R. M., Stiller, J. D., & Lynch, J. H. (1994). Representations of relationships to teachers, parents, and friends as predictors of academic motivation and self-esteem. *Journal of Early Adolescence, 14,* 226–249.

Saarni, C., Mumme, D. L., & Campos, J. J. (1998). Emotional development: Action, communication, and understanding. In W. Damon (Editor-in-Chief) & N. Eisenberg (Vol. Ed.), *Handbook of child psychology: Vol. 3. Social, emotional, and personality development* (5th ed., pp. 237–309). New York: Wiley.

Sadker, M. P., & Sadker, D. (1994). *Failing at fairness: How our schools cheat girls.* New York: Touchstone.

Sagi, A., & Lewkowicz, K. S. (1987). A cross-cultural evaluation of attachment research. In L. W. C. Tavecchio & M. H. van Ijzendoorn (Eds.), *Attachment in social networks* (pp. 427–459). Amsterdam, The Netherlands: Elsevier.

Savin-Williams, R. C., & Demo, D. H. (1984). Developmental change and stability in adolescent self-concept. *Developmental Psychology, 20,* 1100–1110.

Schimmoeller, M. A. (1998, April). *Influence of private speech on the writing behaviors of young children: Four case studies.* Paper presented at the annual meeting of the American Educational Research Association, San Diego, CA.

Schliemann, A. D., & Carraher, D. W. (1993). Proportional reasoning in and out of school. In P. Light and G. Butterworth (Eds.), *Context and cognition: Ways of learning and knowing.* Hillsdale, NJ: Erlbaum.

Schneider, W., & Pressley, M. (1989). *Memory development between 2 and 20.* New York: Springer-Verlag.

Schneider, W., & Shiffrin, R. M. (1977). Controlled and automatic human information processing: I. Detection, search, and attention. *Psychological Review, 84,* 1–66.

Schommer, M. (1994a). An emerging conceptualization of epistemological beliefs and their role in learning. In R. Garner & P. A. Alexander (Eds.), *Beliefs about text and instruction with text.* Hillsdale, NJ: Erlbaum.

Schommer, M. (1994b). Synthesizing epistemological belief research: Tentative understandings and provocative confusions. *Educational Psychology Review, 6,* 293–319.

Schommer, M. (1997). The development of epistemological beliefs among secondary students: A longitudinal study. *Journal of Educational Psychology, 89,* 37–40.

Schonert-Reichl, K. A. (1993). Empathy and social relationships in adolescents with behavioral disorders. *Behavioral Disorders, 18,* 189–204.

Schraw, G., Potenza, M. T., & Nebelsick-Gullet, L. (1993). Constraints on the calibration of performance. *Contemporary Educational Psychology, 18,* 455–463.

Schreibman, L. (1988). *Autism.* Newbury Park, CA: Sage.

Schroth, M. L. (1992). The effects of delay of feedback on a delayed concept formation transfer task. *Contemporary Educational Psychology, 17,* 78–82.

Schunk, D. H., & Zimmerman, B. J. (1997). Social origins of self-regulatory competence. *Educational Psychologist, 32,* 195–208.

Schwartz, G. M., Izard, C. E., & Ansul, S. E. (1985). The 5-month-old's ability to discriminate facial expressions of emotion. *Infant Behavior and Development, 8,* 65–67.

Seligman, M. E. P. (1991). *Learned optimism.* New York: Knopf.

Selman, R. L. (1980). *The growth of interpersonal understanding.* San Diego, CA: Academic Press.

Shaffer, D. R. (1988). *Social and personality development* (2nd ed.). Pacific Grove, CA: Brooks/Cole.

Sheingold, K. (1973). Developmental differences in intake and storage of visual information. *Journal of Experimental Child Psychology, 16,* 1–11.

Short, E. J., Schatschneider, C. W., & Friebert, S. E. (1993). Relationship between memory and metamemory performance: A comparison of specific and general strategy knowledge. *Journal of Educational Psychology, 85,* 412–423.

Shuell, T. J. (1996). Teaching and learning in a classroom context. In D. C. Berliner & R. C. Calfee (Eds.), *Handbook of educational psychology.* New York: Macmillan.

Shulman, S., Elicker, J., & Sroufe, L. A. (1994). Stages of friendship growth in preadolescence as related to attachment history. *Journal of Social and Personal Relationships, 11,* 341–361.

Siegler, R. S. (1976). Three aspects of cognitive development. *Cognitive Psychology, 8,* 481–520.

Siegler, R. S. (1978). The origins of scientific reasoning. In R. S. Siegler (Ed.), *Children's thinking: What develops?* Hillsdale, NJ: Erlbaum.

Siegler, R. S. (1981). Developmental sequences within and between concepts. *Monographs of the Society for Research in Child Development, 46*(2, Serial No. 189).

Siegler, R. S. (1989). Mechanisms of cognitive growth. *Annual Review of Psychology, 40,* 353–379.

Siegler, R. S. (1991). *Children's thinking* (2nd ed.). Upper Saddle River, NJ: Prentice Hall.

Siegler, R. S. (1996a). A grand theory of development. In R. Case & Y. Okamoto, in collaboration with S. Griffin, A. McKeough, C. Bleiker, B. Henderson, & K. M. Stephenson (1996). The role of central conceptual structures in the development of children's thought. *Monographs of the Society for Research in Child Development, 61*(1, Serial No. 246).

Siegler, R. S. (1996b). *Emerging minds: The process of change in children's thinking.* New York: Oxford University Press.

Siegler, R. S., & Ellis, S. (1996). Piaget on childhood. *Psychological Science, 7,* 211–215.

Siegler, R. S., & Jenkins, E. (1989). *How children discover new strategies.* Hillsdale, NJ: Erlbaum.

Siegler, R. S., & Richards, D. D. (1982). The development of intelligence. In R. J. Sternberg (Ed.), *Handbook of human intelligence.* Cambridge, England: Cambridge University Press.

Siever, L., & Davis, K. (1985). Overview: Toward a dysregulation hypothesis of depression. *American Journal of Psychiatry, 142,* 1017–1031.

Silver, E. A., & Kenney, P. A. (1995). Sources of assessment information for instructional guidance in mathematics. In T. Romberg (Ed.), *Reform in school mathematics and authentic assessment.* Albany: State University of New York Press.

Simmons, R. G., & Blyth, D. A. (1987). *Moving into adolescence: The impact of pubertal change and school context.* New York: Aldine de Gruyter.

Slaby, R. G., & Frey, K. S. (1975). Development of gender constancy and selective attention to same-sex models. *Child Development, 52,* 849–856.

Slater, A. M., Mattock, A., & Brown, E. (1990). Size constancy at birth: Newborn infants' responses to retinal and real size. *Journal of Experimental Child Psychology, 49,* 314–322.

Slater, A. M., & Morison, V. (1985). Shape constancy and slant perception at birth. *Perception, 14,* 337–344.

Slusher, M. P., & Anderson, C. A. (1996). Using causal persuasive arguments to change beliefs and teach new information: The mediating role of explanation availability and evaluation bias in the acceptance of knowledge. *Journal of Educational Psychology, 88,* 110–122.

Smith, C., Maclin, D., Grosslight, L., & Davis, H. (1997). Teaching for understanding: A study of students' preinstruction theories of matter and a comparison of the effectiveness of two approaches to teaching about matter and density. *Cognition and Instruction, 15,* 317–393.

Smith, N. R., Cicchetti, L., Clark, M. C., Fucigna, C., Gordon-O'Connor, B., Halley, B. A., & Kennedy, M. (1998). *Observation drawing with children: A framework for teachers.* New York: Teachers College Press.

Solomon, D., Watson, M., Battistich, E., Schaps, E., & Delucchi, K. (1992). Creating a caring community: Educational practices that promote children's prosocial development. In F. K. Oser, A.

Dick, & J. L. Patry (Eds.), *Effective and responsible teaching: The new synthesis.* San Francisco: Jossey-Bass.

Sorce, J. F., Emde, R. N., Campos, J., & Klinnert, M. D. (1985). Maternal emotional signaling: Its effects on the visual cliff behavior of 1-year-olds. *Developmental Psychology, 21,* 195–200.

Sosniak, L. A., & Stodolsky, S. S. (1994). Making connections: Social studies education in an urban fourth-grade classroom. In J. Brophy (Ed.), *Advances in research on teaching: Vol. 4. Case studies of teaching and learning in social studies.* Greenwich, CT: JAI Press.

Spelke, E. S. (1994). Initial knowledge: Six suggestions. *Cognition, 50,* 431–445.

Spencer, M. B., & Markstrom-Adams, C. (1990). Identity processes among racial and ethnic minority children in America. *Child Development, 61,* 290–310.

Sroufe, L. A. (1983). Infant-caregiver attachment and patterns of adaptation in preschool: The roots of maladaptation and competence. In M. Perlmutter (Ed.), Development and policy concerning children with special needs. *Minnesota Symposium on Child Psychology, 16,* 41–83. Hillsdale, NJ: Erlbaum.

Sroufe, L. A., Carlson, E., & Shulman, S. (1993). Individuals in relationships: Development from infancy through adolescence. In D. C. Funder, R. D. Parke, C. Tomlinson-Keasey, & K. Widaman (Eds.), *Studying lives through time: Personality and development* (pp. 315–342). Washington, DC: American Psychological Association.

Stein, R. (1996). Physical self-concept. In B. A. Bracken (Ed.), *Handbook of self-concept: Developmental, social, and clinical considerations* (pp. 374–394). New York: Wiley.

Steiner, J. E. (1979). Human facial expression in response to taste and smell stimulation. In H. W. Reese & L. P. Lipsitt (Eds.), *Advances in child development and behavior* (Vol. 13). New York: Academic Press.

Stenberg, C., & Campos, J. (1990). The development of anger expressions in infancy. In N. Stein, B. Leventhal, & T. Trabasso (Eds.), *Psychological and biological approaches to emotion* (pp. 247–282). Hillsdale, NJ: Erlbaum.

Stevens, R. J., & Slavin, R. E. (1995). The cooperative elementary school: Effects of students' achievement, attitudes, and social relations. *American Educational Research Journal, 32,* 321–351.

Stevenson, H. W., Chen, C., & Uttal, D. H. (1990). Beliefs and achievement: A study of black, white, and Hispanic children. *Child Development, 61,* 508–523.

Stipek, D. J. (1981). Children's perceptions of their own and their classmates' ability. *Journal of Educational Psychology, 73,* 404–410.

Stipek, D. J. (1993). *Motivation to learn: From theory to practice* (2nd ed.). Needham Heights, MA: Allyn & Bacon.

Stipek, D. J. (1996). Motivation and instruction. In D. C. Berliner & R. C. Calfee (Eds.), *Handbook of educational psychology.* New York: Macmillan.

Stodolsky, S. S. (1974). How children find something to do in preschools. *Genetic Psychology Monographs, 90,* 245–303.

Strike, K. A., & Posner, G. J. (1992). A revisionist theory of conceptual change. In R. A. Duschl & R. J. Hamilton (Eds.), *Philosophy of science, cognitive psychology, and educational theory and practice.* Albany: State University of New York Press.

Strutt, G. F., Anderson, D. R., & Well, A. D. (1975). A developmental study of the effects of

irrelevant information on speeded classification. *Journal of Experimental Child Psychology, 20,* 127–135.

Sullivan, R. C. (1994). Autism: Definitions past and present. *Journal of Vocational Rehabilitation, 4,* 4–9.

Sund, R. B. (1976). *Piaget for educators.* Columbus, OH: Charles E. Merrill.

Susman, E. J., Inoff-Germain, G., Nottelmann, E. D., Loriaux, D. L., Cutler, J., Gordon, B., & Chrousos, G. P. (1987). Hormones, emotional dispositions, and aggressive attributes in young adolescents. *Child Development, 58,* 1114–1134.

Sutton-Smith, B. (Ed.). (1979). *Play and learning.* New York: Gardner Press.

Swann, W. B., Jr. (1997). The trouble with change: Self-verification and allegiance to the self. *Psychological Science, 8,* 177–180.

Swanson, H. L. (1993). An information processing analysis of learning disabled children's problem solving. *American Educational Research Journal, 30,* 861–893.

Swanson, H. L., & Cooney, J. B. (1991). Learning disabilities and memory. In B. Y. L. Wong (Ed.), *Learning about learning disabilities.* San Diego, CA: Academic Press.

Sylvester, R. (1995). *A celebration of neurosis: An educator's guide to the human brain.* Alexandria, VA: Association for Supervision and Curriculum Development.

Takahashi, K. (1990). Are the key assumptions of the "Strange Situation" procedure universal? A view from Japanese research. *Human Development, 33,* 23–30.

Tamburrini, J. (1982). Some educational implications of Piaget's theory. In S. Modgil and C. Modgil (Eds.), *Jean Piaget: Consensus and controversy.* New York: Praeger.

Taylor, M., Esbensen, B. M., & Bennett, R. T. (1994). Children's understanding of knowledge acquisition: The tendency for children to report that they have always known what they have just learned. *Child Development, 65,* 1581–1604.

Tellegren, A., Lykken, D. T., Bouchard, T. J., & Wilcox, K. J. (1988). Personality similarity in twins reared apart and together. *Journal of Personality and Social Psychology, 54,* 1031–1039.

Thomas, J. W. (1993). Promoting independent learning in the middle grades: The role of instructional support practices. *Elementary School Journal, 93,* 575–591.

Thomas, S. P., Groër, M., & Droppleman, P. (1993). Physical health of today's school children. *Educational Psychology Review, 5,* 5–33.

Thompson, R. A. (1998). Early sociopersonality development. In W. Damon (Editor-in-Chief) & N. Eisenberg (Vol. Ed.), *Handbook of child psychology: Vol. 3. Social, emotional, and personality development* (5th ed., pp. 25–104). New York: Wiley.

Thornton, M. C., Chatters, L. M., Taylor, R. J., & Allen, W. (1990). Sociodemographic and environmental correlates of racial socialization by Black parents. *Child Development, 61,* 401–409.

Tobias, S. (1977). A model for research on the effect of anxiety on instruction. In J. E. Sieber, H. F. O'Neil, Jr., & S. Tobias (Eds.), *Anxiety, learning, and instruction.* Hillsdale, NJ: Erlbaum.

Tourniaire, F., & Pulos, S. (1985). Proportional reasoning: A review of the literature. *Educational Studies in Mathematics, 16,* 181–204.

Trainor, L. J., Austin, C. M., & Desjardins, R. N. (2000). Is infant-directed speech prosody a result of the vocal expression of emotion? *Psychological Science, 11,* 188–195.

Trawick-Smith, J. (1997). *Early childhood development: A multicultural perspective.* Upper Saddle River, NJ: Merrill/Prentice Hall.

Treffert, D. A. (1989). *Extraordinary people: Understanding Savant syndrome.* New York: Harper & Row.

Turnbull, A., Turnbull, R., Shank, M., & Leal, D. (1999). *Exceptional lives: Special education in today's schools* (2nd ed.). Upper Saddle River, NJ: Merrill/Prentice Hall.

Urban, J., Carlson, E., Egeland, B., & Sroufe, L. A. (1991). Patterns of individual adaptation across childhood. *Development and Psychopathology, 3,* 445–460.

U.S. Department of Education (1996). *To assure the free appropriate public education of all children with disabilities: Eighteenth annual report to Congress on the implementation of the Individuals with Disabilities Education Act.* Washington, DC: Author.

Uttal, D. H., Marzolf, D. P., Pierroutsakos, S. L., Smith, C. M., Troseth, G. L., Scudder, K. V., & DeLoache, J. S. (1998). Seeing through symbols: The development of children's understanding of symbolic relations. In O. N. Saracho & B. Spodek (Eds.), *Multiple perspectives on play in early childhood education.* Albany: State University of New York Press.

Vandenberg, B. (1978). Play and development from an ethological perspective. *American Psychologist, 33,* 724–738.

van Laar, C. (2000). The paradox of low academic achievement but high self-esteem in African American students: An attributional account. *Educational Psychology Review, 12,* 33–61.

Vaughn, B. E., Egeland, B., Sroufe, L. A., & Waters, E. (1979). Individual differences in infant-mother attachment at twelve and eighteen months: Stability and change in families under stress. *Child Development, 50,* 971–975.

Vosniadou, S. (1991). Conceptual development in astronomy. In S. M. Glynn, R. H. Yeany, & B. K. Britton (Eds.), *The psychology of learning science.* Hillsdale, NJ: Erlbaum.

Vosniadou, S. (1994). Universal and culture-specific properties of children's mental models of the earth. In L. A. Hirschfeld & S. A. Gelman (Eds.), *Mapping the mind: Domain specificity in cognition and culture.* Cambridge, England: Cambridge University Press.

Vosniadou, S., & Brewer, W. F. (1987). Theories of knowledge restructuring in development. *Review of Educational Research, 57,* 51–67.

Vygotsky, L. S. (1962). *Thought and language* (E. Haufmann & G. Vakar, Eds. and Trans.). Cambridge, MA: MIT Press.

Vygotsky, L. S. (1978). *Mind in society: The development of higher psychological processes.* Cambridge, MA: Harvard University Press.

Vygotsky, L. S. (1987). *The collected works of L. S. Vygotsky* (R. W. Rieber & A. S. Carton, Eds.). New York: Plenum Press.

Vygotsky, L. S. (1997). *Educational psychology.* Boca Raton, FL: St. Lucie Press.

Waters, E., Merrick, S., Treboux, D., Crowell, J., Albersheim, L. (2000). Attachment security in infancy and early adulthood: A twenty-year longitudinal study. *Child Development, 71,* 684–689.

Waters, H. S. (1982). Memory development in adolescence: Relationships between metamemory, strategy use, and performance. *Journal of Experimental Child Psychology, 33,* 183–195.

Way, N. (1998). *Everyday courage: The lives and stories of urban teenagers.* New York: New York University Press.

Webb, N. M., & Palincsar, A. S. (1996). Group processes in the classroom. In D. C. Berliner & R. C. Calfee (Eds.), *Handbook of educational psychology.* New York: Macmillan.

Webster-Stratton, C., & Hammond, M. (1999). Marital conflict management skills, parenting style, and early-onset conduct problems: Processes and pathways. *Journal of Child Psychology & Psychiatry & Allied Disciplines, 40,* 917–927.

Weinfeld, N. S., Sroufe, L. A., & Egeland, B. (2000). Attachment from infancy to early adulthood in a high-risk sample: Continuity, discontinuity, and their correlates. *Child Development, 71,* 695–702.

Weissglass, J. (1998). *Ripples of hope: Building relationships for educational change.* Santa Barbara, CA: Center for Educational Change in Mathematics and Science, University of California.

Wellman, H., Harris, P. L., Banerjee, M., & Sinclair, A. (1995). Early understanding of emotion: Evidence from natural language. *Cognition and Emotion, 9,* 117–149.

Wellman, H. M. (1985). The child's theory of mind: The development of conceptions of cognition. In S. R. Yussen (Ed.), *The growth of reflection in children.* San Diego, CA: Academic Press.

Wellman, H. M. (1988). The early development of memory strategies. In F. Weinert & M. Perlmutter (Eds.), *Memory development: Universal changes and individual differences.* Hillsdale, NJ: Erlbaum.

Wellman, H. M. (1990). *The child's theory of mind.* Cambridge, MA: MIT Press.

Wellman, H. M., & Estes, D. (1986). Early understanding of mental entities: A reexamination of childhood realism. *Child Development, 57,* 910–923.

Wellman, H. M., & Gelman, S. A. (1992). Cognitive development: Foundational theories of core domains. In M. R. Rosenzweig & L. W. Porter (Eds.), *Annual review of psychology* (Vol. 43). Palo Alto, CA: Annual Reviews, Inc.

Wellman, H. M., & Hickling, A. K. (1994). The mind's "I": Children's conception of the mind as an active agent. *Child Development, 65,* 1564–1580.

Wellman, H. M., & Woolley, J. D. (1990). From simple desires to ordinary beliefs: The early development of everyday psychology. *Cognition, 35,* 245–275.

Werner, E. E., & Smith, R. S. (1982). *Vulnerable but invincible: A longitudinal study of resilient children.* New York: McGraw-Hill.

Wertsch, J. V. (1984). The zone of proximal development: Some conceptual issues. *Children's learning in the zone of proximal development: New directions for child development* (No. 23). San Francisco: Jossey-Bass.

Whiting, B. B., & Edwards, C. P. (1988). *Children of different worlds.* Cambridge, MA: Harvard University Press.

Whiting, J. (1981). Environmental constraint on infant care practices. In R. H. Munroe, R. L. Munroe, & B. Whiting (Eds.), *Handbook of cross-cultural development.* New York: Garland STPM Press.

Wiesel, T. N., & Hubel, D. H. (1965). Extent of recovery from the effects of visual deprivation in kittens. *Journal of Neurophysiology, 28,* 1060–1072.

Wigfield, A. (1994). Expectancy-value theory of achievement motivation: A developmental perspective. *Educational Psychology Review, 6,* 49–78.

Wigfield, A., & Eccles, J. S. (1994). Children's competence beliefs, achievement values, and general self-esteem: Change across elementary and middle school. *Journal of Early Adolescence, 14,* 107–138.

Wigfield, A., Eccles, J. S., & Pintrich, P. R. (1996). Development between the ages of 11 and 25. In D. C. Berliner & R. C. Calfee (Eds.), *Handbook of educational psychology.* New York: Macmillan.

Wigfield, A., & Karpathian, M. (1991). Who am I and what can I do? Children's self-concepts and motivation in achievement situations. *Educational Psychologist, 26,* 233–262.

Williams, D. (1996). *Autism: An inside-outside approach.* London: Kingsley.

Williams, D. E., & D'Alessandro, J. D. (1994). A comparison of three measures of androgyny and their relationship to psychological adjustment. *Journal of Social Behavior and Personality, 9,* 469–480.

Wimmer, H., & Perner, J. (1983). Beliefs about beliefs: Representation and constraining function of wrong beliefs in young children's understanding of deception. *Cognition, 13,* 103–128.

Winer, G. A., Craig, R. K., & Weinbaum, E. (1992). Adults' failure on misleading weight-conservation tests: A developmental analysis. *Developmental Psychology, 28,* 109–120.

Winne, P. H. (1995a). Inherent details in self-regulated learning. *Educational Psychologist, 30,* 173–187.

Winne, P. H. (1995b). Self-regulation is ubiquitous but its forms vary with knowledge. *Educational Psychologist, 30,* 223–228.

Wong, B. Y. L. (Ed.). (1991). *Learning about learning disabilities.* San Diego, CA: Academic Press.

Wood, D., Bruner, J. S., & Ross, G. (1976). The role of tutoring in problem-solving. *Journal of Child Psychology and Psychiatry, 17,* 89–100.

Wood, E., Motz, M., & Willoughby, T. (1997, April). *Examining students' retrospective memories of strategy development.* Paper presented at the annual meeting of the American Educational Research Association, Chicago.

Wood, E., Willoughby, T., McDermott, C., Motz, M., Kaspar, V., & Ducharme, M. J. (1999). Developmental differences in study behavior. *Journal of Educational Psychology, 91,* 527–536.

Wood, E., Willoughby, T., Reilley, S., Elliott, S., & DuCharme, M. (1994, April). *Evaluating students' acquisition of factual material when studying independently or with a partner.* Paper presented at the annual meeting of the American Educational Research Association, New Orleans, LA.

Wood, J. W., & Rosbe, M. (1985). Adapting the classroom lectures for the mainstreamed student in the secondary schools. *The Clearing House, 58,* 354–358.

Woody-Ramsey, J., & Miller, P. H. (1988). The facilitation of selective attention in preschoolers. *Child Development, 59,* 1497–1503.

Yu, S. L., Elder, A. D., & Urdan, T. C. (1995, April). *Motivation and cognitive strategies in students with a "good student" or "poor student" self-schema.* Paper presented at the annual meeting of the American Educational Research Association, San Francisco.

Zervigon-Hakes, A. (1984). Materials mastery and symbolic development in construction play: Stages of development. *Early Child Development and Care, 17,* 37–47.

Zimmerman, B. J., & Bandura, A. (1994). Impact of self-regulatory influences on writing course attainment. *American Educational Research Journal, 31,* 845–862.

Zimmerman, B. J., & Risemberg, R. (1997). Self-regulatory dimensions of academic learning and motivation. In G. D. Phye (Ed.), *Handbook of academic learning: Construction of knowledge.* San Diego, CA: Academic Press.

Zuckerman, G. A. (1994). A pilot study of a ten-day course in cooperative learning for beginning Russian first graders. *Elementary School Journal, 94,* 405–420.